HITLER'S BATTLESHIPS

HITLER'S BATTLESHIPS

by
Edwyn Gray

LEO COOPER
LONDON

First published in Great Britain in 1992 by
LEO COOPER
190 Shaftesbury Avenue, London WC2H 8JL
an imprint of
Pen & Sword Books Ltd,
47 Church Street, Barnsley, South Yorkshire S70 2AS

A CIP catalogue record for this book is available
from the British Library

Typeset by Yorkshire Web, Barnsley, South Yorkshire
in Plantin 10 point

Printed by
Redwood Press,
Melksham, Wiltshire

CONTENTS

AUTHOR'S NOTE

GERMANY'S BATTLESHIPS FOUGHT in the arctic blizzards and sub-zero temperatures of the Barents Sea and the Kara Sea. They probed the mists and ice-floes of the Greenland coast and, during the bombardment of Spitzbergen, were operating within 750 miles of the North Pole. They prowled the convoy routes of the North Atlantic and pushed beyond the equator searching for prey in raiding sorties that took them from the shores of Brazil and Uruguay to those of West Africa. One, the *Admiral Scheer*, penetrated as far east as the Seychelles in the Indian Ocean. Another, the *Bismarck*, sank the Royal Navy's most famous ship, *HMS Hood* − while the *Scharnhorst* and *Gneisenau* destroyed the carrier *Glorious* off Norway and humbled English pride by breaking through the Dover Straits in broad daylight.

Churchill considered them an even greater threat to Britain's sea supremacy than the U-boats. And the fact that six very gallant men were awarded the Victoria Cross − four posthumously − for trying to sink them, is a measure of the importance which the British Government placed upon this determined handful of fighting ships.

Yet, despite their tactical victories and their undoubted strategic value in tying down substantial numbers of Allied warships and aircraft for the major part of the war, their nebulous role as 'a fleet in being' was never fully appreciated by Germany's Nazi leadership. And, indeed, at one critical point in the conflict, Hitler even demanded that they should be demilitarized and scrapped.

Some readers may question my classification of these seven vessels as battleships. But, realistically, no other description adequately fits the bill. Admittedly the original 'pocket-battleships' were rated as *panzerschiffes* − armoured ships − by the German Navy when they were built. But despite their treaty-imposed 10,000-tons displacement, the 11-inch guns which they mounted made them far too powerful to be classed as mere cruisers. Similarly although the *Scharnhorst* and *Gneisenau* were described as battlecruisers by the Royal Navy they were always referred to as battleships by the *Kriegsmarine*. And certainly no battlecruiser − an already outmoded concept by 1939 with the advent of the fast battleship − could have survived the punishment which these two vessels sustained during the war.

This volume has gestated over a period of many years and it is impossible to name every source that has contributed to my understanding of this period of naval warfare. I must, however, acknowledge my debt to three specific books which have been of great value in providing a comprehensive and reliable background against which I could check facts and dates: Ludovic Kennedy's *Pursuit* and its sequel *Menace*; and Richard Garrett's *Scharnhorst and Gneisenau – the Elusive Sisters*. In addition the late Erich Raeder's autobiography, *Struggle for the Sea*, yielded a valuable insight into the political battle between the German naval high command (OKM) and the Führer for control of the *Kriegsmarine*.

I would like to place on record my special thanks to: the late David Woodward, former naval correspondent of the *Daily Telegraph*; the late Grand Admiral Karl Doenitz with whom I corresponded in 1972; Anthony Brown; Wilhelm Gerlach; Sandford Hunt; Elizabeth Knox; Paul Launberg; Hans Schmidt; and Karl Stutz. My thanks too, to the US Navy and the National Archives in Washington, for their ever-willing and efficient help in tracing photographs.

Finally may I express my appreciation to the following publishers for the use of copyright material: Ian Allan; Atheneum Verlag; Cassell & Co; Leo Cooper; Coward McCann; David & Charles; Peter Davies; Doubleday; Hodder & Stoughton; Herbert Jenkins; William Kimber; Naval Institute Press; Secker & Warburg; Gerhard Stalling Verlag; and HM Stationery Office. My apologies to any original copyright owners whom I have failed to trace.

Germany's battleships fought a long and hard war. The *Graf Spee* sailed for her combat station in the Atlantic ten days before Hitler's tanks rolled over the Polish border. The *Lützow* was still firing her guns at Russian troops four days after the Führer had committed suicide in his Berlin bunker. None, sadly, were destined to survive the conflict. This book tells the story of their births, their lives and, ultimately, their deaths.

I offer it as a salute to the men who fought and died in them.

EDWYN GRAY
Attleborough, Norfolk
November, 1991.

PROLOGUE

The DESTRUCTION of the Imperial German Navy began at 1900 hours on the evening of Friday, 15 November, 1918. And, with every detail carefully stage-managed for maximum theatrical effect, the scene aboard Admiral Sir David Beatty's flagship, *Queen Elizabeth*, reflected the drama of the occasion. Even the Almighty contributed to the atmosphere of Gothic tragedy by throwing a cloak of thick impenetrable fog over the waters of the Firth of Forth and the damp gloom echoed with the banshee wail of sirens from the anonymous ships inching their way cautiously through the murk.

Two sword-bedecked senior officers were standing at the rails of the flagship ready to receive Admiral Franz von Hipper's representative, Rear-Admiral Hugo Meurer, and escort him to the Commander-in-Chief's quarters. Behind them a ring of Royal Marines with fixed bayonets sealed off the quarterdeck like a palisade of spiked railings while, hidden from view in the darkness, more than a thousand sailors looked down on the historic scene from various vantage points high up on the superstructure hoping to catch a glimpse of the German party as it came aboard.

Despite the fog the *Königsberg* arrived from Wilhelmshaven at precisely 1400 hours and, shepherded by the cruiser *Cardiff*, felt her way up-river to the Inchkeith light where, in obedience to a signal from her escort, she dropped anchor. Some four hours later a steam barge was lowered and, with the admiral's ensign overtopped by a white flag of truce fluttering limply from its stern, it shuttled Meurer to the destroyer *Oak* in which he was to make the 12-mile passage up the Firth to the 27,000-ton flagship of the Grand Fleet.

A grim-faced Beatty, sitting behind a massive table and flanked by Vice-Admiral Sir Charles Madden, his second-in-command, and Rear-Admiral Sir Osmond de B. Brock, the Chief of Staff, was waiting for him in his dining cabin aboard the *Queen Elizabeth*. A brass lion, symbolic of British sea power and a treasured souvenir from the Commander-in-Chief's former flagship *Lion*, bestrode the green baize of the table cover and, as a further pointed reminder of the Royal Navy's long tradition of victory, a full-length painting of Lord Nelson hung on the bulkhead immediately behind Beatty's head. The remainder of the spacious cabin was austerely bare. Plain grey armoured-steel walls, gleaming brass-rimmed scuttles, and a selection of good quality mahogany dining chairs interspersed with commodious leather sofas. Finally, and discreetly hidden from view behind 'a mass of flowers' in the left-hand corner of the cabin, the official war artist Sir John Lavery waited to commit the scene to canvas for posterity.

In a private letter to his friend Mrs Eugenie Godfrey-Faussett★ the Admiral confided his personal recollections of the occasion: 'It all began with the advent of Admiral Meurer. You would have loved that, it was dramatic and tragic to a high degree. He arrived onboard at 7pm, pitch dark aided by a thick fog in which he could see nothing and had no idea he was surrounded by the Greatest Fleet in the World. I arranged a most beautiful setting, my Dramatic Sense was highly developed at the moment. When he marched up the gangway he was met by a blaze of light ... which lighted the gangway and the path to be trod from there to my hatchway. Outside the Path of Light, half in and half out, was a line of the fattest marine sentries, about two paces apart, with fixed bayonets upon which the light gleamed. Wherever he looked he met a bayonet. He was met by Tommy Brand and Chadfield★★ who were frigidity itself. The wretch nearly collapsed on the Quarter Deck, and his party was led to my cabin.

Beatty's gloating and somewhat unwholesome description of Meurer's carefully orchestrated humiliation offers a revealing insight into his character. As, indeed, did many other aspects of the events that were to follow.

Meurer's task was made no easier by the straits in which the Imperial Navy found itself as a direct consequence of the mutiny that had crippled the High Seas Fleet's will to fight and which had given a new urgency to Germany's first tentative moves to bring an end to hostilities. And, having presented his credentials in response to Beatty's abrupt demand for documentary confirmation of his authority to negotiate, the German Admiral listened in miserable silence as the British Commander-in-Chief read out a prepared list of instructions. When Beatty had finished, Meurer took the opportunity to explain the effects of the blockade on Germany and to remind the assembled officers that mutiny and revolution had reduced the nation to near anarchy. Then, stumbling over his words, he apologized for his own embarrassing situation:

'I must inform the Herr Admiral that three plenipotentiaries from the Sailors' and Workers's Soviet of the North Sea Command are aboard the *Königsberg* and have been authorized by the Provisional Government to attend all conferences.'

★ Quoted p 277 *Earl Beatty, The Last Naval Hero*, Stephen Roskill, Atheneum, New York, 1981

★★ Rear-Admiral the Hon. Hubert G. Brand (Captain of the Fleet) and Captain Ernle Chatfield (Beatty's flag-captain).

'Tell them to go to hell,' Beatty growled at his interpreter.

Commander W.T. Bagot worded his translation in more diplomatic language than that employed by the Commander-in-Chief. But the meaning was the same. 'Admiral Beatty refuses to see the plenipotentiaries of the Sailors' and Workers' Soviet,' he informed the German representatives blandly. Meurer, on hearing Beatty's reply visibly relaxed. And he made no attempt to conceal his relief that someone was at last prepared to put the mutineers in their place. Perhaps honour could yet be salved from the bitter embers of defeat.

Deprived of victory in open battle by the reluctance of the Kaiser's fleet to leave harbour, Beatty had for some weeks insistently urged the British Government to demand the surrender of the German Navy as part and parcel of any general armistice terms. His uncompromising attitude was supported by the First Sea Lord, Admiral Sir Rosslyn Wemyss, and virtually every other senior office in the Royal Navy. But the politicians had different ideas. First and foremost it was imperative for the war to be brought to an immediate conclusion before the entire fabric of Western society collapsed and they were afraid that the German request for a ceasefire − first made to America's President Woodrow Wilson on 5 October − might be withdrawn if a demand for the total surrender of their fleet proved to be unacceptable. It was possible, too, that the United States might accede to a ceasefire on its own terms and leave its European allies to continue the war against Germany alone. It was a risk that few were prepared to take.

Beatty, however, remained unequivocal and in a memorandum submitted to the British War Cabinet on Monday, 21 October, headed *The Naval Terms of an Armistice*, he made no effort to mince his words and, in the concluding paragraph of his submission he stated with characteristic bluntness: 'To achieve the destruction of German Sea Power and reduce Germany to the status of a second-rate Naval Power, it is necessary to lay down in the Naval Terms of the Armistice, conditions which would be commensurate with the result of a naval action' − in the circumstances a somewhat complacent and over-confident statement bearing in mind the heavy losses sustained by the Royal Navy during the only major sea battle of the war at Jutland on 31 May, 1916. 'Remove the power of the High Seas Fleet now, and ... reduce the continental nation of Germany to that of second-rate Naval Power, corresponding to her geographical position and requirements, and *our* [Beatty's italics] position at sea is at once secured ... Great Britain in the future will be spared a race with Germany for sea supremacy.'*

Beatty's demand for a total naval surrender did not go down well with the

* Extracts quoted from *The Life and Letters of David Beatty*, W.S. Chalmers, Hodder & Stoughton, 1951, p 332

politicians — especially those from France and Italy. And his insistence that the island fortress of Heligoland should also be yielded up by the Germans was considered to be unrealistic. Indeed by the time the German delegates took their places at the table in the railway carriage at Rethondes on 8 November the naval terms of the proposed armistice had already been watered down considerably — the Allies now demanding the surrender of 160 U-boats but only the *internment* of the enemy's surface fleet. Furthermore all mention of Heligoland had been deleted. In fact Paragraph 23, the clause pertaining to the Imperial Navy's surface ships as agreed and signed by the German delegates, fell very far short of Beatty's requirements:

'The following German surface warships [are] to be disarmed and thereafter *interned* [author's italics] in neutral or allied ports, [with] only care and maintenance parties being left on board: six battle-cruisers, ten battleships, eight light cruisers (including two minelayers), and fifty destroyers of most modern type. All other warships and auxiliaries to be disarmed and placed under Allied supervision. Vessels for internment to leave German ports within seven days.'

Smarting under the imagined injustice of Clause 23 and thwarted in his demand for the total surrender of Germany's surface fleet, Beatty resolved to ignore the strict terms of the Armistice agreement. Meurer was provided with details of the British Admiral's proposals and was then sent back to the *Königsberg* to consider his response overnight.

Powerless to resist Beatty's demands, Meurer returned to the flagship the following morning to signify his assent to the humiliating ceremony which the Grand Fleet's staff officers had drawn up at the Commander-in-Chief's instigation. Although Beatty's Flag Lieutenant, Ralph Seymour, described the Admiral's treatment of the German delegation as 'courteous in the extreme but firm as a rock' the Commander-in-Chief's private correspondence suggests that he revelled in the discomfiture of his former enemy.

'Generally speaking, they would agree to anything, they raised points here and there which were firmly squashed,' he wrote to Eugenie. 'They prated about the honour of their Submarine Crews being possibly assailed [a reference presumably, to the enforcement of Clause 22 which required the *surrender* of *all* submarines] which nearly lifted me out of my chair. However, I scathingly replied that their personal safety would be assured, which would doubtless satisfy their Honour. In any case, it [German honour] was different to ours and we wouldn't waste time over it' — a sarcasm somewhat out of place on such an occasion. 'When it came to signing the documents,' Beatty's letter continued, 'I thought he [Meurer] would collapse, he took two shots at it, putting his pen down twice, but we got him over it and they retired into the fog in grim silence.'

Another version of the final meeting based on German sources supports the details of Beatty's description: 'Beatty signed swiftly, his sprawling signature flowing into the document. Meurer took the pen. The man was in great anguish. He tried to touch the point to the paper, but his hand shook so violently that he must lift it again. For a moment, as he struggled to control himself his face was contorted with pain too acute to look upon. By a powerful effort of will he mastered mind and muscle, and made the marks of script that seemed the very blood of the Navy he loved. Then the German [Rear-Admiral] went, as stiffly, as misunderstood, as beaten and, as humiliated, as he had come.'*

Beatty's plan for receiving the German Navy into internment on 21 November was simple in concept and flamboyant in execution. And the stigma of abject surrender was apparent in every finely-tuned detail. The enemy fleet − forlorn, dirty and dispirited, but still a formidable force of nine battleships, five battle-cruisers, seven cruisers, and forty-nine modern destroyers − was met at sea by the British cruiser *Cardiff* which, taking the van position at the head of the long, almost interminable, line of ships, proceeded to lead it into the Firth of Forth.

Waiting to receive it was the Grand Fleet which had been formed up into two parallel columns − a vast assembly of 370 vessels comprising thirteen squadrons of British capital ships and cruisers, the US Navy's 6th Battle Squadron, and myriad shoals of fast-moving destroyers. But even in his supreme moment of self-glorification Beatty remained prudently watchful. And as a precaution against any last-minute attempt by the Germans to give battle, every British warship had its weapons loaded and its crews, wearing anti-flash gear, closed up at action stations, although, to avoid provocation, the guns themselves were kept trained fore-and-aft.

As the snaking line passed clear of May Island the *Cardiff* guided the enemy ships between the jaws of the two approaching columns of British dreadnoughts and, at the appropriate moment, Beatty's battleships reversed course by turning through 180° with faultless precision. Then, taking station on either side of the enemy vessels like armed guards escorting a file of prisoners, they shepherded the German ships to their anchorage off Aberlady Bay. For the victims it was an unnecessarily humiliating experience that few ever forgot or forgave. For the British, however, it was tangible proof that they had won the war at sea. And, of equal importance in Beatty's eyes, his carefully scripted exhibition convinced the world that the German fleet had *surrendered* to the Royal Navy.

It was, nevertheless, very much of a one-man show. Neither Lord Fisher, the man who had, almost single-handed, created the superb fighting machine that Beatty now commanded, nor Sir John Jellicoe, his predecessor as

---

* *Death of a Fleet*, Schubert and Gibson, Coward-McCann, New York, 1932, p 201

Commander-in-Chief of the Grand Fleet who had forced the High Seas fleet to fly for its life at Jutland, were present to witness the fruits of their endeavours − the failure to send invitations to them being excused as 'an oversight' − while the First Sea Lord, Wester Wemyss, declined to attend the ceremony because he said it pained him to watch the humiliation of fellow officers, even Germans.

His Majesty King George V was also conspicuous by his absence despite having visited the fleet only the previous day. It was said that he had refused Beatty's invitation as he did not wish to detract from the Admiral's day of triumph. But, somewhat strangely, no trace of an invitation, either formal or informal, has ever been discovered in the Royal archives. In fact only one other person was allowed to share the limelight − Beatty's wife, the American heiress Ethel Field — who, ignoring the constraints of protocol, and behaving like a saucer-eyed sightseer on a cheap-day excursion trip, cruised past the German ships in her luxury steam-yacht *Sheelah*. To her consternation, however, she was rewarded with a chorus of cat-calls and similarly vulgar noises from the mutinous and indisciplined crew of the *Seydlitz*. It was not quite what Beatty had intended!

Later that morning, at 11.04, the *Queen Elizabeth* made a General Signal to all ships: *The German flag will be hauled down at 3.57pm [sunset] today, Thursday, and will not be hoisted again without permission.* It was Beatty's final defiance of the armistice. And in the light of Clause 23 it was, of course, totally illegal. Rear-Admiral Ludwig von Reuter promptly lodged a strong complaint in which he pointed out that interned ships had the right to fly their national ensigns. But he was predictably snubbed for his pains and the insult rankled in German breasts.

Perhaps the last word should be given to Britain's pre-eminent modern naval historian, the late Captain Stephen Roskill:

'Beatty would have been wiser to have shown magnanimity towards his late enemies rather than a desire to humiliate them; since he probably thereby sowed some of the seeds which came to harvest later through the propagation of the "stab in the back" legend − that the German armed forces had never been defeated but had been betrayed by the civil authorities; and that contributed to the resurgence of German militarism in the 1920s, with consequences which all the world knows'.*

Unloved and unwanted − for the presence of the German fleet in the busy waters of the Firth of Forth proved to be something of an embarrassment to the Allies − the surrendered ships were escorted northwards by their British jailors to the inhospitable obscurity of Gutter Sound in Scapa Flow

---

* *Earl Beatty, the Last Naval Hero*, p 280

where they were left under guard to await the outcome of the peace negotiations at Versailles. During the long and demoralizing months of incarceration that lay ahead von Reuter and his senior officers passed the time by preparing detailed contingency plans for the destruction of the interned warships if, and when, a situation arose that demanded positive action. But although nerves on both sides grew tauter as the delegates continued to wrangle in Versailles the German Admiral was denied both the opportunity and the psychological trigger necessary to bring his clandestine scheme to reality.

By May of 1919 the delegates at Versailles had finally hammered out mutually acceptable terms for ending the war. Von Reuter, however, did not learn the details until Friday, 20 June and, sitting in his cabin, the Admiral read the naval provisions of the draft treaty with growing horror. According to *The Times* − his only source of reliable information − Germany was to *surrender* all warships that were at present subject to internment; the island fortress of Heligoland was to be demilitarized; and the numerical strength of the post-war German fleet was to be restricted in terms of both ships and personnel. Failure to accept the provisions would result in the Allies revoking the Armistice with all the dire consequences such a momentous step would entail. Denied the victory at sea which he had craved, Beatty, it seemed, had won the equally important diplomatic battle. And Germany's Navy, which in 1914 had been the second largest in the world, was to be reduced in status to that of a 4th-rate maritime power.

Von Reuter shrugged wearily as he put the newspaper down on his desk. It was too late for recriminations. After nearly seven months of covert planning the time for action had finally arrived. The honour of the Germany Navy could now only be retrieved by denying the victor his spoils. And when, on the very next day, Sir Sydney Fremantle's 1st Battle Squadron left the Flow to carry out torpedo exercises, the German Admiral took swift advantage of his jailor's absence to implement his carefully prepared secret operation.

As Fremantle's ships were swallowed up by the morning mists in Hoxa Sound a string of flags ran up *Emden*'s foremast: *Paragraph 11 −Acknowledge*. The coded order was relayed from ship to ship by repeater flags, semaphore, signal lamps and word of mouth. And as grim-faced officers hurried below decks to open the sea-cocks, petty officers mustered the maintenance crews at pre-selected assembly points to await the order to abandon ship.

'Water poured into the hulls in solid blue-green jets, full streams of the sea − rising, luring, embracing in the wet caress of destruction. An inch ... a foot ... a tide − bubbling and washing − the gurgle of it like torrents under spring rains' was how one contemporary author described the scene.

Slowly and inexorably the great ships settled deeper into the black waters of Gutter Sound.*

The 24,380-ton *Friedrich der Grosse* — the former flagship of the High Seas Fleet at Jutland — was the first to succumb. With a thunderous rush of escaping air she rolled over like a dying whale just before noon and, sixteen minutes later, slipped quietly beneath the surface. Others followed, some eagerly embracing the sea, others reluctant to take the final plunge, and within a few hours the surface of the Flow was littered with upturned and sinking warships. A group of Royal Navy trawlers did their best to stem the rising tide of disaster. German seamen were ordered back to their vessels at gunpoint. Shots were fired. Men died. But nothing could now stop the momentum of von Reuter's act of self-immolation.

The last to sink was Germany's most modern and powerful battle-cruiser, the 26,180-ton *Hindenburg*. She settled slowly and her death agony lasted many hours until she, too, joined her sisters on the seabed during the late afternoon. In all, no fewer than fifty of the seventy-four warships interned at Scapa Flow had gone to the bottom — useless rusting hulks fit only for scrap when they were finally raised. Indeed the subsequent salvage operation proved to be a mammoth task and an incredible nineteen years were to pass before the last battleship, the *Kronprinz Wilhelm*, was brought back to the surface to begin her final passage to the ignominy of the breakers' yard. Von Reuter's men had done their job well.

A further twenty-four vessels, including the battleship *Baden*, the cruisers *Emden*, *Frankfurt* and *Nürberg*, and eighteen destroyers were beached by the British in a successful last-ditch attempt to prevent them from suffering the same fate as the rest of the fleet. Only two small destroyers survived and as the shadows of dusk embraced the sullen waters of Gutter Sound armed parties of Royal Navy seamen boarded them to prevent any further treachery. It was, in the words of Winston Churchill in connection with another British débâcle, a case of too little, too late.

'I rejoice,' Admiral Reinhold Scheer, the last Commander-in-Chief of the Kaiser's High Seas Fleet, commented on hearing the news. '...the stain of surrender has been wiped from the escutcheon of the Germany Navy. The sinking of these ships has proved that the spirit of the Fleet is not dead. This last act is true to the best traditions of the German Navy.'**

Honour had been restored. But the traumas of 1918 were to remain a festering sore in the body politic of German militarism for the next twenty-seven years.

* *Death of a Fleet*, p 261.

** Quoted from *The Collapse of Power*, David Woodward, Arthur Barker, 1973, p 184

CHAPTER ONE

'Battleships or Child Welfare'

ADMIRAL VON REUTER'S decision to scuttle the vessels interned at Scapa Flow may have cost the German Navy its most modern battleships. But the success of the operation served to take the sting out of the Peace Treaty when it was signed a week later at the Palace of Versailles. For Part V of the document which the German delegates stepped forward to ratify at 3.12 pm on that historic Saturday afternoon required the handing over to the Allies of *all* existing battleships and cruisers. Thanks to von Reuter, however, the majority of these were now quietly rusting on the bottom of Gutter Sound. And the victors were forced to leave Versailles empty-handed.

Article 181 of the Treaty allowed the new Republic to retain only six battleships on the active list plus a further two in reserve; six small cruisers with a similar pair in reserve; and twelve destroyers and twelve torpedo boats plus appropriate reserve units. In addition the construction and use of submarines and naval aircraft was forbidden. It was a bitter pill for the world's second largest navy to swallow.

The restriction imposed on battleship strength was, in fact, far more crippling than the figures at first suggested for the eight vessels to be retained: *Braunschweig, Elass, Hanover, Hessen, Schleswig-Holstein, Lotheringen, Preussen,* and *Schlesien,* had all been launched between 1902 and 1906 and predated Britain's revolutionary all-big-gun *Dreadnought* design. They were already obsolete in 1914 although some had fought at Jutland in Rear-Admiral Mauve's 2nd Squadron.

Although strictly members of two separate classes, the eight vessels were virtually identical in appearance and specification. Measuring 413 feet overall and displacing 12,100 tons, each ship was armed with four 11-inch guns and fourteen 6.7-inch weapons. And with a top speed of only 18 knots they were inferior to ships of post-*Dreadnought* design in every respect. The cruisers were even older and, dating from 1899, ranged from 2,600 to 3,250 tons with a comparatively weak armament of 4.1-inch guns. Modern British light cruisers were some 7 knots faster and mounted 6-inch weapons that could blow their puny adversaries out of the water with effortless ease.

But, of course, the task of the post-Versailles fleet was not to challenge the Royal Navy for command of the world's oceans. Its sole purpose was to defend the Baltic coastline of the new German republic from the bolshevik threat from the east. And, weak though it was, it was probably adequate for the purpose, bearing in mind the chaotic state of the Russian fleet after the 1917 revolution.

Ships, however, represent only one aspect of a navy's strength and the enforced reduction in personnel to just 15,000 men — with a maximum of 1500 officers — was, perhaps, a more serious threat to the future potential of the fleet than the restrictions on ship numbers. Thousands of highly trained and experienced seamen, engineers and technicians found themselves on the scrapheap. And to ensure that the naval establishment was not inflated by artificially short-period service contracts, the Allies shrewdly required officers to serve a minimum of 25 years and ratings 12 years — a ruling that effectively prevented Germany from building up a large reserve of trained men.

There were changes, too, in the higher levels of command. On 26 March, 1919, Admiral Adolph von Trotha was appointed head of the Admiralty while Meurer, the victim of Beatty's bullying tactics five months earlier, was given command of the High Seas Fleet. However, when it was realized that the latter force was likely to be interned at Scapa Flow for an indefinite period he was subsequently given the less imposing but more realistic appointment of Flag Officer, Baltic.

Germany's new navy, the *Reichsmarine*, was formally established by the National Assembly of the Weimar Republic on 16 April. But continued indiscipline quickly wrecked this initial attempt to bring order from chaos. And to make matters worse many officers, who should have known better, allowed themselves to become involved in politics. Meurer himself was removed from his Baltic command early in 1920 following a public dispute with Matthias Erzberger, a leading government minister, and in March units of the new navy erupted in mutiny — the second in the space of eighteen months — when a group of right-wing officers supported a bid for power by Wolfgang Kapp. The attempt failed but it was to have disastrous repercussions. Admiral von Trotha was arrested for complicity in the *putsch*, together with 171 other naval officers who had given Kapp their active support. When the dust had settled the majority were either dismissed from the service or prematurely retired. But the affair did little to boost morale in the new *Reichsmarine* or inspire confidence amongst the ordinary enlisted seamen. There were troubles, too, at Kiel where communist-led strikers attacked the naval arsenal and seized control of the dockyard in an outbreak of violence that ended with the unauthorized arrest of the port admiral, von Levetzow, and four hundred of his officers by the militant workers. Similar disturbances occurred at Wilhelmshaven where two torpedo-boats were scuttled by mutinous and disaffected sailors.

Otto Gessler, the Minister of Defence, finally managed to bring the situation under control and, deciding that none of the flag officers on the Active List had the ability to heal the grievous wounds that were splitting the navy asunder, he recalled Vice-Admiral Paul Behncke from retirement and made him Chief of Naval Staff. At the same time he appointed Rear-Admiral Zenker as Flag Officer, North Sea.

During the war Zenker had captained the battle-cruiser *Von der Tann* which, as a part of Vice-Admiral Franz Hipper's First Scouting Group, had met and outfought Beatty's ships in the opening stages of the Battle of Jutland. Hipper's Chief of Staff from 1913 until 1918 had been a young up-and-coming officer by the name of Erich Raeder. It was therefore possibly no coincidence that, in the wake of Zenker's promotion, Raeder found himself placed in charge of the Central Division of the Admiralty in Berlin with the task of reorganizing the officer corps of the *Reichsmarine*. But his promising career was blighted when, as an adviser to Admiral von Trotha, he came under suspicion in the wake of the Kapp *putsch* and was relegated to the naval archives branch − an uninspiring post which nevertheless afforded him a unique opportunity to study all aspects of cruiser warfare and commerce raiding. The knowledge he acquired was to pay handsome dividends when he rose to become, firstly, Commander-in-Chief of the *Reichsmarine* and then, five years later, Hitler's senior naval adviser and supreme commander of the *Kriegsmarine*.

Karl Dönitz, the man destined to succeed Hitler in the dying days of the Third Reich, also had a passing involvement in the events of the Kapp *putsch*. Taken prisoner by the British in October, 1918, after his submarine, *UB-68*, had been sunk during a convoy attack, he had resumed duty in the post-war navy as an *Oberleutnant* following his repatriation to Germany in the summer of 1919. When the communist-led workers rampaged through Kiel dockyard he was acting as temporary captain of a 'loyal' torpedo-boat and, in the confusion of revolution and counter-revolution, he found himself relieved of his short-lived command by the self-appointed Workers' Soviet. Dönitz somehow survived the chaos that ensued and finally, on 31 May, after the legitimate government had regained control, he was reinstated as an officer of the *Reichsmarine* and given command of the torpedo-boat *T-157*.

Although of only local significance at the time, 1920 saw another very minor political coup in Bavaria some 400 miles to the south of strife-torn Kiel. But despite its obscurity it was destined to have a traumatic effect on the professional careers of both *Käpitan zur See* Erich Raeder and the eagerly ambitious *Oberleutnant* Karl Dönitz.

At the beginning of 1919, as part of a scheme to counteract the seditious influence of communist and other left-wing agitators, the Army had appointed a number of reliable NCOs for duties as propagandists and instructors. After a brief period of training they were sent to transit camps where they gave counter-revolutionary and patriotic lectures to returning prisoners-of-war and acted, generally, as political spies.* In September of that year a 30-year-old corporal attached to the 2nd Infantry Regiment as a *V-mann* was instructed to attend a meeting of the German Workers' Party — the *Deutsche Arbeiter Partie* or DAP — at the Sterneckerbraü beer hall in Munich to ascertain whether its aims were subversive. The corporal, a veteran from the trenches of the Western Front who had won the Iron Cross 2nd Class for gallantry under fire and who was still recuperating from the effects of an Allied poison gas attack, went to the beer hall as ordered. But instead of making notes for a report to his superiors he quickly found himself sympathizing with the nationalistic arguments of the various speakers at the meeting. A few days later the *V-mann* accepted an invitation to join the DAP — the obscurity of which can be judged by the fact that his party membership card was only the seventh to be issued.

The soldier's skill as an orator and his violent anti-semitic sentiments soon brought him a measure of notoriety in Munich and on 1 April — only a fortnight after the collapse of the Kapp *putsch* — Corporal Adolf Hitler quit the army to enter the world of politics. On the very same day DAP changed its name to the National Socialist German Workers' Party — usually abbreviated to NSDAP or, as it became more generally known, the Nazi party. In the months that followed two further significant steps were taken towards the creation of the Third Reich. The swastika emblem worn by Hermann Erhrhardt's naval brigade when it had fought in support of Kapp during the March *putsch* was adopted by Hitler as the Nazi party's symbol. And a short time later the new leader organized the *Sturmabteilung* — the brown-shirted stormtroopers — a force which grew rapidly into a private army of armed and uniformed thugs to whom Hitler delegated the task of quelling his political opponents.

By October, 1922, the *Reichsmarine* had come to terms with its reduced status and was tentatively exploring the future. A new flag, issued to replace the old Imperial Ensign, symbolized the change and, having completed its

---

* The *Vertrauensmann* or V-mann was employed solely as a low-ranking political instructor and propagandist. He was not a *Bildungsoffizier* or Education Officer as later historians have often suggested.

initial task of clearing the wartime minefields laid by the Kaiser's fleet, the Supreme Naval Staff, or *Seekriegsleitung* (*SKL*) began to rationalize its resources within the restricted limits imposed by the Treaty of Versailles.

The first step was to form two miniscule fleets for the defence of Germany's coasts — one based in the North Sea and the other in the Baltic. Each comprised a single obsolete battleship supported by two even older cruisers and a flotilla of eleven veteran destroyers. Dönitz, now a three-ringed *Kapitanleutnant*, served with the newly formed Baltic Fleet for a year before being moved to a shore job in Kiel while Raeder, who had gained flag-rank as a Rear-Admiral on 1 July, 1922, left the backwaters of the archives section to take up the influential post of Inspector of Training and Education — an appointment which lasted until July, 1924, when he was given command of Light Forces in the North Sea. Three months later he was promoted to Vice-Admiral and hoisted his flag as Commander-in-Chief, Baltic Fleet.

Although Article 181 of the Peace Treaty expressly banned the *Reichsmarine* from either building or operating submarines, senior officers were already seeking ways to evade the embargo. And it did not take long to find a loophole. For, while the construction of submarines was forbidden in the Fatherland, there was nothing in the Treaty to prevent German designers from keeping abreast with current technological advances by building the prohibited vessels abroad. And so in 1922 — eleven years before Hitler achieved power — a company was formed in Holland, the *Ingenieurskantoor voor Scheepsbouw*, the sole purpose of which was the development of the new submarine designs. Other experts left Germany for the Far East where they helped the Japanese Navy to build up its own formidable underwater fleet.

The Treaty also set down rules for replacing the ships which the *Reichsmarine* had been allowed to retain — the most important of which only permitted the replacement of battleships after twenty years of service. This, however, was not quite such an onerous restriction as it may have first appeared, for the twenty-year yardstick had also been freely adopted by most of the world's major navies when determining the replacement dates for their own battleships. Of far more concern to Admiral Behncke and his senior advisers in the *SKL* was Article 190 which stipulated that the standard displacement of any future battleships which Germany chose to build must be limited to 10,000 tons. As contemporary battleships in Britain, the United States, and Japan were already exceeding 30,000 tons and a new upper displacement limit of 10,000 tons had been set for *cruisers* by the Washington Treaty signed at the end of 1921, it was apparent that, if Germany adhered to the conditions of the Versailles Treaty, she would never again be able to achieve parity on a ship-to-ship basis with the rest of the world's fleets.

There were similar restrictions on the size of German cruisers which were limited, by Article 190, to a maximum standard displacement of 6,000 tons. And as the *Reichsmarine*'s cruisers were even older and more decrepit than its battleships it was decided that their replacement must take priority. The first ship, *Emden*, was laid down in December, 1921, only 30 months after signature of the Peace Treaty — a remarkably determined achievement by Admiral Behncke and his staff in the circumstances. But, despite being announced as measuring 5,700 tons, the new cruiser, when finally commissioned on 15 October, 1925, displaced 6,700 tons — an excess of more than 10% above the 6,000- ton limit set by Article 190 of the Treaty. And the cruisers that followed, *Karlsruhe*, *Köln* and *Königsberg*, launched between 1927 and 1928, all showed similar discrepancies. Although officially declared to have displacements of 6,000 tons the true figure was, in fact, 6,650 tons. When considering the deceit with which Germany flouted the restrictions of the Peace Treaty, it is worth noting that Hitler and the Nazis did not come to power until *twelve* years after the keel of the *Emden* was laid.

Unlike the later ships, the *Emden* boasted no revolutionary design features and was, in most respects, inferior to contemporary cruisers of other navies. She was coal-fired* and her armament of eight 5.9-inch guns was mounted singly with two weapons on each broadside and four on the centreline. The three ships that followed, however, were a marked improvement. Their nine 5.9-inch guns were mounted in three triple-gunned turrets — Germany was in fact the first nation to employ triple turrets on cruisers — while mixed turbine and diesel propulsion provided a greater than average cruising radius, although this still fell well short of the range of comparable British light cruisers. Nevertheless, they were good ships even though the weight of armament on such a low displacement hampered their sea-keeping qualities and they had to be modified at a later date.

In addition to the new cruisers a number of modern destroyers were laid down in the same period. These also exceeded the Treaty limits by an equally handsome margin. The first, *Möwe*, authorized in 1923, laid down in 1924 and launched on 24 March, 1926, displaced 924 tons instead of its official measure of 800 tons and, at full load, reached 1,290 tons. Even so the new vessels were too small for the demands of modern destroyer warfare and they were subsequently reclassified as torpedo-boats when the large Z-class boats joined the fleet in the mid-thirties.

Having successfully launched a programme of cruiser replacement, the Navy now turned its attention to the more difficult task of designing new battleships that complied with the Versailles Treaty's twin limitations of a 10,000 tons standard displacement and a maximum gun calibre of 11 inches.

---

* Converted to oil-burning in 1934.

The ensuing problems seemed insurmountable and plan after plan was considered, argued over, and then finally rejected. The first draft design, produced in 1923, envisaged a lightly armoured vessel mounting four 15-inch guns with a speed of only 18 knots but was coldly received by the top brass and, in any case, exceeded the restriction on gun calibre. And an alternative proposal for a heavily-protected coast-defence monitor with large guns and slow speed was swiftly rejected.

A modified design, identified cryptically as B2, produced a ship with thinner armour, six 12-inch guns, and a speed of 21 knots and this initially found favour with both Zenker* and Raeder as it was highly suitable for Baltic operations. But a further set of plans produced in 1927 projected a revolutionary new type of warship which, aided by electrically-welded hull construction and the use of diesel engines, would be able to combine six 11-inch guns with a 4-inch armour belt and a speed of 26 knots without, in theory, exceeding a displacement of 10,000 tons.

Zenker immediately came down in favour of the Type C design, as the new plans were designated. The large calibre guns could see off all foreign cruisers that dared to come within their range while the relatively high speed of 26 knots meant that it could outrun any contemporary battleship which had guns large enough to out-range and out-fight it. In addition the MAN diesel engines provided the ship with sufficient radius of action to make it an ideal vessel for commerce raiding. And it was this latter attribute that persuaded Raeder to support Zenker in the political struggle to get the new vessel approved.

The lead ship of the class – rated in Germany as a *Panzerschiff* or armoured ship rather than a full-blown battleship – was needed as a replacement for the ageing *Preussen*. But although the *Reichstag* voted the first building credit in 1927 there was considerable political opposition to the new vessel and construction was delayed until the election for a new *Reichstag* had taken place on 20 May, 1928. Even then, it was November before the project received final approval – and then only after fierce opposition from the Socialists who adopted the emotive slogan: 'Battleships or Child Welfare!'. The 1928 election is, however, of interest for another reason for a total of 810,000 people voted for the National Socialist party and the Nazis emerged with twelve seats in the *Reichstag* – their first success in national as opposed to regional politics. But their support represented only 2.63% of the total vote and, with Hitler discredited with the middle classes following his imprisonment in February, 1924, after his failed Munich *putsch* in November of the previous year, a long uphill struggle lay ahead if political supremacy was

* Hans Zenker replaced Behncke as Commander-in-Chief of the *Reichsmarine* in 1924.

to be achieved. Nevertheless, with the voting in favour of the new battleship amounting to only 255 with 203 against, the Nazi party's 12 votes were both welcome and appreciated in the circles that mattered.

Germany's first pocket-battleship, *Deutschland*, was launched by President Paul von Hindenburg at Kiel's *Deutsche-Werke* shipyard on 19 May, 1931, with all the traditional pomp and circumstance of waving flags, brass bands and patriotic speeches. And it fell to Chancellor Heinrich Brüning to voice the nation's pride in its achievement: 'In this ceremony,' he told an enthusiastic crowd of dignitaries and workers, 'witnessed by the entire world, the German people have demonstrated that, despite the shackles imposed upon them and all their terrible economic problems, they have the strength to guard their peaceful co-existence with the rest of Europe.'

By the time the new *panzerschiffe* was commissioned into the fleet on 1 April, 1933, Heinrich Brüning and his two immediate successors, Franz von Papen and Kurt von Schleicher, had vanished from the political stage and the *Reich* had a new Chancellor — the former army corporal who had launched the National Socialist German Workers' Party in April, 1920. By chance, rather than by design, the *Deutschland* had become the first of Hitler's battleships!

German propagandists made much of the special features incorporated into the *Deutschland*'s design which had enabled the builders to keep the completed vessel inside the 10,000-ton Versailles Treaty limitation. The electrically-welded hull, they pointed out, had made a substantial contribution to weight-saving, as, too, had the 56,800 BHP diesel engines — a revolutionary means of propulsion for so large a warship — although, in reality, all three pocket-battleships suffered continual engine problems during the war and the power units were not quite so successful as their admirers liked to claim. But although the welded hull helped to reduce the overall displacement, many of the other so-called weight-saving features were little more than a façade designed to conceal the truth. For, in reality, the standard displacement of the *Deutschland* on completion was 11,700 tons — almost 20% in excess of the Treaty Limit — while at full-load she displaced a massive 15,900 tons. But the propaganda and flood of false statistics achieved the desired aim and it was not until 1945, when the war was over, that the Allies discovered the extent to which the proverbial wool had been pulled over their eyes.

It can be argued that the Allies themselves were in part to blame for the deceit because of the totally unrealistic restrictions which they imposed on the German navy in the Peace Treaty. Indeed the terms of the Versailles Treaty provided Hitler with a grievance which he could exploit and with which the German people could identify. And, closing their eyes to the violent anarchy of the SA stormtroopers and the growing brutality of Hitler's anti-Jewish pogroms, the German electorate pushed the Nazi vote up to 6,409,600 in the 1930 election — a victory that won them the second most powerful single block of deputies in Germany's parliament.

The *Reichsmarine* failed to enjoy similar success. In 1928, when the first political steps were being taken to obtain the *Reichstag*'s approval for the *Deutschland*, a financial scandal erupted. It was not a matter of individual corruption or the lining of personal pockets. But it involved a high-level conspiracy to conceal from parliament the true destination of monies voted for the use of both the army and the navy — funds which were urgently needed for the clandestine purchase of arms from Italy and secret development work on projects forbidden by the terms of the Treaty. As a result the Defence Minister, Otto Gessler, and Admiral Zenker were forced to resign and Raeder, waiting in the wings as C-in-C Baltic, was appointed Head of the Navy, a post he was to hold for the next fourteen years.

The son of a public school headmaster, Erich Raeder was born at Wandsbeck near Hamburg on 24 April, 1876, and, joining the Imperial Navy in 1894, had been commissioned as a Sub-Lieutenant in 1897. After service at sea in various ships, he was appointed to the Information Section as a Press Officer where his experiences in handling reporters and foreign journalists taught him the value of good public relations — a lesson he was never to forget throughout his long years of service to the Fatherland. His next appointment as the navigating officer of the Kaiser's yacht *Hohenzollern* in 1911 brought him into close contact with courtiers, leading politicians and admirals, and gave him the self-confidence necessary to mix easily in the highest circles of state. By 1913 he had become Chief Staff Officer to Admiral Hipper, the C-in-C of the High Seas Fleet's elite Scouting Force and, as such, he took part in both the Dogger Bank action and the Battle of Jutland — privately expressing a personal view that the latter had been a strategic defeat for Germany.

Raeder was a strict disciplinarian and was not particularly popular with the junior officers and enlisted men he commanded in the Baltic Fleet where he gained a ribald notoriety with an Order of the Day which 'prohibited officers' wives from bobbing or shingling their hair, using rouge or other cosmetics, wearing short skirts, or having [painted] fingernails'.* Later, in 1937, he issued other unpopular orders which imposed strict closing times for officers' canteens together with a ban on drinking in public bars and smoking when in uniform. He was nevertheless well-liked by his senior colleagues and, despite his arrogant and dictatorial manner, venerated by his personal staff. At heart Raeder was a simple kindly man whose patriotic

* *Hitler's Generals*, W.E Hart, Cresset Press, 1944.

loyalty to Germany blinded him to the evils of Nazism. Although he was a devout Christian, he did not consider it to be his duty to make moral judgements on matters of state policy. As an officer 'he obeyed orders as strictly as he demanded obedience from others'* and when Hitler ordered total war Raeder obeyed without question. It was an excuse that found little favour with the judges at the Nuremberg War Crimes tribunal who, after considering the evidence, ruled him guilty of waging a war of aggression. It was a sad end to an otherwise brilliant career.

By the time Adolf Hitler became Chancellor on 30 January, 1933, the construction of Germany's new navy was gaining momentum. The *Deutschland* was about to join the fleet; her sister-ship *Admiral Scheer*, laid down in 1931 and launched on 1 April, 1933, would be in service by November, 1934; while the *Admiral Graf Spee* was scheduled for completion in January, 1936. Five modern light cruisers, *Emden*, *Köln*, *Königsberg*, *Karlsruhe* and *Leipzig*, were already in commission with a sixth, *Nürnberg*, to follow in 1935. In addition twelve 900-ton destroyers had been completed and, although the Navy still possessed no U-boats of its own, German designers were busily producing submarines in foreign yards for the Finnish and Turkish navies and gaining valuable experience in the process.

Raeder met Hitler for the first time on 2 February, 1933, when the recently appointed Chancellor made a two-hour speech to senior officers from both services in the course of which he promised that, under his leadership, Germany would launch a massive programme of rearmament. And, in a private conversation with Raeder after the main meeting had ended, he assured the Admiral that 'under no circumstances would he contemplate war with Britain, Italy, or Japan'.** Raeder was favourably impressed with Germany's new Chancellor and expressed himself as being surprised by Hitler's wide-ranging grasp of naval affairs. Nevertheless, both men accepted that the Nazi leader lacked any practical knowledge of sea warfare and, in the first few years of their professional relationship, the Führer was more than willing to seek, and rely upon, the Admiral's advice on matters relating to maritime strategy.

Hitler paid his first official visit to the fleet at Kiel in May, 1933, and no doubt swayed by Raeder's enthusiasm, subsequently gave his approval to the inclusion of a fifth pocket-battleship — a fourth had already been authorized by the *Reichstag* — in the 1934 naval programme. There were, however, certain areas of disagreement. Raeder favoured a main armament of 15-inch

* *Hitler and his Admirals*, Anthony K. Martienssen, Secker & Warburg, 1948, p 159.

** *Struggle for the Sea*, Grand Admiral Erich Raeder, William Kimber, 1959, p 63.

guns while Hitler, politically sensitive to world opinion and still uncertain of his personal position, realized that this was not the moment for open defiance and refused to allow the use of any weapons larger than the 11-inch calibre permitted by the Treaty, although he was seemingly prepared to countenance an increase in displacement substantially in excess of the Versailles limits.

Even so, he decided to keep the construction of the additional fifth vessel, Battleship E, secret. During a meeting on 27 June, 1934, he chided Raeder for publicly referring to the proposed 26,000-ton displacement of the two new ships — their construction having by that time been announced — and advised him to refer to them as 'improved 10,000-ton ships' in future speeches. Finally, and although he did not fully concur with his senior naval adviser's recommendations, he agreed that the two projected ships should mount a third turret — an addition that would give them a 50% increase in firepower over the earlier under-gunned pocket-battleships.

In April, 1934, and prior to this latter meeting, the *Deutschland* earned herself a special place in Nazi iconography when she provided the backdrop to a secret deal between Hitler and Germany's armed services — an agreement referred to in Party history as the '*Deutschland* Pact'. Hitler and leading members of the Nazi party, General Werner von Blomberg, the Defence Minister and Commander-in-Chief of the *Oberkommando der Wehrmacht* or *OKW*, and a number of other top-ranking officers, had assembled on board the battleship to observe a set-piece military exercise in the western Baltic. Taking advantage of the opportunity, Hitler called them all together in the *Deutschland*'s spacious conference cabin and asked for the support of the armed forces in his bid to succeed to the Presidency of the Reich when the ailing 87-year-old von Hindenburg died — an event expected within a matter of weeks. In return he offered to reduce the strength of his private brown-shirt army, the SA, by two-thirds and to guarantee that in future only the army and the navy would have authority to bear arms.

Seizing the chance to rid the nation of the hated stormtroopers, Raeder accepted the offer without hesitation, although the more cautious General von Fritsch first sought the approval of his fellow generals before throwing the weight of the army behind Hitler's ambitions. The political agreement which the Nazi leader had obtained on board the *Deutschland* was the final constitutional hurdle. When von Hindenburg died in August Hitler was able to combine the two principal offices of state, those of President and Chancellor, to become the undisputed Führer of the Reich — an accession that bestowed upon him the absolute dictatorial powers he needed in his quest for world supremacy. Swept off their feet by Hitler's mesmeric oratory, none of the officers seated around the table realized that, in due course, Hitler's black-uniformed bodyguard, the Waffen SS, would pose a far greater threat to the freedom of the ordinary German citizen than the brawling SA thugs ever had. By the time they came to their senses it was too late.

1934 also witnessed the launch of the *Admiral Graf Spee*, the last of Germany's trio of pocket-battleships. Raeder was present at the ceremony on 30 June at the *Marinewerft* shipyard in Wilhemshaven and the launch itself was performed by the late Vice-Admiral Graf von Spee's daughter, Fraulein Huberta von Spee. But even while the celebratory champagne corks were popping in Wilhelmshaven the purge of the SA, which Hitler had promised the generals at the meeting on board the *Deutschland*, had begun. More than 150 SA leaders were rounded up on the orders of Hermann Goering and Heinrich Himmler and, lined up against a wall, were shot by SS firing-squads. The precise number of persons murdered was never officially revealed but several historians have placed the total as being in excess of a thousand. Among the victims was the Führer's one-time closest associate, Ernst Roehm, who had been one of the original seven members of the German Workers' Party in 1919. As Raeder himself was to discover many years later, loyalty and friendship offered little protection once the Führer had decided on a particular course of action.

Although Hitler continued to espouse the cause of peace, his growing stranglehold on the German political system increased his hunger for power. And the navy, now known as the *Kriegsmarine* or War Fleet, was among the first to benefit. The keel plates of the 31,800-ton Battleship D (*Scharnhorst*) were laid down at Wilhelmshaven's naval dockyard in March, 1935, to be followed, two months later, by those of the still-secret Battleship E (*Gneisenau*) at the *Deutsche Werke* in Kiel. Both, of course, had been authorized in total defiance of the 10,000-ton displacement limit which was still legally in force.

They turned out to be excellent and handsome vessels armed with nine 11-inch and twelve 5.9-inch guns with fourteen 4.1-inch AA weapons — the latter supplemented by sixteen 37-mm semi-automatic pom-poms. In addition each ship mounted six torpedo tubes and carried four floatplanes with two launching catapults. Fed by twelve Wagner boilers, the 160,000 SHP Brown-Boveri geared turbines were capable of powering the vessels at a maximum of 32 knots — although they proved to be disappointingly unreliable in service. Nevertheless, as the coming conflict was to demonstrate, they were tough ships capable of absorbing considerable punishment from torpedoes, shells, mines and bombs, without impairment of their fighting ability.

On 16 March, a few days before the *Scharnhorst*'s keel was laid, Hitler publicly proclaimed Germany's repudiation of the Versailles Treaty and the introduction of compulsory military service. At the same time he officially established the *Luftwaffe* whose ambitious commander, Hermann Goering, promptly upset Raeder by claiming that 'everything that flies' came under his control — including naval aviation.

Raeder had shown himself equally ready to ride roughshod over the Treaty as early as November, 1934, when he suggested that six U-boats which had already been partially prefabricated abroad should be brought back to Germany for assembly. Hitler initially vetoed the proposal but apparently withdrew his objections some time later and the project was soon underway behind the locked doors of three heavily-guarded sheds at the *Deutsche Werke* in Kiel.

By 1935 the diplomatic climate was more encouraging and, even before Hitler's repudiation of the Treaty, both Britain and France had expressed a willingness to renegotiate its terms. Although the British government lodged a half-hearted protest when it received details of Hitler's speech of 16 March, it nevertheless suggested that talks should take place with the object of agreeing a jointly acceptable basis for German rearmament. On 25 March Sir John Simon, the British Foreign Secretary, together with Anthony Eden, met Hitler in Berlin. The German dictator surprised his guests by voluntarily offering to limit the strength of Germany's new fleet to 35% of that of the Royal Navy — an offer which the British Government was happy to accept in recompense for the failure of earlier diplomatic efforts with other countries, notably France and Japan, to control naval armaments.

Events moved rapidly in the wake of the meeting and the Anglo-German Naval Treaty was signed in London on 18 June, 1935. In addition to the general 35% limitation already agreed in Berlin, there were special provisions for submarine construction. Germany was to be allowed parity with the Royal Navy's underwater fleet, but, somewhat curiously, she accepted that the *Kriegsmarine*'s submarine force would not exceed 45% of British tonnage unless the situation warranted an increase to full parity. If such circumstances were to arise further talks would be held.

Raeder regarded the treaty as 'a great success for us'* for it bestowed British approval on Hitler's unilateral renunciation of the Treaty. But the underlying hypocrisy of Hitler's diplomacy and the ruthless nature of the Nazi rearmament programme was starkly exposed on 28 June when, just ten days after the London naval agreement had been signed, the first U-boat was commissioned at Kiel — tangible and indisputable proof that

* *Struggle for the Sea*, p 52.

Germany had been building the nucleus of its new underwater fleet in secret for many months and a fact carefully concealed from the British during the treaty negotiations.

'Today is the happiest day of my life,'* Hitler had told Raeder when a telephone call from London confirmed that the Treaty had been ratified. And the C-in-C of the *Kriegsmarine*, accepting the Führer's statement at face value, regarded it as a further confirmation of Hitler's frequently professed peaceful intentions towards Britain. Indeed, Raeder believed so implicitly that war with England was impossible that he would not permit the naval staff to include any reference to Britain as a potential future enemy when they were drawing up the scenarios for their war-game exercises. And when, on 27 May, 1936, the fleet's contingency war plans were issued, British involvement was specifically left out of account. According to Hitler only France and Russia were Germany's enemies. Raeder was content to accept the dictator's assurance without question.

Germany soon took advantage of her new freedom to build and the *Kriegsmarine*'s first full-sized battleship, *Bismarck*, was authorized as part of the 1935 construction programme. Her maximum displacement was announced as being 35,000 tons, in line with the five *King George V*-class battleships which the Royal Navy was preparing to lay down.** In reality it was 41,700 tons. When it came to deceit it was clear that the Nazis had nothing to learn from their predecessors in the Weimar government. Finally, on 9 July, Berlin officially confirmed that the *Scharnhorst* and the hitherto secret *Gneisenau* were already under construction.

By January of 1936 there were twelve U-boats in commission with *Kapitan zur See* Karl Dönitz — last encountered as the commander of the torpedo boat *T-157* at Kiel in 1920 — as Commander-in-Chief U-boats (*Befehlshaber der Unterseebootes* or *BdU*). And later that year the *Reichstag*, by now no more than a compliant tool of the Nazi machine, authorized the construction of Hitler's seventh battleship, the *Tirpitz*. Once again her announced standard displacement was 35,000 tons. And, once again, the figure was handsomely exceeded — topping even that of the *Bismarck* at 42,900 tons. Both battleships, as was only to be expected, were magnificent vessels combining heavy armour with high speed. And the 15-inch guns making up their main armament ensured that they had nothing to fear from any other contemporary capital ship.

---

* Quoted in *Hitler's Naval War*, Cajus Bekker, Doubleday, New York, 1974, p 26.
** For various technical and legal reasons Germany was not subject to the 35,000-ton displacement limit which had been accepted by all major naval powers with the exception of Japan following the expiry of the 1921 Washington Treaty.

The outbreak of the Spanish Civil War on 18 July, 1936, threw the regular peacetime programmes of exercises, training cruises and routing visits to friendly neighbours to show the flag into turmoil. In fact the *Graf Spee* was on her way back to Wilhemshaven after a shake-down cruise to the Canary Islands where General Franco, the Islands' governor, had been received on board the pocket-battleship as an honoured guest, when an insurrection in Spanish Morocco triggered the conflict. According to his memoirs Raeder was initially in favour of sending warships to Spain to protect German interests — as indeed did other nations, notably Britain, France and Italy — but Hitler had reservations and feared that a chance provocation could provoke an international incident. However, guided by Raeder's advice, he gave his consent to the plan and on 23 July Vice-Admiral Rolf Carls sailed for the war zone with the pocket-battleships *Deutschland* and *Admiral Scheer*.

Eighteen days later the communist-controlled Spanish government declared a blockade of rebel-held ports and on 20 August a Republican cruiser, the *Libertad*, stopped the German freighter *Kamerun* at sea in breach of International Law. Raeder's response was to ask Hitler whether Germany intended to support Franco's insurgents by breaking the blockade. At the same time he warned the Führer that untoward action could easily lead to a general European war, although he insisted that, if support was to be given, 'it must be carried out effectively'.

Any doubts which Hitler may have entertained were resolved when Franco was proclaimed Head of the National Government — a somewhat presumptuous act with the outcome of the war far from decided — and both Germany and Italy promptly recognized his administration. Equally promptly Soviet Russia and France announced their continued support for the Republican government. With the gauntlet down all four nations openly backed their own favoured factions with force of arms. Britain meanwhile maintained a strictly impartial stance, although Raeder noted that 'some British naval officers made no secret of their sympathy with General Franco'. On one noteworthy occasion three foreign warships which were lying at anchor at Palma were asked to leave the harbour before Republican ships carried out a bombardment of the port. Britain's Vice-Admiral Sir James Somerville happened to be the senior officer present and, flying his flag in the cruiser *Galatea*, he led the *Deutschland* and the Italian destroyer *Marocello* out to sea where he manoeuvred the three vessels as a single squadron.

When the ships subsequently returned to harbour Somerville issued an appreciative signal to his two foreign colleagues: 'The station-keeping, signalling, and manoeuvring of the International Squadron has aroused my warmest admiration.' To which Vice-Admiral Carls replied: 'When all ships of these three navies would be joined in a squadron like that one today, it would be very good in many ways.' The German Admiral's command of the

English language may have left much to be desired, but no one could fault the sentiment which he expressed.

But Germany's undisguised support for Franco's forces and the sufferings of Spanish refugees fleeing from German and Italian air attacks lost the *Kriegsmarine* much sympathy. Worse was to come when, on 29 May, 1937, the *Deutschland* was heavily bombed by Republican aircraft while anchored off Ibiza — an attack that left 31 sailors dead and a further 78 wounded. Germany's response was a typical example of Nazi brutality. The battleship *Admiral Scheer* was despatched south and, two days later, her 11-inch guns opened fire on the defenceless town of Almeria. Hundreds of civilians died in the bombardment and an estimated 8,000 Spaniards were left homeless; structural damage was estimated at many millions of pounds.

Yet despite public outrage in the left-wing press Britain continued to maintain friendly relations with Germany and even allowed the *Kriegsmarine* to bury the seamen killed on the *Deutschland* in the military cemetery at Gibraltar, although, on Hitler's personal orders, they were later exhumed and returned to the Fatherland as part of a propaganda exercise. A week before the bombing incident the *Graf Spee* represented the Third Reich at the Spithead Coronation Review where her smart appearance and disciplined efficiency brought much favourable comment.

The reconciliation between the two former foes seems to have been genuine enough at government level, although Hitler's ambivalent attitude makes it difficult to assess his private feelings. Certainly at one time he seemed anxious to have Britain as an ally and showed a marked reluctance to become involved in an outright war with England. But this may have been merely a convenient front to conceal his hatred for the nation which had already once thwarted Germany's ambitions for world domination. In Raeder's case, however, it seems clear that he both respected and admired Britain and, in particular, the Royal Navy. When Admiral of the Fleet Earl Jellicoe died on 28 November, 1935, he ordered all ships of the *Kriegsmarine* to fly their flags at half-mast and sent a select group of senior officers to represent the German Navy at the funeral. It is also on record that he kept a framed photograph of Jellicoe on his desk when he worked in the Archives Section. Significantly, he did not accord Beatty a similar place of honour!

The two new vessels, Battleship D and Battleship E, were launched after the outbreak of the Spanish Civil War. The first, *Scharnhorst*, took to the water on Saturday 4 October, 1936, and Field-Marshal Werner von Blomberg made use of the ceremony to deliver an appropriately eulogistic speech: '*Scharnhorst*,' he told a distinguished audience that included both Hitler and Raeder, was 'an emblem of reawakened German prestige on the seas... our first thoughts are owed today to the man to whom we owe the new armed forces and, within them, the new Navy — our Führer and supreme commander. This vessel... is an achievement of Adolf Hitler.' But von Blomberg's deliberate public display of sycophancy proved to be of little avail when in November, 1937, he opposed Hitler's proposed use of force to gain control of Austria and Czechoslovakia. Three months later, on the basis of a trumped-up scandal, he was dismissed from the army and retired into obscurity.

By a strange coincidence Colonel-General Freiherr Werner von Fritsch, the Commander-in-Chief of the army, who delivered the keynote speech at the launching of the *Gneisenau* at Kiel on 8 December, 1936, suffered a similar fall from grace. He had already offended Hitler by his failure to give his immediate agreement to the *Deutschland* pact and he was also one of the generals who supported von Blomberg's objections to the use of force against Austria. Accused of an illicit homosexual relationship by the Gestapo — the charge was, in fact, completely baseless — he was dismissed from the army by Hitler even though he had been acquitted by a specially convened court martial at which both Goering and Raeder served as judges.

This sorry sequence of events still lay in the future, however, when Frau Maerker smashed the traditional bottle of champagne against *Gneisenau*'s bows in the presence of Hitler, Rudolf Hess, von Blomberg and Raeder. But on this particular occasion the customary teutonic efficiency was lacking. The battleship went down the slipway too fast. Two drag chains snapped and she careered across the muddy estuary of Kiel fjord and smashed her stern against a sea wall on the opposite bank. General von Fritsch rose to the occasion, however, and his speech did much to relieve the red-faced embarrassment of the assembled dignitaries.

'Be loyal!' he thundered. 'Let foreigners on their distant shores witness the power and prestige of the Third Reich. Prepare in time of peace for the day of destiny — a day which we do not desire but which will find us ready.' It was all good rabble-rousing stuff, but like von Blomberg's earlier speech at Wilhelmshaven, it was not enough to save the General from Hitler's rage a year later.

Although Raeder wisely kept his mouth shut and thus avoided the same fate as his two army colleagues, he admitted in his memoirs that he was equally upset by Hitler's speech of 5 November when, in the course of a four-hour oration to the leaders of the armed services, the Führer referred to 'those odious enemies, Britain and France'. Goering told him not to take Hitler's words too seriously as they were only intended to create a favourable political climate for Germany's massive rearmament programme. But, in truth, the Führer meant exactly what he had said. And in May of the following year Raeder was summoned to the Chancellery to be informed by Hitler for the first time that Britain was now to be regarded as a future enemy. Then, having delivered his bombshell, the Nazi leader ordered

Raeder to go away and prepare plans for an immediate increase in warship construction.

It was not, of course, as easy as that. There were many matters to be discussed and considered before any building could begin: whether, for example, to produce a balanced fleet capable of meeting the Royal Navy on equal terms in conventional battle, or to construct a force of heavy surface ships to launch an all-out attack on Britain's seaborne commerce, or, perhaps, to concentrate all available resources on a U-boat war. Raeder left the problem to others. He set up a committee under Vice-Admiral Gunther Gruse to consider the options and ordered his youngest staff officer, Commander Hellmuth Heye, to prepare a plan for waging a successful war against the British Empire. Then he sat back and awaited results, content that time was on his side, for the Führer had assured him that the new fleet would not be needed before 1946.

The preliminary groundwork was completed in September and the committee met on the 23rd to consider the first proposal − or Plan X − which comprised an exhaustive schedule of all the ships and logistical facilities needed to make up a balanced fleet. Rear-Admiral Werner Fuchs, the Chief of Naval Construction, hastily poured cold water over the idea by pointing out that the massive numbers envisaged were utterly beyond the capability of Germany's shipbuilding industry. Heye, too, opposed the scheme but for a different reason. He argued that any future Battle of Jutland was unlikely to improve Germany's strategic situation and that, in any event, the prospects for achieving success against Britain with a conventional battle fleet were virtually zero. Heye's conclusion did not please the senior admirals. To expand the navy without building newer and more powerful battleships was tantamount to an act of sacrilege and the young Commander was told to think again.

A second exercise, Plan Y, was considered and rejected and, in October, Heye produced two alternative Z plans each of which was based on a sustained attack on Britain's oceanic trading routes. One version − which enjoyed the twin advantages of being both cheap and quick to implement − proposed a joint operation using pocket-battleships, U-boats, and surface raiders. The other visualized a hard-hitting and fast surface fleet designed to carry out raiding operations against convoys in the Atlantic and merchant shipping anywhere in the world. And as such a fleet must be able to fight its way through the British blockade, it followed that it must consist of the largest and most powerful battleships that Germany could design and build.

The two alternative Z plans were submitted to Raeder on 31 October and, the following day, he placed them before Hitler. The Führer had always favoured battleships, partly because of the mind-blowing impression that *Deutschland*'s 11-inch guns had made upon him the first time he saw them fired during exercises in the Baltic in 1934 and, on a more mundane level, partly because he was less prone to seasickness on larger vessels which were usually more stable. And as a battle-cruiser veteran of the High Seas Fleet Raeder naturally had no hesitation in recommending the alternative big-ship version of the plan. Having repeated his earlier assurance that war with Britain was impossible before 1946, Hitler accepted and approved Raeder's recommendation. There was, he pointed out, adequate time to build the proposed ships.

The Z plan as drawn up by Commander Heye was breathtaking in its scope, for when completed, the expanded German fleet would consist of no fewer than six 56,200-ton battleships each mounting eight 16-inch guns: three 32,300-ton battle-cruisers and two aircraft carriers. The first of these, *Graf Zeppelin*, had been authorized some time earlier and was launched on 8 December, 1938, almost two months before Hitler approved Heye's Z plan. In the event she was never completed – a victim of the power struggle between Raeder and Goering for control of naval aviation – and all work on her was finally suspended in 1943. In addition to these major units, the Z plan also included six light cruisers of 7,800 tons displacement armed with eight 5.9-inch guns, and a number of large and powerful destroyers.

These new vessels were, of course, additional to the three pocket-battleships, the two battle-cruisers and the two battleships already in service or under construction. To increase the firepower of the *Gneisenau* and *Scharnhorst* – the two ships having joined the fleet on 21 May, 1938, and 7 January, 1939, respectively – it was decided to replace their nine 11-inch guns with six 15-inch weapons. However, like the rest of the overly ambitious Z plan, the war came too quickly for the work to be carried out.

The first of Germany's true battleships, *Bismarck*, was launched on 14 February, 1939, but not before Hitler and Raeder had participated in a blazing row the previous November during which the admiral had offered his resignation following the Führer's unfounded criticisms of the new ship's design and combat ability. But all was sweetness and smiles at the launching ceremony at the Blohm & Voss yards at Hamburg at which, in addition to Hitler and Raeder, all the leading members of the Party – Goering, Goebbels, Hess, Ribbentrop, Himmler and Bormann – were present.

This outward display of harmony was, however, more than a little misleading. For although Raeder had accepted Dönitz's demands for 300 U-boats as part and parcel of the Z plan, the two men had differing ideas on the types of submarines to be built and the former had pulled rank to over-ride the U-boat chief's wishes. He had also, in the face of Dönitz's protestations, put all experimental work on the back-burner and accorded it only the lowest priority for resources. The resulting delay in perfecting the hydrogen-peroxide gas turbine was to cost Germany victory in the U-boat war.

There were problems, too, with Goering. In 1935, following the creation of the *Luftwaffe*, Raeder and Goering had agreed that the Naval Aviation Branch should be controlled by the *Kriegsmarine* although the Air Force would provide the machines – a total of sixty-two squadrons comprising more than 700 aircraft to be completed and delivered by 1942. But in January, 1939, the *Luftwaffe* took over all aspects of marine aviation – minelaying, attacks on enemy shipping, reconnaissance, and even the provision of aircraft and crews for the two new carriers. In fact the only branch of the old Naval Air Service which was allowed to remain under the direct control of the *Kriegsmarine* was that responsible for the floatplanes carried by the fleet's battleships and cruisers. And even these were to be supplied, maintained and crewed by the *Luftwaffe*. It was, as events were to demonstrate, a recipe for disaster and it was, in part, to lead to the loss of at least two of the navy's battleships in the war that now lay only months away.

Finally, when Hitler unilaterally abrogated the Anglo-German naval treaty in the course of a speech to the *Reichstag* on 28 April, he did so without any prior consultation with Raeder. Yet, only four weeks earlier and as a token of esteem for the C-in-C of the *Kriegsmarine*, the Führer had promoted him to the rank of Grand Admiral and had once again told the navy chief 'clearly and definitely' that he would do nothing to provoke a war with Britain before completion of the Z plan's construction programme.

The launch of the battleship *Tirpitz* on 1 April, 1939, offered the opportunity to conceal this internal dissent with another public display of solidarity, although, as with the *Scharnhorst* and *Gneisenau*, the main personage involved in the ceremony – in this instance Frau von Hassel, the grand-daughter of Admiral von Tirpitz – suffered a similarly dramatic fall from grace five years later. Frau von Hassel was the wife of Ulrich von Hassel, at one time Germany's Ambassador to Italy, who was executed by the Nazis for his part in the bomb attempt on Hitler's life in July, 1944.

Battleships remained very much in the news in the months leading up to the outbreak of war. The first two 56,200-ton leviathans authorized under the Z plan, Battleships H and J, were laid down respectively at Hamburg on 15 June and Bremen on 15 August. Meanwhile, in a speech to members of the Hitler Youth Movement at Brunswick on 20 May Grand Admiral Raeder had stressed that: 'Battleships alone are able to win or defend the supremacy of the seas' – a boast clearly intended to provoke both Goering and Dönitz.

But it was not all rhetoric and ceremony. On 18 April the *Graf Spee* and the *Deutschland* — the latter having just returned to the fleet after taking a very sea-sick Adolf Hitler to Lithuania to make a triumphal entry into the newly annexed city of Memel on 23 March — together with three cruisers and a flotilla of destroyers, sailed for a spring cruise in the Atlantic. Significantly, in the light of Raeder's strategic plan to attack British seaborne commerce in the event of war, five days were to pass before the Royal Navy realized that the German ships were at sea. They were first sighted, not by a warship or a reconnaissance aircraft, but by a cross-Channel steamer peacefully wending its way from Dover to Calais.

Raeder, confidently convinced that war between Germany and Britain was unlikely before 1944 at the very earliest, allowed the *Gneisenau* to proceed into the Atlantic for a shakedown cruise with only practice ammunition in her magazines and, during the same month, gave approval for Commodore Friedrich Ruge, the leader of the *Kriegsmarine*'s minesweeping forces, to go on extended leave. Even more remarkably, on the conclusion of the annual U-boat exercises in the Baltic, which he attended in person, he raised no objections when Dönitz proposed to go on holiday as well.

In a speech to U-boat officers on 22 July to mark the end of the Baltic exercises, Raeder repeated that he had the Führer's personal assurance that there would be no war with Britain in the near future. This, of course, did not mean that he was unaware of the planned attack on Poland for he had, like the other service chiefs, seen Hitler's directive of 11 April which set out the details of *Fall Weiss*, the operational codename for the assault, scheduled for 1 September. But, mesmerized by the Führer, he believed implicitly that neither France nor England would respond to Germany's military actions in the east.

That, at least, was Raeder's story as recounted to the judges at Nuremberg and in his memoirs. But certain shipping movements in August scarcely support his plea of lily-white innocence. For the battleship *Graf Spee* left Wilhelmshaven on 21 August, followed, three days later, by the *Deutschland*. Both vessels, fully stored and ammunitioned, were under orders to proceed to their war stations and, on arrival, to await further instructions. At the same time the supply ships *Altmark* and *Westerwald* were directed into the Atlantic in a support role. According to Raeder, the dispositions were a normal part of contingency planning. But the secrecy shrouding the movements of the ships concerned once they had left port suggested a more sinister purpose.

Nevertheless, in a speech to senior generals and admirals at Obersalzberg on 22 August Hitler did not see fit to amend his opinion on British involvement. 'England's position is much too precarious,' he told them confidently. 'I believe it is impossible that a responsible English statesman, given this situation [the use of force against Poland], would incur the risk of war.' It was a political miscalculation that was ultimately to destroy the Third Reich.

But despite the smokescreen of excuses put forward by the Führer, Raeder and many pro-Nazi historians, the fact remains that one of Hitler's battleships, the *Graf Spee*, sailed for her war station ten clear days before the first German soldier crossed the Polish border. And of the 1124 officers and men who waved farewell to their relatives and friends standing on the quayside at Wilhemshaven that morning 38, including the battleship's commanding officer Captain Hans Langsdorff, would never see the Fatherland again.

CHAPTER TWO

'Battleships Are Supposed To Shoot ...'

DESPITE THE GRANDIOSE ambitions of the Z plan the *Kriegsmarine* entered the war with only four battleships fit for operational service: the *Deutschland, Admiral Graf Spee, Scharnhorst* and *Gneisenau.* The *Bismarck* and *Tirpitz* were still fitting-out, while the *Admiral Scheer* was at Wilhemshaven undergoing a lengthy overhaul and reconstruction following months of intractable engine problems. The two giant, and as yet unnamed, 56,200-tonners had scarcely progressed beyond the laying of their keel plates.

The shortage of first-line heavy ships led to the gunnery-training vessel *Schleswig-Holstein* – one of the original eight battleships retained by the *Reichsmarine* under the Treaty of Versailles – being returned to combat service and despatched to the Baltic to provide inshore support to the army as it advanced into Poland. On the very first day of the war, 1 September, her ancient 11-inch guns opened fire on the Polish fortress of Westerplatte and she maintained her relentless bombardment until the 7th when the shell-shocked defenders finally surrendered. Then, having been joined by the *Schlesien*, Germany's other surviving pre-Dreadnought battleship, the two vessels carried out a series of devastating bombardments on troop concentrations and defensive positions at Oxhoft, Ostrowogrund and Hexengrund, before moving on to support the final offensive against the Polish army in the Hela peninsula. By the end of the month their task had been accomplished and, like elderly workhorses being pensioned off to pasture, the two veteran warships returned to Germany to resume their unglamorous careers as harbour service and training ships.

According to Raeder* who had been summoned to the Reich Chancellery on the morning of 3 September and informed that Britain and France had declared war on Germany, Hitler was embarrassed by his misjudgement of the British response to Germany's attack on Poland and admitted apologetically, 'I was not able to avoid war with England after all'.

The Führer would have been even more embarrassed had he seen the

* *Struggle for the Sea*, p 133.

private memorandum that Raeder was to write later the same day. For, having placed on record Hitler's repeated assurances that war against Britain was unlikely before 1944 the Grand Admiral observed bluntly: 'The surface forces [of the German Navy] are so inferior in numbers and power to those of the British fleet that, even at full strength, they can do no more than show that they know how to die gallantly.' He concluded: 'The pocket-battleships ... can never play a decisive part in the outcome of the conflict.'

The RAF wasted little time in coming to grips with its old adversary and on 4 September, less than 24 hours after Raeder had attended the Chancellery to see Hitler, a force of Blenheims arrived over Wilhemshaven where the *Admiral Scheer* was lying at anchor in the Schillig Roads. The planned high-level bombing attack had to be aborted at the last minute due to weather conditions and the first five machines, all from 110 Squadron, were forced to approach at low altitude.

Coming in at masthead height, they caught the Germans by surprise and scored one direct hit with three near misses, two of their 500-pound GP bombs actually striking the deck of the *Scheer* before bouncing off into the water. Unfortunately all of the bombs that hit the ship failed to explode and the battleship suffered no damage. One machine from the first wave was lost to German flak. The five Blenheims of 107 Squadron that followed were denied the advantage of surprise and the anti-aircraft defences sent four of the machines crashing into the sea, a foretaste of the *Kriegsmarine*'s gunnery expertise which was, at the beginning of the war, immeasurably superior to that of the Royal Navy. One of the lost machines, however, achieved a modicum of involuntary success in its dying moments. Hit by anti-aircraft gunfire from the cruiser *Hipper*, the Blenheim cartwheeled in flames into the bows of the *Emden*, killing a dozen German seamen in addition to its own three-man crew.

Nine Wellingtons also reached Brunsbüttel and attempted to launch a high-level attack on the *Scharnhorst* and *Gneisenau* which were moored to buoys in the River Elbe. But, intercepted by fighters, they failed to hit their targets and two bombers were shot down by the *Luftwaffe*. Although the *Kriegsmarine* was more than satisfied with the 23.3% loss rate inflicted on the enemy the raids had exposed an unexpected threat. For it was now apparent that, unlike the High Seas Fleet in the First World War, Germany's battleships were no longer able to escape attack by remaining in harbour. And, as the war progressed, Raeder was to discover to his cost that no hiding place was safe from the long arm of the Royal Air Force.

For the moment, however, there were no more raids. Chastened by the heavy losses, Bomber Command held back from launching further attacks on naval bases while its experts assessed the problem. The next raid, on 29 September, was against warships at sea off Heligoland when six Hampden bombers made an abortive attack on a pair of destroyers without loss. But a second wave of five aircraft from 144 Squadron was intercepted by Messerschmitt fighters and every machine was shot down. Faced by such slaughter, the RAF abandoned daylight raids on warships in defended anchorages and inshore waters and nearly five months were to pass before Bomber Command tried again, this time under cover of darkness.

The *Graf Spee*, which had cleared Wilhelmshaven on 21 August, was already off Bergen two days later, and, using a convenient fog to conceal her movements, she swung south and increased speed. Forging ahead in the worsening weather, her bows dug deep into the cresting waves, and a maelstrom of tumbling green seas surged down her fo'c'sle to crash against the breakwater protecting her forward 11-inch gun turret, sending up a wall of icy-cold spray that blinded the bridge lookouts. But, undeterred by the conditions, *Kapitan zur See* Hans Langsdorff, the *Graf Spee*'s 45-year old commanding officer who had succeeded Konrad Patzig, the vessel's first captain, in 1938, maintained speed and held to his southerly course.

By 25 August the battleship had passed east of Iceland to enter the North Atlantic. But the storm still showed no sign of abating and, during the forenoon watch, the *Graf Spee* suffered the trauma of losing a man overboard. The heavy seas made it impossible to launch a boat. Although Langsdorff turned back and spent more than three hours vainly quartering the area he was finally forced to abandon the search at dusk. The unfortunate victim, Bosun's Mate Matzke, had become the *Kriegsmarine*'s first official war casualty, six days before the outbreak of hostilities.

The *Deutschland* and her supply ship passed through the Denmark Strait into the Atlantic on 28 August and the two vessels reached their assigned waiting area as the first Panzer units were rolling over the Polish border on 1 September. On the same day the *Graf Spee* rendezvoused with her own supply ship, the *Altmark*, and replenished her bunkers before continuing south. The next forty-eight hours passed without incident but at 11 am GMT on the 3rd the battleship's radio room picked up the signal GERMANY TOTAL from the British Admiralty's transmitting station at Rugby, a coded warning to all Royal Navy ships that a state of war now existed with Hitler's Germany. And the interception was confirmed a short while later when Langsdorff, no stranger to war and a veteran of Jutland where he had served on the *Grosser Kurfürst*, received a signal from the *Kriegsmarine*'s radio link at Nauen, near Berlin. He was also instructed, at the same time, not to attack ships flying the French flag, British vessels apparently being considered fair game.

At this stage of the conflict Hitler was still hopeful of concluding peace with both Britain and France, and on 5 September, as part of a plan to avoid the dangers of any untoward incidents, the *SKL* instructed Langsdorff not to attack *any* shipping — British, French or Polish — and to withdraw the *Graf Spee* away from the main trade routes into an area of the Atlantic where contact with other vessels was unlikely. *Deutschland*'s captain, Paul Wennecker, received a similar signal and was told to remain hidden from sight among the ice floes of the Arctic.

Refuelling continued at intervals as the *Graf Spee* moved south and, each time the battleship stopped to take on oil from the *Altmark*, her Arado floatplane was catapulted off to guard against a surprise encounter with British patrols. After topping-up her bunkers on the 6th the battleship crossed the equator two days later when Langsdorff unwisely neglected to pay the traditional tribute to King Neptune and his Court by organizing the customary ceremonies to celebrate 'crossing the line' and entering the southern hemisphere. It was a slight for which the oceanic monarch was to exact a bloody revenge in due time.

Langsdorff's caution in flying-off *Graf Spee*'s aircraft yielded dividends on the 11th when it sighted the British cruiser *Cumberland* steaming to join Commodore Henry Harwood's squadron which was patrolling off the estuary of the River Plate. *Oberleutnant* Spiering, the floatplane's naval observer — its pilot was a *Luftwaffe* officer — sent an urgent warning back to the ship and Langsdorff was able to avoid contact with the enemy vessel. The *Cumberland*, whose lookouts had failed to see the tiny dot of the Arado in the sky, maintained course and speed, her captain unaware that he had been within striking distance of the raider.

The *Graf Spee* had by now assumed the guise of her sister-ship *Admiral Scheer*, the similarity in design of the three pocket-battleships making such changes in identity a simple matter. Indeed, when the *Graf Spee* and the *Deutschland* first began claiming victims several weeks were to elapse before the British realized that there was not one, but *two*, raiders loose in the Atlantic.

Finally, on 26 September, the *SKL* in Berlin transmitted radio orders to both battleships instructing them to resume combat operations, a direct result of Raeder constantly badgering the Führer to strike while the iron was hot and before the enemy had fully implemented his convoy system. The new policy was also due in part to Hitler's realization that his tortuous diplomatic initiative to achieve a peace agreement with Britain and France over the Polish question had failed.

Langsdorff knew that there would be an abundance of worthwhile targets among the homeward-bound freighters and cargo liners sailing from the Plate estuary with their holds crammed full with frozen meat and grain. Like a terrier scenting a rabbit, he turned the battleship westwards.

The *Graf Spee* found her first victim shortly before 11.30 on the morning of 30 September when she encountered the 5,051-ton Booth Line steamer *Clement* off Bahia. Hoisting the blue and yellow flag denoting the letter *K* in the international alphabet − the code for *Stop Immediately* − she closed the vessel while her Arado floatplane circled overhead and machine-gunned the bridge by way of gentle persuasion. Captain Harris, the *Clement*'s Master, initially confused the battleship's single smokestack with that of the British cruiser *Ajax* which he knew was in South American waters. But the blood-red Nazi ensign flying from the *Graf Spee*'s stern quickly exposed his mistake. Realizing that resistance was futile, he ordered the *Clement*'s crew to abandon ship and instructed his radio operator to transmit an urgent distress signal.

Many writers have accused Langsdorff of violating the Pan-American Security Zone which banned any warlike acts inside an area extending up to 600 miles from the American continent's coasts. But this is an unjustified charge. The conference at Panama at which delegates from twenty-one American republics authorized the establishment of the exclusion zone was not convened until 3 October. At the time of the *Clement* incident the German battleship's movements were only circumscribed by the universal three-mile limit of territorial waters laid down by International Law.

The captain and chief engineer of the *Clement* were taken back to the battleship where Langsdorff greeted them with a salute and a handshake before sending the engineer to the ship's hospital for medical attention to a bullet wound in his hand. Then, turning to Captain Harris, he said apologetically, 'I am sorry that I have to do this, but I must sink your ship.' He shrugged sympathetically: 'It is war.'

What followed proved to be something of an embarrassing anti-climax. The *Graf Spee* fired two torpedoes, both of which missed. She then opened fire with her main secondary armament with results that were only marginally better. According to Commander Rasenack, the raider's ordnance officer, despite being presented with a sitting target the battleship's gunners demonstrated a surprising ineptitude and it took a total of five 11-inch shells and twenty-five rounds of 5.9-inch to send the unfortunate steamer to the bottom. But, despite the loss of his ship, the *Clement*'s captain showed no animosity towards Langsdorff whom he described as a fine sailor of the best type − a man of innate decency'.* It is now conceded that the brutal machine-gun attack on the defenceless merchant ship was carried out by the seaplane's *Luftwaffe* pilot without Langsdorff's authority.

Although Captain Harris and his Chief Engineer were retained on board the *Graf Spee* as the battleship moved eastwards away from the scene, the crew of the *Clement* were left to fend for themselves in the ship's lifeboats.

* *The Battle of the Plate*, A.B Campbell, Herbert Jenkins, 1940, p 33.

But they were not far from the South American coast, the weather was good, and an officer from the *Graf Spee*, having checked their water and provisions, gave them a course to steer. Five hours later the battleship intercepted the Greek steamer *Papelemos* and Langsdorff transferred his two prisoners to the neutral ship after first extracting a solemn promise from her master to maintain radio silence until his vessel reached the Cape Verde Islands.

One of the *Clement*'s boats was subsequently picked up by the Brazilian *Itatinga*, the survivors landing at Maceio on 1 October, and the rest of the crew arrived safely the following day. News of the sinking was promptly flashed to London but the signal caused considerable confusion at the Admiralty because the survivors had reported the raider as being the *Admiral Scheer*. For the time being, however, it was enough to know that a raider was loose in the Atlantic and by 5 October, in co-operation with the French navy, a total of eight powerful hunting groups had been formed to track down the battleship, still wrongly, if understandably, identified as the *Admiral Scheer*, while two Home Fleet capital ships were detached to bolster the escort forces covering the homeward-bound convoys from Halifax, Nova Scotia. Raeder's shrewd prophecy that one or two well-armed raiders could virtually tie up an entire fleet of enemy ships, an assessment he had arrived at while studying the records in the archives section in the early 'twenties, was already proving to be well-founded.

Realizing that he had aroused a hornet's nest with his attack on the *Clement*, Langsdorff prudently shifted to a new operational area off the coast of West Africa where, on 5 October, he stopped the 4,651-ton *Newton Beech*. Although his victim succeeded in transmitting a distress signal before the *Graf Spee*'s boarding party could silence her radio the weak and fading call was only picked up by one other ship, who in turn, passed it visually to the *Cumberland* some hours later. However, for various reasons the cruiser did not repeat the SOS to naval HQ at Freetown and the C-in-C South Atlantic, Vice-Admiral D'Oyly Lyon, was unaware that a German raider was operating on his doorstep.

With an armed boarding-party in control of the freighter, Langsdorff decided to retain her in company for the time being for use as an accommodation ship. So, with the captured vessel trailing astern, the *Graf Spee* set off in search of another victim, a task made all the easier by the treasure trove of confidential Sailing Instructions and other Admiralty documents which the Germans had found on the freighter. From these Langsdorff learned that distress calls were prefixed *R-R-R* if the vessel was under attack by a surface raider; *S-S-S* if her assailant were a U-boat; and *A-A-A* in the case of an aircraft. Even more importantly the papers showed that all distress calls were acknowledged with the prefix *CT*. This vital piece of intelligence meant that the battleship's team of civilian *B-Dienst* experts could monitor the appropriate British naval wavelengths and warn him if shore stations had picked up his victim's signals.

Two days later, in the early morning of 7 October, the *Graf Spee* met up with the 4,222 ton *Ashlea* and boarded her. Having removed the crew to safety, the unfortunate freighter and her cargo of raw sugar was despatched to the bottom by means of demolition charges, a more economical and efficient method of destruction than gunfire. On the 9th the *Graf Spee* rendezvoused with the *Altmark* and, having first replenished the battleship's depleted bunkers, the crews from the two British vessels were transferred to the supply ship for safe keeping. At the same time, because its heavy funnel smoke made it something of a liability when the element of surprise was all-important, the *Newton Beech* was scuttled. Langsdorff had so far certainly enjoyed an amazing run of good luck and he had every reason to be satisfied with the results of the *Graf Spee*'s first ten days of active operation. Three ships had been destroyed but, even better, the enemy had not only no clear idea of where he was, they were even uncertain *who* he was. As Commander Rasenack observed, it had been 'an excellent beginning'.

The *Deutschland* also claimed her first victim on 5 October, the day that the *Graf Spee* had seized the *Newton Beech*, and this had added to the uncertainty and confusion in London. Like her sister-ship, the *Deutschland* had been unleashed on 30 September and was soon prowling the main shipping route between Bermuda and the Azores. She had intercepted the 5,044-ton cargo ship *Stonegate* some 5,600 miles east of Bermuda, but the British vessel, despite the threat of the battleship's guns, valiantly transmitted an *R-R-R* distress signal before the *Deutschland* opened fire and sank her. Realizing that the SOS would bring British warships hotfoot to the scene Captain Wennecker wasted no time and, almost before the *Stonegate* had disappeared beneath the waves, the pocket-battleship was already steering north at high speed in search of fresh victims.

The presence of two raiders, even if their precise identity was a matter of conjecture, running amok in the Atlantic was bad enough, but on 8 October Raeder compounded the British Admiralty's problems by sending Admiral Hermann Boehm on a provocative sortie towards Norway with the *Gneisenau*, the cruiser *Köln*, and nine destroyers. The *Scharnhorst*, who should have accompanied her sister on the operation, remained behind in Kiel where she was undergoing remedial surgery on her chronically troublesome high-pressure boilers. An RAF Coastal Command aircraft sighted the squadron the next day and, alarmed by the unexpected appearance of enemy surface units so close to home, Admiral Sir Charles

Forbes hurried his fleet to sea to intercept. But the *Gneisenau* and her flock were safely back at their moorings at Wilhelmshaven by the time the Home Fleet had left Scapa Flow and as Forbes' ships headed out into the North Sea they came under heavy air attack from the *Luftwaffe*. Happily no damage was done but the British admiral was sufficiently worried by the strength and determination of the German Air Force that he took the fleet back to Loch Ewe, out of range of enemy bombers, leaving only the *Royal Oak* to return to Scapa. Five days later the 29,150-ton battleship was torpedoed and sunk by Gunther Prien's *U-47* with the loss of 833 lives.

The sortie also led to repercussions on the German side of the North Sea, repercussions that were a direct result of the somewhat bizarre command structure which Raeder had instituted shortly before the war. Overall control of naval operations was vested in the *Seekriegsleitung*, the Supreme Naval Staff or *SKL*, based in the Admiralty building on Berlin's *Tirpitzufer* which, in turn, received its directions from the *Oberkommando der Kriegsmarine*, the Supreme Naval Command, more usually referred to as the *OKM*.

Day-to-day control rested, however, with two separate shore-based commands: Navy Group West, under Admiral Alfred Saalwachter, which was responsible for operations in the North Sea area, and Navy Group East, commanded by Admiral Conrad Albrecht, who looked after the Baltic. The fleet commanders thus had to take their orders from their respective Groups and the system quickly led to friction when the sea commanders found the admirals ashore dictating their movements, dispositions, and even tactics, instead of being left to make their own decisions on the spot where they were in a better position to judge events. Boehm, the fleet commander, soon found himself in dispute with Saalwachter, the immediate issue being the use of the *Kriegsmarine*'s battleships as a covering force for minelaying operations off the English coast by destroyers. Raeder intervened in the wrangle and, in the interests of discipline, was forced to support the more senior admiral, Saalwächter, even though he had a high regard for Boehm and sympathized with his views. Angered by a tactlessly worded order from Raeder, Admiral Boehm offered his resignation which the former accepted 'with a heavy heart' and Vice-Admiral Wilhelm Marschall was appointed to take his place as Fleet Commander, Group West, on 21 October. With the war less than two months old it was not a good omen for the future.

In the meanwhile the *Deutschland* had created a diplomatic furore when, on 8 October, Wennecker stopped the US freighter *City of Flint* and, putting a prize crew on board, ordered her to be taken to Murmansk and then on to Germany. The United States government issued a strong protest as soon as details of the incident reached Washington and, anxious not to antagonize American public opinion, the policy-makers in Berlin ordered the ship to put into a Norwegian port where the members of the prize crew were interned and the freighter released unharmed to its rightful owners. The episode drew Hitler's attention to the battleship and, worried that the *Deutschland* might be brought to action by the Royal Navy and sunk, he urged Raeder to recall her before his fears were realized.

Two days after the *Deutschland*'s interception of the *City of Flint*, the *Graf Spee* captured the 8,300-ton British-owned *Huntsman* just south of the equator. According to Captain Brown, the *Huntsman*'s master, the *Graf Spee* was flying the French flag as she approached, but, on closing her victim, the tricolour was hauled down and a swastika ensign was hoisted in its place — a perfectly legal deception providing the German vessel did not open fire. A prize crew was put aboard and three days later, having trailed across the empty ocean behind the pocket-battleship, she was brought alongside the *Altmark* to off-load part of her cargo and to transfer Captain Brown and his crew into the custody of Captain Heinrich Dau aboard the supply ship. At the same time over 80 tons of stores were transhipped from the *Altmark* to the *Graf Spee*.

Now that the British vessel had served its purpose it was scuttled and, taking leave of the supply ship, Langsdorff moved off in search of another victim. In the meanwhile, on 14 October, the *Deutschland* had sunk the neutral Norwegian freighter *Lorenz W. Hansen* east of Newfoundland and, leaving her crew adrift in lifeboats, had callously abandoned them to their fate. By now, however, Hitler was insisting almost daily that the battleship should be recalled and although Raeder procrastinated for more than three weeks he finally bowed to the Führer's demands and ordered Wennecker to return.

The pocket-battleship passed through the Denmark Strait on 8 November and reached the Norwegian coast three days later. Successfully escaping detection by RAF patrols she entered the Skagerrak on the 14th and berthed at Gdynia* the next day. Her level of success had been poor and despite nearly twelve weeks at sea she had sunk only two ships; her third victim, the *City of Flint*, having been taken as a prize, was later released.

But Hitler's genuine relief at her safe return blinded him to the failure of her sortie. His abiding fear that a ship bearing the name of the Fatherland might be sunk by the enemy had literally kept him awake at nights. Now that the battleship was home he took steps to ensure that he would never face the same mental torment again. On 15 November, the day on which the *Deutschland* arrived in Gdynia, and without first consulting Raeder, the Führer ordered the ship to be renamed *Lützow*.

Despite Wennecker's meagre success, the *Deutschland*'s sortie had

* The Germans changed the name of Gdynia to Gotenhafen following its occupation in 1939.

achieved exactly what Raeder had intended – a fact confirmed by no less an authority than Winston Churchill who was to write in his memoirs: 'The mere presence of this powerful ship upon our main trade route had ... imposed ... a serious strain upon our escorts and hunting groups in the North Atlantic. We should ... have preferred her activity to the vague menace she embodied' – a sentiment no doubt shared by the Home Fleet's C-in-C, Admiral Forbes, who, unaware of the *Deutschland*'s safe return to Germany, continued to search for her until the middle of December!*

On 22 October the *Graf Spee* exploited the use of false French colours again to snare the 5,299-ton *Trevanion* which was en route to Britain with a cargo of concentrates. When the vessel's radio operator defied orders to remain silent and began transmitting a raider distress call, the *Graf Spee* opened fire on the bridge and upperworks but, undeterred, he remained at his post until a German boarding party physically removed him and the rest of the crew back to the battleship. Happily his valour was not in vain. The signal was picked up by the *Llanstephan Castle* which passed it on to Freetown. Vice-Admiral D'Oyly Lyon responded immediately and Force H and Force K** were despatched to hunt down and destroy the raider. Langsdorff, forewarned by the telltale *CT* prefix that the distress call had been picked up and acknowledged, knew he had to move quickly. After scuttling the *Trevanion*, he headed south, meeting up again with the *Altmark* six days later at a pre-arranged rendezvous well clear of the main shipping lanes.

While the *Altmark* was pumping fuel into the battleship's depleted bunkers there was an exchange of signals with Berlin in the course of which Raeder suggested that the *Graf Spee* might find it both safer and more advantageous to extend her area of operations into the Indian Ocean, a fruitful hunting ground for raiders like the *Emden* in 1914. It was sound advice and it had been offered at just the right moment, for the survivors from the *Lorenz W. Hansen* had come ashore in the Orkneys on 21 October and, a day later, the *City of Flint* had arrived at the Russian port of Murmask. These two events confirmed what the British Admiralty had suspected – that there were *two* of Hitler's battleships operating in the Atlantic: one, the *Deutschland*, in northern latitudes and a second, still wrongly identified as the *Admiral Scheer*, prowling the sea lanes south of the equator. With the situation clarified, it was certain that the Royal Navy would redouble its efforts to catch both ships.

The Second World War, Winston Churchill, Cassell & Co, 1948, Vol 1, p 464.
**Force H: heavy cruisers *Shropshire* and *Sussex*. Force K: battle-cruiser *Renown* and aircraft carrier *Ark Royal*.

Langsdorff concurred with Raeder's suggestion and, as soon as refuelling had been completed, he took his leave of the *Altmark* and set course south-east with the intention of passing well to the south of the Cape of Good Hope before swinging northwards to enter the Indian Ocean. A few days later a signal from Berlin informed him that the Führer had awarded 100 Iron Crosses to the ship's company, leaving Langsdorff, who had told his officers that 'every man aboard deserves this decoration', with the onerous task of deciding which members of his crew should get the medal. That same evening the officers and enlisted men crowded onto the quarterdeck to enjoy an open-air film show, the ship's entertainment officer having chosen for their delectation the somewhat mawkish *Ninon*, a colourful period romance set in the Court of Louis XIV. Unsuitable it may have been, but the sailors loved it.

The battleship entered the Indian Ocean on 3 November but continual rough seas and poor visibility forced *Graf Spee*'s captain to abandon his original intention of trawling the Cape Town — South Australian trade route for potential victims and, cutting his losses, he headed for Madagascar in search of better conditions. The state of the weather, however, was the least of Langsdorff's problems.

The *Graf Spee*'s Arado floatplane on which he relied for reconnaissance had been suffering with engine trouble for some time and on 8 November, rebelling at the constant stress of landing alongside the battleship in a heavy swell, the spare engine developed a cracked cylinder block and *Oberleutnant* Bongard, the *Luftwaffe* pilot, reported that no further flying was possible. It was a bitter blow but there was nothing Langsdorff could do about it. Happily, although deprived of his long-range eyes, he still had his ears, for, having penetrated the Royal Navy's codes, thanks to the documents seized from his earlier victims, he could intercept and decipher enemy signals traffic, which meant that he knew the movements of most of the warships that were attempting to hunt him down. The key word, however, was *most*. For unless *all* Allied warships could be tracked and identified there was always the danger of being caught by surprise, especially now that he lacked the protection of an air patrol.

Langsdorff arrived off Lourenço Marques on 14 November, a mere 300 miles from the British naval base at Durban. Yet, despite being on the enemy's doorstep, the ocean remained depressingly empty. At 11.15 the following morning, however, the *Graf Spee*'s luck changed. Running close inshore, the bridge lookouts sighted a small tanker, the Shell Oil Company's 706-ton *Africa Shell*. The tanker's master, Captain Patrick Dove, examined the approaching warship through his binoculars and recognized what he thought was the French tricolour flying at the masthead. Nevertheless he had a gut feeling that the vessel was an enemy raider— his personal guess was the *Deutschland* — and he made a desperate effort to reach the neutral territorial waters of Portuguese East Africa which he estimated to be no more than three miles ahead.

The little *Africa Shell* was making her best speed, all of 10 knots, with the *Graf Spee* closing rapidly from astern at 26 knots. Suddenly a string of brightly coloured flags ran up the battleship's yardarm: *Heave to. I am going to board you.* Captain Dove tried to buy time by getting his own signal flags in a muddle but Langsdorff was not easily bluffed. A puff of smoke erupted from one of the 5.9-inch guns and a geyser of dirty water rose high into the air a few hundred yards astern of the tanker. With the odds stacked against him, Captain Dove obeyed the order to stop and, as the *Africa Shell* lost speed, he and his Second Officer carefully checked the bearings of the lighthouses at Cape Zavora and Quessico Point, which, according to their reckonings, put them half a mile inside the limit of Portuguese territorial waters and therefore, in theory, immune from hostile attack.

Many writers have claimed that the *Africa Shell* was caught by surprise and had insufficient time to transmit a distress call, a somewhat ludicrous conclusion in the light of the *Graf Spee*'s pursuit of her prey. The lack of a signal, however, had a far more prosaic explanation. The coastal tanker did not possess a radio. Unable to warn the authorities of the attack, the Royal Navy remained unaware of the incident until the *Africa Shell*'s crew rowed ashore some hours later.

Dove himself was taken aboard the *Graf Spee*, but although he claimed that his ship had been stopped in territorial waters, Langsdorff politely disagreed. He nevertheless allowed the disgruntled Master to lodge a formal protest in writing which he countersigned. And then, having done so, he sent the little *Africa Shell* to the bottom with demolition charges. There was, however, nothing piratical about Langsdorff's actions. In the course of *Graf Spee*'s raiding cruise in which she sank a total of nine ships totalling 50,089 tons, not a single civilian officer, seaman or passenger lost their lives at his hands. It was an honourable record and certainly comparable with that of the other great gentleman raider, Karl von Müller, the captain of the cruiser *Emden* in the First World War.

On the day following the *Africa Shell* incident Langsdorff intercepted the Dutch steamer *Mapia*. Recognizing her neutral status, and observing the strict rules of war, he allowed the vessel to continue on her way. His forbearance earned its own reward for the *Mapia*'s master made no attempt to report the encounter until his ship reached Sumatra, by which time the *Graf Spee* was once again safely back in the South Atlantic.

The pocket-battleship had by this time steamed some 30,000 nautical miles since leaving Germany on 21 August and, returning to the desolate wastes of empty ocean that comprised his waiting area on 23 November, Langsdorff spent the next four days in enforced idleness while his engineers overhauled the diesel motors and carried out essential maintenance. Taking advantage of the hiatus, the *Graf Spee* was disguised to resemble the British battle-cruiser *Renown* by the addition of a second funnel, made up from canvas around a wooden frame, and a third turret. It was not entirely convincing but it was enough to mislead the inexperienced eye of an untrained lookout on the bridge of a merchant ship in poor visibility. The *Altmark* arrived on 26 November and, having refuelled and stored the battleship, arrangements were made to redistribute the prisoners being held on the two vessels. Ships' masters and key officers such as chief engineers were transferred to the *Graf Spee* in readiness for the return passage to Germany, while the seamen and stokers were accommodated on the *Altmark*, Captain Dau being instructed to disembark them at the nearest neutral port when convenient. Meanwhile Langsdorff had sent a detailed signal to Berlin reporting the poor state of the *Graf Spee*'s engines, which he said needed a dockyard overhaul, and his intentions of moving to a new area of operations off the River Plate on or around the 6 December before returning to Germany in the New Year.

Raeder, fully aware of the problems facing Langsdorff, had already taken steps to relieve the pressure on the *Graf Spee*'s captain some time before the *Africa Shell* episode. Informed early in November that the *Scharnhorst*'s boiler problem had been cured, he ordered the battleship and her sister-ship *Gneisenau* to be transferred to Wilhemshaven via the Kiel Canal, the passage evincing a certain amount of local excitement as the two ships were, at the time, the largest vessels to have used the waterway which the Kaiser had widened before the First World War for just such a contingency.

The strategic thinking behind Raeder's decision to use the *Scharnhorst* and *Gneisenau* to draw British forces away from their pursuit of the *Graf Spee* was encapsulated in the directive he issued on 13 November when, having ordered Vice-Admiral Wilhelm Marschall to take the two ships to a position south of Iceland, he instructed him to 'maintain strategic pressure on the enemy's North Atlantic sea routes [and to launch] successful strikes against inferior forces whenever the occasion offered.'

On Tuesday, 21 November, as the *Graf Spee* was passing through the Roaring Forties on her way back into the South Atlantic after her Indian Ocean sortie, a small but formidable fleet of surface ships left Wilhemshaven and headed northwards. Marschall flew his flag in the *Gneisenau* which was accompanied by the *Scharnhorst*, the cruisers *Köln* and *Leipzig*, the destroyers *Bernd von Arnim*, *Karl Glaster* and *Erich Giese*, and three torpedo-boats. The cruisers and light forces were detached the following day and headed for the Skagerrak where, on the 24th, they were joined by the battleship *Lützow* (the former *Deutschland*) for an anti-shipping sweep which, in the event, yielded no significant successes.

Gneisenau and *Scharnhorst*, however, maintained course northwards in the teeth of gale-force winds which, on occasions, gusted to hurricane strength while their crews, mostly young and inexperienced sailors, suffered the agonies of seasickness as the worsening conditions forced Marschall to reduce speed to 12 knots. There was little improvement the following day but the bad weather at least shielded the two battleships from British air and surface patrols, for the poor visibility conditions made it virtually impossible to sight anything that was more than a mile away. Nevertheless Marschall was taking no chances, and, for added protection, he ordered his ships to fly the White Ensign.

The appalling weather continued for a further 36 hours as the ships hammered their way through the heavy seas towards the Iceland-Faeroes passage. Suddenly, during the late afternoon of the 23rd, Marschall saw the *Scharnhorst* increase speed and alter course northwards. A few minutes later the Admiral was handed a signal clip: *Scharnhorst to Fleet Commander. Large steamer sighted on parallel course. Distance plus 25 kilometres. Have altered course to 355°.*

Captain Kurt Hoffman, who had taken over from the battleship's first commanding officer, Otto Ciliax, early in 1939, continued to close the target which was soon identified as being an armed merchant cruiser. Nevertheless, although convinced that he was approaching a hostile warship, Hoffman gave the other vessel the benefit of the doubt and signalled: Stop. What ship? The identification letters flashed by the suspect vessel meant nothing to the *Scharnhorst*'s captain but an alteration in course and a perceptible increase in speed by the stranger suggested hostile intent. And with the range down to 4½ miles, far too close for comfort, the battleship fired a warning shot across the vessel's bows.

The enemy ship was, in fact, the 16,697-ton *Rawalpindi*, a former passenger liner taken over by the Admiralty at the beginning of the war and fitted with eight 6-inch guns for service as an auxiliary cruiser on the Northern Patrol. Against the overwhelming power of a modern battleship she stood no chance at all. Her inferior speed made it impossible for her to run away even if she had wanted to, her obsolete guns were out-ranged and her high vulnerable superstructure offered a massive unprotected target for the enemy's weapons. True to the traditions of the Royal Navy, Captain Edward Kennedy ignored the odds and prepared to fight. But the chemical canisters which he ordered to be thrown over the side to generate a protective smokescreen proved to be faulty and, failing to ignite, they fizzled miserably and ineffectively when they hit the water. In a desperate attempt to escape Kennedy altered course to bring the battleship on to his starboard quarter.

And, at 17.03, he opened fire with the *Rawalpindi*'s 6-inch guns, a latterday David fending off the Nazi Goliath. The *Scharnhorst* replied only moments later and her second 11-inch salvo knocked out the merchant cruiser's electrical system leaving the ship in darkness and disabling the electrically-powered ammunition hoists. Thanks to an emergency generator the radio was still functioning and the operator tapped out an urgent distress signal that the ship was being fired upon by a single battle-cruiser, a message amended on Kennedy's personal instructions to: *Under attack by the Deutschland*.

At 17.06 the *Scharnhorst*'s fourth salvo struck the forward superstructure killing Captain Kennedy and most of the ships' officers, as well as destroying the wireless office abaft the bridge. The *Gneisenau* was also now within range and, passing astern of the British vessel, began to fire at her previously disengaged port side. The *Rawalpindi*, torn asunder by high-explosive shells, was ablaze from stem to stern by this time, yet, miraculously, her guns maintained a steady if inaccurate fire on the enemy until, one by one, they fell silent as the men serving the weapons were struck down and killed at their posts.

Such an unequal contest could only have one ending and when, after some thirty minutes, the battered and burning auxiliary cruiser could no longer defend herself, the order was given to abandon ship. High up on the blazing superstructure an anonymous hero with a hand-held Aldis signal lamp flashed a laconic request to the enemy: *Please send boats*. Marschall responded immediately and *Scharnhorst* was ordered to pick up survivors. The errand of mercy was unfortunately short-lived. After dragging 27 men* from the sea the rescue operation was aborted when lookouts detected the approach of a British warship, the cruiser *Newcastle* which had occupied the adjacent billet to the *Rawalpindi* in the patrol line and which was responding to Kennedy's first attack signal.

But she, too, failed to recognize the two battleships and at 18.17 she reported: *Have sighted cruiser (sic) Deutschland distance 13,000 yrds*. And a minute later: *Lights of a second ship … approaching from dead ahead*. But Marschall had already taken to his heels. Unwilling to risk interception by enemy heavy units he had turned away under cover of a smokescreen and vanished into the darkness.

The *Funkbeobachtungsdienst*, the German Navy's radio intelligence service more commonly known as the *B-Dienst*, had broken British naval codes as early as 1936 and was able to read the Royal Navy's signal traffic with considerable accuracy. Indeed, throughout the action and its aftermath,

---

* A further 11 members of the *Rawalpindi*'s crew were rescued from a raft by *HMS Chitral* the following day.

Marschall was kept informed of all relevant Admiralty signals, often receiving information about enemy movements as rapidly as his British counterparts. It was a *B-Dienst* interception of the *Rawalpindi*'s last signal that revealed Captain Kennedy's mistaken identification of the *Scharnhorst* as the *Deutschland*, the latter vessel, as noted earlier, being engaged on the anti-shipping sweep of the Skagerrak under her new name of *Lützow* at the time of the *Rawalpindi* sinking. To compound his enemy's confusion Raeder ensured that when German radio stations broadcast reports of the action no mention was to be made of either the *Scharnhorst* or the *Gneisenau*. It would serve to keep the British guessing, and it was the nearest thing to a joke of which the Admiral was capable.

When the shore station at Wilhemshaven informed Marschall that the Home Fleet was at sea and that the cruisers *Delhi* and *Newcastle* had been detached from the Northern Patrol to join the hunt for the ship or ships responsible for sinking the *Rawalpindi* the German Admiral realized that his intended sortie against the North Atlantic convoy routes would have to be aborted. But with the battle-cruiser *Hood* and the French battleship *Dunkerque* reported as approaching from the south it would clearly be unwise to double-back to Germany immediately. Bad weather, in fact, was his only hope of escaping the steel-jawed trap which the Royal Navy was closing around his two battleships. Acting on no more than a hunch, Marschall steered north towards the Arctic, a fortuitous squall enabling him to give the slip to the *Newcastle*, which, without the advantages of radar, was endeavouring to shadow the enemy ships visually.

A German weather-ship reported that a storm was developing off south-west Greenland and the information was passed on to the Fleet Meteorological Officer, Dr Hartnung, who correctly forecast that the front would reach the coast of Norway at around dawn on the 26th. Marschall altered course accordingly and was rewarded with atrocious weather, exactly as Hartnung had predicted. It may not have been welcomed by the seasick seamen aboard the two battleships but, from the admiral's viewpoint, it was just what the Doctor had ordered, or, more accurately on this occasion, just what the Doctor had forecast. Under cover of driving rain, a south-westerly gale and minimal visibility Marschall made his way down the Norwegian coast to arrive at Wilhemshaven in time for lunch on the 27th to the acclaim of the Nazi-controlled press. 'England has been forced to abandon the North Sea and North Atlantic,' boasted one editorial. GREAT NAVAL VICTORY OFF ICELAND shrieked banner headlines in another. But Raeder's earlier orders remained in force and all specific references to either the *Scharnhorst* or the *Gneisenau* were carefully removed by the censor.

At Staff level the appraisal of the sortie was more realistic. Firstly, the intended break-out into the Atlantic had not taken place and, secondly,

46

Raeder's plan to roll up the Northern Patrol had failed. The *Kriegsmarine*'s Chief of Operations, Rear-Admiral Kurt Fricke, was more scathing. On learning that Marschall had fled from the cruiser *Newcastle* under cover of smoke, he observed coldly: 'Battleships are supposed to shoot − not lay smokescreens.' Marschall, however, defended his actions vigorously by pointing out that, although his ships could have destroyed the shadowing cruiser, he could not take the risk of a night action as he had no destroyers in company. More importantly, he could not afford the loss of, or even substantial damage to, either the *Scharnhorst* or the *Gneisenau*. Germany had only two other battleships operational and one of these, the *Graf Spee*, was only 7,000 miles away in the South Atlantic. Indeed, on the day that Marschall's squadron was passing through the Skagerrak on the final leg of its return passage to Wilhemshaven, the *Graf Spee* was lying alongside the *Altmark* and topping up her bunkers in readiness for another sortie against the enemy's trade routes. On 29 November the pocket-battleship dipped her swastika ensign in farewell to the tanker and set course north-eastwards for the busy shipping lanes off the west coast of Africa.

This time a victim was found without undue delay when, shortly after noon on 2 December, the battleship's powerful rangefinder detected smoke over the port bow at a distance of 33 miles, well beyond the pathetically short range of the *Graf Spee*'s primitive 80cm *Seetakt* radar scanner which was virtually useless for targets more than nine miles away. This time, for some unknown reason, Langsdorff departed from his usual practice of approaching under cover of the French flag and, shortly after sighting the vessel, one of the battleship's 11-inch guns fired a warning shot that exploded uncomfortably close to its target. Captain William Stubbs, the Master of the 10,085-ton Blue Star refrigerator ship *Doric Star*, said later that he had not observed the raider when the first shell exploded unexpectedly off the steamer's beam, but 'at about 1.10 pm a second shell exploded within two hundred yards of the starboard bow, and the [approaching] vessel was seen to be a battleship'.

Langsdorff's new and seemingly misguided tactics gave Stubbs time to transmit a raider distress call and his radio-operator continued tapping out the *R-R-R* alarm until the *Graf Spee* flashed an imperative order by searchlight: *Stop your wireless or I will open fire*. Stubbs obeyed − his ship's solitary 4-inch anti-submarine gun on the poop was no match for the *Graf Spee*'s massive firepower − and a motorboat carrying three officers and a party of thirty armed seamen came alongside to board the Blue Star steamer which was now rolling gently in the Atlantic with her engines stopped.

The *Doric Star*'s distress signal was picked up by several other ships in the vicinity and the *Port Chalmers* passed it on to the British naval base at Simonstown from where it was, in turn, relayed to Vice-Admiral Lyon at

Freetown and to the Admiralty in London. For the first time in several weeks the British now knew exactly where the *Graf Spee* was, even though there was continued confusion over her identity due to Captain Stubbs reporting her as being the *Admiral Scheer*. Lyon, with the prey in his sights at last, reacted swiftly to the news and sent Force K on a sweep up the West African coast northwards from Cape Town while directing Force H to search the trade routes running between South Africa and the island of St Helena.

Force G, under Commodore Henry Harwood and based in the Falklands, was responsible for covering the shipping lanes of Rio de Janeiro and the River Plate estuary even though, at that particular moment, the four-ship squadron was widely dispersed with the *Exeter* refitting at Port Stanley, the *Achilles* refuelling in Montevideo and the *Cumberland* on her way south to join the *Exeter* in the Falklands, the latter's recent departure leaving Force G reduced to a single 6-inch gunned cruiser, Harwood's own flagship, the *Ajax*.

The Commodore had spent many weeks exercising his tiny squadron for just such an opportunity, and when, on 2 December, he received Vice-Admiral Lyon's signal reporting the sudden appearance of an enemy pocket-battleship off West Africa, he reviewed the three most likely scenarios: a German attack on the trade routes north of Rio, an assault on the mass of shipping that left the Plate estuary at regular and frequent intervals, or a raid on the Falkland Islands to mark the 35th anniversary of Vice-Admiral Maximilian Graf von Spee's sortie against Port Stanley in December, 1914. Even these three alternatives were precariously based on the further supposition that Langsdorff intended to move south and west rather than to break north and return to the Fatherland.

Harwood's intuition, aided by an uncanny ability to read his opponent's mind, led him to conclude that the middle option, an attack on the River Plate shipping lanes, would be the *Graf Spee*'s most likely objective. Having made his choice, the Commodore acted swiftly. Ordering the *Exeter* to leave the Falklands on 9 December, the day on which the *Cumberland* was due to arrive at Port Stanley, and recalling the New Zealand cruiser *Achilles* from Montevideo, he instructed their captains to concentrate with the *Ajax* at a point on the chart some 150 miles east of the Plate estuary on the 12th.

It was a bold decision. Some might even describe it as a calculated gamble. But it proved to be the death-knell for Captain Hans Langsdorff and the battleship *Graf Spee*.

CHAPTER THREE

'To Die For The Honour Of The Flag'

LANGSDORFF REALIZED THAT HIS ATTACK on the *Doric Star* had stirred up a hornet's nest. The *B-Dienst* experts monitoring the 500kc/s wavelength in the *Graf Spee*'s radio room had warned him that the steamer's distress call had been acknowledged and there was little doubt in his mind that the Royal Navy had already started to close in. Yet, despite the urgency of the situation, he was powerless to respond for the pocket-battleship could not leave the scene until her boarding-party had been recovered, and the latter seemed to be in no hurry to quit their prize.

As sailors, armed with rifles and sub-machine guns, checked the *Doric Star*'s cargo, rather ineptly failing to discover some 8,000 tons of refrigerated meat and dairy produce which the raider's depleted larder sorely needed, the officers searching Captain Stubbs' quarters had found a quantity of silver bars. Forgetting the necessity of speed in their excitement, they ignored the increasingly terse and impatient recall signals from the *Graf Spee* as they stowed their haul of treasure in the motorboat.

Langsdorff also faced another unenviable dilemma. Shortly before the *Doric Star* was sighted the battleship's Arado seaplane, now repaired and airworthy again thanks to the efforts of *Oberleutnant* Bongard's *Luftwaffe* technicians, had been catapulted off on a reconnaissance sortie. But an empty petrol tank forced the machine down in the sea and, only minutes after the *Doric Star* had transmitted her distress signal, the *Graf Spee* received an SOS from Bongard and, while Langsdorff fretted impatiently over the delay in the return of the boarding party, valuable minutes were ticking away. He could not begin his search for the missing floatplane until the British steamer had been destroyed, and he could not make his escape until the lost aviators had been located and rescued.

With the hoard of silver bars and the captured crew of the *Doric Star* both safely aboard, the motorboat finally returned to the battleship and, wasting no further time, Langsdorff used his 5.9-inch secondary armament plus a single Type *G-7a* torpedo to send his victim to the bottom. The rest of the day was taken up with a vain search for the missing aircraft, but, as dusk fell and hopes of success were fading, a flare suddenly streaked up into the twilight sky. *Graf Spee* switched on her powerful searchlights and the silvered beams settled on the Arado wallowing forlornly in the Atlantic swell. The battleship was brought carefully alongside the waterlogged machine and, just after 19.00, both crew and aircraft were winched safely back on board.

As if responding telepathically to Harwood's assumptions, Langsdorff now set course for the River Plate and, soon after dawn the next morning, Advent Sunday, the rangefinder picked up the smoke of a steamer some thirteen miles astern off the port quarter. Closing to within six miles of his prey, the Furness Withy Company's 7,983-ton *Tairoa*, Langsdorff ordered her to stop. But, like Captain Stubbs of the *Doric Star*, her master was not easily frightened and her radio began transmitting the familiar *R-R-R* raider distress call, even though the *Graf Spee* had, on this occasion, reverted to the earlier ruse of flying a French ensign to mislead her intended victim.

Langsdorff, however, was at last beginning to show symptoms of stress, occasioned, no doubt, by the mounting pressures under which he was labouring. And when the *Tairoa*'s radio continued to transmit he uncharacteristically ordered the battleship's 37mm guns to open fire, the exploding shells inflicting considerable damage to the steamer's port superstructure as well as destroying the bridge wing and several of the ship's boats on that side of the vessel. Five members of the crew were wounded in the bombardment but Captain W.B.S. Starr nevertheless considered that 'the humanity [shown by] the captain of the *Graf Spee* who used only his smallest guns to achieve his purpose helped to keep casualties to a minimum'.

The fog of mistaken identity that pursued the *Graf Spee* right up to the moment of her arrival at Montevideo on 13 December, when an American press agency report still referred to her as the *Admiral Scheer*, took on an almost farcical twist at this juncture. As already noted, Langsdorff had added a dummy third turret together with a wood and canvas second funnel in an attempt to disguise the raider as the British battle-cruiser *Renown*. But Captain Starr was not easily deceived. 'The *Graf Spee* was disguised as the *Deutschland* [when] she captured us,' he told a leading naval writer in 1940. He was, it seems, unaware that the *Deutschland*, a sister-ship to the *Graf Spee*, had only one funnel and two turrets and was so similar in appearance to Langsdorff's ship it needed a trained eye to tell them apart.

Three days later, when the battleship met her faithful supply ship to take on more oil, the opportunity was taken to dismantle the dummy funnel and turret which Captain Starr had apparently failed to notice. Langsdorff also used the occasion to reallocate his prisoners yet again, their numbers now swollen by the men from the *Doric Star* and the *Tairoa*. Twenty-nine officers, together with three wounded deckhands from the latter ship, were retained on board the *Graf Spee* with the intention of taking them back to Germany as prisoners-of-war at the end of the cruise, while the remainder were sent to join the other merchant seamen being held in improvised cells on the *Altmark*. But, with sympathetic understanding, Langsdorff allowed both Captain Brown of the *Huntsman* and Captain Starr of the *Tairoa* to remain behind on the *Altmark* so that they could look after their bewildered lascar crews, Captain Starr later observing that the *Graf Spee*'s commanding officer 'impressed me as a man of great humanity, with a distaste for his job of raiding unarmed vessels'.*

The raider bade farewell to her supply ship for the last time shortly before dawn on 7 December, and, gathering speed, vanished over the western horizon. Later the same day, at 17.46 in the afternoon, smoke was sighted and closer investigation showed it to be coming from the 3,895-ton freighter *Streonshalh* whose master prudently obeyed the battleship's signal not to use his radio. Having taken off the officers and crew Langsdorff proceeded to sink the vessel by gunfire, somewhat oddly choosing to employ his 4.1-inch anti-aircraft weapons for the purpose. The *Graf Spee* then resumed her interrupted passage and continued towards her next area of operations some 300 miles east of the Plate estuary.

With Langsdorff's promise that they would soon be returning home fresh in their minds the crew were relaxed and cheerful. The officers, too, were optimistic of more successes, for radio intelligence from Berlin revealed that the 14,000-ton *Highland Monarch* was scheduled to leave the Plate on or about the 5th while an equally important prize, the Blue Star Line's *Andalusia Star*, was sailing from Buenos Aires three days later. If everything went to plan both ships would be within striking distance of the *Graf Spee* on 10 December. And although the whereabouts of the Royal Navy's hunting groups remained uncertain Berlin was able to confirm from its consular sources that the cruiser *Achilles* was still safely berthed alongside the oil wharf at Montevideo on the 9th. Prospects looked encouragingly bright as the *Graf Spee* headed west.

The next few days were uneventful, although Langsdorff's optimism was somewhat deflated on the 11th when the battleship's floatplane, which had been a constant source of trouble throughout the cruise, cracked its only remaining cylinder block and had to be written off as incapable of further flying. It was a serious setback. Indeed, it was possible that, had the seaplane been able to undertake its usual routine reconnaissance flights during the subsequent 48 hours, it may have seen the approaching British cruisers in time for the *Graf Spee* to have taken evasive action. Oddly enough, although Harwood had four aircraft at his disposal, he was so intent on preserving

* *Battle of the Plate*, Commander A.B. Campbell, Herbert Jenkins, 1940 p 68.

51

their engine life that he made no use of the machines to supplement the eyes of his lookouts. As it happened the lack of air reconnaissance may have given the British an unforeseen advantage, for had Langsdorff seen a seaplane in the distance he would have undoubtedly cut his losses and fled for his life.

The three cruisers making up Harwood's Force G had concentrated 150 miles east of the Plate estuary at 0700 on 12 December as planned and soon after 0600 the following morning a thin wisp of smoke was sighted on the horizon. According to Harwood's official despatch he ordered the *Exeter* to investigate and, at 0614, Captain Frederick Bell signalled the flagship: *I think it's a pocket-battleship*. The Commodore had been right to trust to his intuition. The calculated gamble had paid off. Langsdorff had walked into the trap which Harwood had so carefully laid.

Thanks to the height of her control tower and the power of her rangefinder the *Graf Spee* nevertheless enjoyed a considerable advantage over her British opponents in the preliminary stages of the battle and the German official account of the action reveals that the masts of the *Exeter* were first sighted at 0552 when she was still some twenty miles away. Moments later the alarm gongs echoed throughout the ship as the men were called to Battle Stations and the German vessel had already cleared for action before the British lookouts had even sighted her funnel smoke. The approaching ships were at first identified as a cruiser and two destroyers, the smaller cruisers being mistaken for the Royal Navy's new J-class destroyers which were just coming into service in 1939 and which also had single funnels. But at 0616, simultaneously with Captain Bell's report to Harwood that the vessel on the horizon was a pocket-battleship, Langsdorff was informed that the two smaller ships were, in fact, the cruisers *Ajax* and *Achilles*.

The raider's captain was undismayed by the news. For, while the enemy squadron outnumbered the *Graf Spee* by three to one, the German battleship completely out-gunned her opponents in both the weight of her shells and the range of her weapons. In addition her armour was thick enough to protect her from the 6-inch shells of the *Ajax* and *Achilles* and she was only vulnerable to the heavier 8-inch weapons of the *Exeter*, a fact that was to determine Langsdorff's tactics in the opening rounds of the impending battle. But there was one serious weakness in the German position. The raider's speed was some six to seven knots slower than that of the British cruisers. And that meant that the *Graf Spee* must stand and fight.

Harwood, however, had anticipated the situation which now faced him and he had prepared his battle plan accordingly. 'My policy with three cruisers in company versus one pocket-battleship,' he had told his captains, '[is to] attack at once by day or night. By day [we] act as two units [with] the 1st Division (*Ajax* and *Achilles*) and *Exeter* diverged to permit flank marking. The 1st Division will concentrate [its] gunfire.' In other words Harwood intended to divide his squadron and force Langsdorff either to concentrate his powerful 11-inch guns on one ship or to split his firepower between the two opposing groups. In an amplifying order which he issued later the Commodore emphasized that all three cruisers were 'to maintain decisive gunnery range' — a reminder that echoed Nelson's exhortation to 'engage the enemy more closely'.

Langsdorff made his decision to give battle without hesitation and as the battleship increased speed he climbed the narrow steel ladder into the foretop where he would have an unimpeded view of action. When the range was down to 20,000 yards he turned the raider to port in order to clear his 'A' arcs — a necessary manoeuvre if both main turrets were to enjoy a clear field of fire — and at 0617 *Graf Spee* loosed her first 11-inch salvo at the *Exeter*. Three minutes later, having altered course to 280° so that all three of his 8-inch turrets could be brought to bear, Captain Bell replied. Harwood, in the meanwhile, had closed up with the *Ajax* and *Achilles* and at 0621 their 6-inch guns joined in the duel.

The *Graf Spee*'s third salvo straddled the *Exeter*, killing the crew of her starboard torpedo tubes and damaging the cruiser's two Walrus aircraft so severely that they had to be jettisoned. But worse was to follow and, although one 11-inch projectile passed clean through the hull without detonating, another heavy shell exploded on B turret, knocking it out of action and killing everyone on the bridge except Captain Bell and two other officers. It also destroyed the wheelhouse and all communications. Bell immediately evacuated the shattered blood-spattered bridge and made his way to the secondary steering position aft where, despite facial wounds, he resumed command of the cruiser by passing his orders verbally via a chain of messengers. During the time it took him to reach the emergency steering position, probably not more than three minutes at most, the *Exeter* had suffered two more direct hits which were seen from the *Graf Spee* and described as 'a column of fire [rising] almost as high as the mast'.

But the German battleship had not emerged unscathed from the duel. Splinters of steel from near misses had pierced the hull below the waterline, while a shell from either the fifth or sixth salvo had torn a gaping hole in the superstructure near the funnel. Langsdorff, too, had been slightly wounded by splinters and needed a temporary dressing to staunch the bleeding. But he remained at his post in the foretop and at 1630 turned one of his 11-inch turrets against the *Ajax* and *Achilles* who were approaching too close for comfort. Seizing the opportunity to strike back, the *Exeter* fired a salvo of torpedoes from her starboard tubes at 1632 followed six minutes later by a repeat salvo from the port tubes. No hits were scored in either attack but at 1637, with the lighter guns of the two smaller cruisers stinging like bees, Langsdorff had been forced to turn 150° to port under cover of smoke in an attempt to ease the pressure on the battleship. When the *Exeter* obtained a second direct hit with one of her 8-inch shells the raider's captain turned his rear turret back on to Captain Bell's heavy cruiser.

Although the shell had only caused superficial damage, it was now becoming clear to Langsdorff that the *Exeter*'s 8-inch armour-piercing projectiles were capable of penetrating the *Graf Spee*'s armour and, appreciating that she represented a far more formidable threat than the more lightly-armed *Ajax* and *Achilles*, he knew that she must be eliminated if the Nazi battleship was to survive. He was surprised, too, by Harwood's offensive tactics. Given the immense superiority of the *Graf Spee*, he had anticipated that the British ships would have remained out of range and merely shadowed the raider until the Royal Navy's heavy ships could arrive on the scene.

A few moments later Langsdorff's hopes of victory were boosted when two of the *Graf Spee*'s 11-inch shells struck home, one knocking out the *Exeter*'s forward turret and the other starting a serious fire in the warrant officers' mess. As the cruiser began to settle by the bows the damage control teams rushed into the fore part of the ship to shore up the sagging bulkheads and seal the leaks, their task hampered by a third shell which penetrated the Navigating Officer's cabin, cut a bloody path through the crowded armaments office, and finally burst against the foremost 4-inch gun of the starboard battery, killing and wounding its crew and igniting the ready-use ammunition. With the fire-control circuits severed, the last remaining turret had to shift to local control, while Captain Bell was forced to steer the cruiser with the aid of a small magnetic compass hastily borrowed from a nearby boat when the gyro repeater system gave up the ghost. But despite the chaos and confusion, the roaring flames and acrid billowing smoke, and the dead and wounded men scattering the decks, the *Exeter* kept up the fight as her sole remaining turret continued to fire at the enemy. Not surprisingly its shells failed to hit their target but the threat they posed helped to distract Langsdorff from the task of eliminating the two light cruisers.

In addition to this daunting catalogue of disaster, several small fires were burning on the *Exeter*'s mess decks and in the highly inflammable paint store, the ship's wireless was no longer working and the internal telephone system had been knocked out. By 0700 the cruiser was listing 10° to port and had shipped 650 tons of water in her forward compartments. In the wrecked shambles of torn steel and smouldering wood sixty-one men lay dead, with a further twenty-three seriously wounded. But despite the carnage Bell steadfastly refused to give up the fight and *Exeter*'s last remaining turret continued firing until 0729 when the electricity supply failed. Yet, in spite of the structural damage she had suffered, the cruiser's engines were still working perfectly and Captain Bell said later that, although the ship had no serviceable weapons left, he fully intended to use his superior speed to ram the *Graf Spee* if an opportunity to do so had presented itself. But this final sacrifice was not to be. At 0730 she broke off the action and at 0750, according to the *Exeter*'s log, the 'enemy disappeared to westward pursued by the *Ajax* and *Achilles*'.

The fate of the *Exeter* demonstrated the wisdom of Germany's designers in equipping the pocket-battleships with the largest calibre weapon that their limited displacement would allow. It also revealed the correctness of Raeder's insistence on giving the two later battleships, *Scharnhorst* and *Gneisenau*, a third turret, an addition which Hitler had strenuously opposed at the time they were laid down. Had Langsdorff been in command of a battleship equipped with three turrets there is little doubt that he could have sunk all three of Harwood's cruisers without suffering any undue damage to himself.

The *Graf Spee*, meanwhile, had been under galling, if ineffective, fire from the *Ajax* and *Achilles*. For although their small six-inch guns were incapable of piercing the raider's armour they were still able to inflict considerable superficial splinter and blast damage to the superstructure. At 0700 Langsdorff tried to minimize the threat by means of a smokescreen and a series of sharp movements of the helm, but at 0710 Harwood decided that he must try to relieve the pressure on the *Exeter* by closing the range, now standing at 17,000 yards as a result of Langsdorff's evasive action. Accepting the reduction of firepower that would follow as his 'A' arcs closed, the Commodore altered course westward and increased speed. Langsdorff thwarted Harwood's intention by turning sharply to port under cover of smoke, but at 0720 he swung to starboard again to open the *Graf Spee*'s own 'A' arcs and turned both of his 11-inch turrets on to the First Division. The range was now down to 11,000 yards and, taking advantage of the situation, the German gunners straddled the cruisers with three successive salvoes.

An 11-inch shell struck the *Ajax* abaft her mainmast, knocking out her two after turrets and causing other damage. But, undeterred, Captain Charles Woodhouse swung his ship to starboard and at 0728 fired a spread of four 21-inch Mark VIII torpedoes at a range of 9,000 yards, forcing Langsdorff to alter course. Once the torpedoes had run clear, however, he resumed his original course and launched a salvo of the *Graf Spee*'s own torpedoes in reply. Fortunately the cruiser's Fairey Sea Fox floatplane was airborne, having been catapulted off at 0637 to spot and report the fall of shot from the *Ajax*'s guns, and a timely warning from the machine's observer enabled the First Division to turn away and 'comb the tracks' of the enemy weapons before resuming the chase.

The battleship was by now steering westwards at high speed and it was becoming increasingly apparent that Langsdorff had little stomach for the fight, despite having crippled the *Exeter* and virtually disabled the *Ajax* which, in addition to losing half of her main armament, had had her W/T aerials shot away, which meant that, until jury-rigged aerials could be improvised, she was unable to either receive or transmit radio signals. In addition to these difficulties Harwood found himself facing another problem when he was informed that his flagship had expended 80% of her ammunition. With his magazines nearly empty a renewal of the gunnery duel was now out of the question and, at 0740, having passed his orders to the *Achilles* by signal lamp, the Commodore led the First Division eastwards under cover of smoke and took up a shadowing position some 15 miles astern of the *Graf Spee* which was now making for Montevideo at a steady 24 knots.

Some while later Harwood learned that he had been misinformed about the ammunition stocks — the figures given to him earlier related only to the flagship's A turret — but, in view of the damage inflicted on his ships, he decided not to alter his plans and the two cruisers continued to shadow their fleeing adversary while *Ajax*'s seaplane was despatched in search of the *Exeter*.

The crippled and burning cruiser was located soon after 0800 and, although 'obviously hard hit', Captain Bell indicated that he was not in need of any immediate assistance, news which the Commodore received with considerable relief. After recovering the flagship's hard-worked seaplane Harwood sent a message to the *Cumberland* at Port Stanley instructing Captain Fallowfield to sail in support as soon as possible. Fortunately the cruiser's commanding officer, having deduced that a sea battle was in progress from intercepted radio traffic, had anticipated Harwood's order. The cruiser had a full head of steam in her boilers some ninety minutes before the Commodore's signal was received and she was able to leave Port Stanley soon after 1000 for the long haul northwards, a passage of some 36 hours, even steaming at maximum speed.

Captain Langsdorff was facing similar problems to those besetting Commodore Harwood. The *Graf Spee* had used up 60% of her 11-inch ammunition and the battleship had barely enough left in her magazines for a renewal of the battle. In addition she had suffered no fewer than twenty direct hits, including three from the *Exeter*'s destructive 8-inch armour-piercing shells. Nevertheless only one shot had penetrated the armoured deck — further confirmation, if any was needed, that the naval architects employed by the old Weimar Republic had got the crucial balance of firepower, protection and speed almost exactly right. The most serious damage was a hole in the bows which would require the attention of expert shipwrights before the battleship could face the rigours of a North Atlantic passage in winter with any degree of confidence. In addition the superficial damage to the unarmoured superstructure had affected several vital departments of the ship which, while not reducing its battle-worthiness, augured ill for the long voyage back to the Fatherland, facilities which included the galleys, bakery and fuel purification plant. Equally grave were the casualties sustained in the battle: 36 dead, 6 seriously wounded and a further 53 with more minor injuries. Yet, incredibly, not a single one of the 62 prisoners being held on board had received as much as a scratch.

The *Graf Spee* continued to steam westwards throughout the day while Harwood's light cruisers shadowed her from a safe distance astern. At 1005 the battleship had fired two 11-inch salvoes at the *Achilles* when she incautiously closed to 23,000 yards and the accuracy of the German guns persuaded Captain Parry to retire out of range under cover of smoke. During the day Langsdorff transmitted a brief battle report to Berlin in which he confided his intention to seek sanctuary in Montevideo so that his ship could be repaired before undertaking the hazardous return voyage to Germany. The *Graf Spee*'s captain did not seem to realize that he was entering a trap from which there could be no possibility of escape, a misjudgement later blamed on the head wound he had suffered early in the action and which, it was alleged, had resulted in mild concussion. But, whether Langsdorff was thinking clearly or not, Raeder nevertheless raised no objections to the proposal, and indeed, radioed his agreement within hours.

Although Harwood found it difficult to believe that Langsdorff would commit the tactical error of entering the Plate estuary he nevertheless despatched a signal to the British naval attaché in Buenos Aires warning him of the *Graf Spee*'s probable destination. He then drew up a fresh plan to ensure that the battleship would not escape undetected if Langsdorff decided to double back into the Atlantic. The *Achilles* was given the task of shadowing her if she passed west of Lobos Island while the semi-crippled *Ajax*, his own flagship, moved south to cover the alternative route.

Despite her headlong flight, the *Graf Spee* was still a force to be reckoned with and at 1915 she fired two 11-inch salvoes at the *Ajax*, forcing Harwood to turn away under cover of smoke. All three ships were, at the time, still safely outside Uruguayan territorial waters and Langsdorff's action was not in breach of International Law. But the situation was looking increasingly alarming to the Uruguayans and, as the *Graf Spee* rounded the Punta del Este, the cruiser *Uruguay* emerged to defend her country's neutrality. She fortuitously arrived just in time to observe the *Achilles* open fire on the battleship while both vessels were, allegedly, inside Uruguayan waters, an attack that provoked Langsdorff to return the compliment.

The true facts behind this brief exchange of fire have never been satisfactorily established. British accounts claim that the *Graf Spee*'s guns spoke first, firing three salvoes at the *Achilles* in an attempt to keep her at a distance. The New Zealand cruiser replied to the challenge with five salvoes of her own. According to an Admiralty appraisal of the incident the *Graf*

Spee fired the first shot at 2048 and the *Achilles* replied some six minutes later at 2054. Langsdorff, however, disputed this British version of events in a letter to the German Minister in Montevideo: 'In spite of a favourable tactical position, and in spite of good visibility, I did not open fire on the British cruiser [which was] standing off the Isla de Lobos until the enemy fired on my ship and his shells had fallen close [to the *Graf Spee*].'

Langsdorff's denial of culpability was confirmed by Captain Fernando Fuentes of the *Uruguay* who claimed that the *Achilles* fired first and that the German vessel had only replied in self-defence. According to his report to the Inspector General of the Navy the following day: 'The English ship [*Achilles*]... opened fire when off Punta Negra about eight miles from the coast and within [Uruguayan] territorial waters... the whole of the action, with the exception of the first few minutes, took place within territorial waters.' To add to the confusion Fuentes reported that the *Achilles* had opened fire at 7.50 pm (1950 hours) which, unless the *Uruguay*'s clocks were an hour slow, was presumably local time.

The question of culpability was a matter of considerable diplomatic importance for the *Graf Spee* was making for Montevideo and would need the active support of the Uruguayan government if she was to carry out the repairs which she so urgently needed. From a propaganda viewpoint it was, of course, in the interest of both belligerents to put the other in the wrong. Harwood countered the German claim by repeating that the *Graf Spee* had fired first and he repudiated Fuentes' evidence by alleging that the *Uruguay* was 'beyond the visual horizon' when the exchange of fire took place and her captain was therefore in no position to know who had fired the first shot.

The British Foreign Office dismissed the Uruguayan claim that the incident had taken place inside territorial waters. Uruguay, it claimed, considered that her territorial waters extended nine miles from the coast, a unilateral declaration that could not be supported by International Law which, at that time, recognized only a three-mile limit. In an attempt to hedge its bets the Foreign Office tried to muddy the already unclear waters by raising such esoteric matters as estuary limits and the legal definition of inland waters. The Admiralty, on the other hand, seemed content to accept the Uruguayan claim and merely argued that passage through territorial waters, even in 'hot pursuit', was not an infringement of either sovereignty or neutrality. Significantly — and the reader may draw his own conclusions — *Achilles*' track plan had been conveniently lost and could not be produced to support the British argument.

There was a further brief rumble of gunfire between 2130 and 2145 when the *Graf Spee* again warned off the *Achilles* when the latter approached too closely and, at 2350, the battleship entered the Montevideo roadstead and dropped anchor. Baulked of his prey, Harwood withdrew outside territorial waters and patrolled to seaward of English Bank while he waited the arrival of the heavy cruiser *Cumberland* from the Falklands. The outcome of the struggle was now in the hands of the diplomats and, for the next seventy-two hours, the battle was to be fought with pens and law-books rather than guns and torpedoes. And, as the British and German representatives in Montevideo, Eugen Millington-Drake and Otto Langmann, sat down at their desks to consider their tactics, the Royal Navy flexed its muscles.

Vice-Admiral Lyon ordered the 8-inch-gunned cruiser *Dorsetshire* to proceed to the Plate estuary with all speed, while the Admiralty, somewhat tardily and 36 hours after news of the battle had reached Whitehall, directed her sister-ship, *Shropshire*, to join Harwood's flag, the latter being promoted to the rank of Rear-Admiral on the 16th in recognition of his victory. The battle-cruiser *Renown* and the carrier *Ark Royal* were despatched to Rio de Janeiro, where, after refuelling, they were to be joined by the cruiser *Neptune* before moving south to reinforce the blockade outside Montevideo. Finally, the veteran carrier *Eagle* and the cruisers *Cornwall* and *Gloucester* were placed under Admiral Lyon's command with orders to cover the *Graf Spee*'s alternative escape route into the Indian Ocean via the Cape in the unlikely event of her breaking out from her temporary refuge in Uruguay.

Article 17 of Convention No XIII of the Second Hague Conference stated that belligerent warships could only remain in a neutral port for a maximum of 24 hours unless a longer period was needed to 'carry out such repairs as are absolutely necessary to render [them] seaworthy'. The Article, however, specifically vetoed any work which would restore or improve a vessel's fighting efficiency. It also laid down that the responsibility for deciding the nature and amount of work to be done, and the time needed for its completion, rested with neutral power in whose waters the ships had sought refuge.

The German Minister, Otto Langmann, promptly submitted that the *Graf Spee* would need fifteen days of intensive repair work to restore her to seaworthy condition while Millington-Drake, the British representative, argued for a rigorous application of Article 17 and demanded that the battleship's stay in Montevideo should be limited to 24 hours. With commendable impartiality, and acting strictly in accordance with Convention No XIII, the Uruguayan government arranged for two of its officers, Commander Jose Varela and Lt-Cdr Fernando Pontana, to go aboard the raider at 1900 that evening (14th) to assess the damage.

Somewhat surprisingly their report, delivered the following morning, indicated that the battleship had suffered rather less damage than

Langsdorff had implied and, significantly, they made no mention of the hole in the bows that was apparently causing him so much concern. Nevertheless they concluded that 'the result of our examination indicates that provisional repairs can be carried out in three days'.

The government considered the report alongside the representations of the diplomats, the latter now increased by a French submission that the *Graf Spee* should be interned. There was also a note from America's President Roosevelt urging Uruguay to intern the battleship if she failed to leave Montevideo within the prescribed 24 hours. After conscientiously weighing up their options, the Uruguayans came to a decision and a formal Presidential Decree was issued on 15 December allowing the *Graf Spee* 72 hours to complete her repairs – 'the time limit to expire at 8pm on the 17th inst.'. It was a compromise that suited nobody.

While the diplomats wrangled and the Uruguayans procrastinated, the crew of the *Graf Spee* started to put their ship in order. One seriously wounded seaman had been landed soon after midnight on the 14th and during the following day Langsdorff received permission to arrange a military funeral for the battleship's dead and, anxious to impress the world's press, a contingent of 320 sailors, resplendent in their white tropical uniforms, were sent ashore to provide a guard of honour and to act as pallbearers. Much was made in British newspapers of the fact that the *Graf Spee*'s captain bade farewell to his former shipmates with a conventional naval salute rather than the upraised arm of the Nazi salute. However, as the latter was not made mandatory in the *Kriegsmarine* until 1944, too much significance should not be attached to the episode.

It was, nevertheless, a hectic period for Langsdorff and the emotional stress of the funeral ceremony did little to ease the pressures under which he was working in Montevideo. He had to deal with the Uruguayan authorities wishing to inspect the *Graf Spee* and he had to attend numerous meetings ashore with Langmann and with senior government officials. In addition he had to keep up the morale of his men, decide which repairs were to be given priority and issue instructions to his officers with regard to the various tasks to be undertaken. Finally, the attitude of the local shipyard workers, who refused point-blank to help the Germans, only served to increase the heavy burden of responsibility which rested on his shoulders.

In his Battle Report to Berlin, despatched at 01.18 on 15 December, Langsdorff accepted that he was running a grave risk of being bottled up in Montevideo, an admission that suggests his reasoning and decision-making ability were in no way impaired by the wounds he had suffered. He informed his superiors in Germany that he had sought refuge in Uruguay because the 'ship cannot be made seaworthy for a breakthrough to the Fatherland with the means available on board'. He also again referred to the 'direct hit on the forecastle' which he claimed would make a winter passage of the North Atlantic too hazardous.

But he had other worries. In his report to Berlin he referred to an unsuccessful submarine attack on the battleship south of Lobos Island and was clearly unaware that the nearest British submarine, the *Clyde*, was some 2,000 nautical miles away patrolling to the west of Freetown. But to Langsdorff the submarine threat was a real one and this undoubtedly added to his anxieties and influenced his plans. The tension heightened when the *Graf Spee*'s gunnery officer, *Fregattenkapitan* Paul Ascher, sighted and positively identified the battle-cruiser *Renown* lying off the Uruguayan coast and thought that he also had caught a glimpse of the *Ark Royal*. Although Langsdorff had not allowed himself to be too much influenced by radio reports of British warships arriving off the Plate, which he rightly suspected were part of a subtle psychological campaign instigated by the enemy to wear down his resistance, he accepted Ascher's report without question. This, not surprisingly, only added to his worries.*

When Langsdorff advised Berlin of the Uruguayan decision to allow him a respite of 72 hours in which to repair the *Graf Spee*, he indicated that he was now actively considering the possibility of fighting his way across the Plate to seek internment in Argentina, a country known to be more sympathetic to Nazi Germany than the anglophile government of Uruguay. The battleship's captain concluded his message with a request for instructions. In particular he asked 'whether [he was] to scuttle the ship... or submit to internment'. The option of coming out and giving battle was not mentioned.

Raeder and his inner circle of advisers considered what should be done next. Although *Fregattenkapitan* Wagner insisted emphatically that neither the *Renown* nor the *Ark Royal* could possibly have reached the Plate as Langsdorff had claimed, they agreed that the *Graf Spee*'s captain, as the man on the spot, was best placed to know the true situation and that he should be given complete discretion to act as he saw fit. When Raeder reported the outcome of the meeting to Hitler the latter grumbled petulantly about the *Kriegsmarine*'s policy of avoiding risks and expressed a personal wish that Langsdorff would fight it out. But, with no firm views on matters of naval strategy, he was content to abide by the Grand Admiral's ultimate decision, whatever it might be. On his return to the Admiralty building on the *Tirpitzufer* Raeder despatched a radiogram to Langsdorff giving him the necessary freedom to act according to his best judgement. *But*, Raeder

---

* It is difficult to know what Ascher, a reliable and respected officer, actually saw. Neither the *Renown* nor the *Ark Royal* were on station off Montevideo at this time.

warned him, there was to be 'no internment in Uruguay'. And he reminded him that 'if the ship is scuttled you must do your best to ensure that she is completely destroyed'. As this sequence of events indicates, the claim made by many historians that Hitler personally ordered the *Graf Spee* to be scuttled is incorrect. The ultimate decision was taken by Erich Raeder. The Führer merely rubber-stamped it.

The die was cast late on the afternoon of the 16th when Langmann failed to secure Uruguay's agreement to an extension of the 72-hour time limit. And when a dispirited Langsdorff returned to the *Graf Spee* after midnight, still convinced that a powerful British squadron was lying in wait off the mouth of the estuary, he started to make arrangements for the battleship to be blown up. His earlier plan to seek internment in Buenos Aires had been aborted when examination of the local pilotage charts had revealed that the River Plate was too shallow for a vessel of the *Graf Spee*'s draught to negotiate in safety. Nevertheless he still intended to exploit Argentina's pro-German sympathies by landing his crew at Buenos Aires in the guise of shipwrecked mariners so that, as provided by International Law, they could be repatriated to Germany instead of being incarcerated in internment camps for the duration of hostilities, a ploy used successfully by the British on a number of occasions in the First World War.

The work began well before dawn. Confidential documents were burned or thrown overboard in weighted sacks; the breech-blocks of the guns were removed, while men with hammers, and in some instances hand-grenades, destroyed the fire-control equipment, rangefinders, radio installations and other delicate instruments. Explosive charges, including the warheads of the *Graf Spee*'s remaining torpedoes, were carefully placed in vital parts of the ship while electricians linked the time fuses to the chronometer in the central control room. Finally, all of the crew, with the exception of eight trusted petty officers who had volunteered to take the battleship to sea when the hour of destiny arrived, were transferred by ship's boats to the German-owned merchant ship *Tacoma*. Amongst the last to leave were the 31 wounded seamen still receiving treatment in the *Graf Spee*'s sick bay who were taken to a hospital ashore in the care of Uruguayan doctors and nurses.

Shortly after 1800 on the evening of Sunday 17 December, watched by vast crowds of curious onlookers ashore and accompanied by a running commentary from the American radio reporter Mike Fowler, whose minute by minute description of events provided useful on-the-spot intelligence for Rear-Admiral Harwood, the battleship *Graf Spee* weighed anchor and steamed slowly out of Montevideo harbour. The Nazi ensign was flying from both the fore and mainmasts and, with most of her battle damage patched up and painted over, she looked ominously warlike as she gathered speed and steered between the buoys marking the limits of the dredged channel.

Was she, after all, about to challenge the British navy and fight her way out of the trap into which Langsdorff had taken her three days earlier? Unaware of the truth — that her crew had been evacuated, her guns rendered unserviceable, and her equipment destroyed — the watching crowd thrilled at the prospect of battle.

But as she passed beyond the Uruguayan three-mile limit and entered international waters she suddenly swung west, *away* from Harwood's waiting cruisers, and, moments later, she let go her anchors. The time fuses of the demolition charges were set and, after hauling down the colours, Langsdorff, with his senior officers and the eight-man volunteer crew, climbed down into a waiting motorboat and headed for Buenos Aires in a dramatic flurry of white spray.

Twenty minutes later, at 2000, and appropriately just after sunset, a series of massive explosions lit the twilight sky and tore the great vessel apart. 'It was quite Wagnerian,' recalled Captain E.D.G. Lewin who, as a young naval pilot, was flying over the scene in the *Ajax*'s Seafox seaplane at the time, '*Graf Spee* was silhouetted against the [setting] sun... and the fantastic series of explosions with which she destroyed herself still stick in my mind.'*
Another British naval officer wrote later: 'The Germans made a very thorough job of it. She burned fiercely with small explosions every few minutes as the flames reached some new compartment.'

Langsdorff's carefully prepared plan to have his crew repatriated to the Fatherland as shipwrecked mariners failed calamitously. A Uruguayan warship intercepted the *Tacoma* before she had even left territorial waters and she was forced to return ignominiously to Montevideo under escort. In anticipation of just such a contingency, however, the *Graf Spee*'s survivors had already been transferred to tugs, specially chartered for the purpose by the German Embassy, which took them safely to Buenos Aires. But the Argentinian government proved to be rather less sympathetic than Langsdorff anticipated and, refusing to recognize the *Kriegsmarine* sailors as shipwrecked mariners, they were accordingly interned for the duration of hostilities. Langsdorff himself was castigated by the Press for cowardice, many newspapers seemingly taking a particular delight in dragging him down to the gutter.

The *Graf Spee*'s captain was tired, dispirited and worn out. He had been at sea continuously from 21 August until 14 December, a total of 115 days without setting foot on dry land, and much of that time had been spent on the run from the enemy. He had been subjected to all the pressures of a

* Quoted in *The Drama of Graf Spee and the Battle of the Plate*, Sir Eugen Millington-Drake, Peter Davies, 1964, p 355.

ship's captain who, alone in his majestic isolation, must take responsibility for each and every decision made aboard his ship. He had been defeated by a weaker force and, under that shadow, had been forced to engage in prolonged negotiations with an unfriendly government who showed sparse sympathy for his predicament. He had received little positive assistance from his Commander-in-Chief, Admiral Raeder, and even less from his Leader, Adolf Hitler. Now his plan to get his crew back to Germany was in ruins and, most hurtful of all, he had been branded as a coward by the world's press. It was more than any honourable man could endure.

Sitting at a small desk he wrote three letters, two to his family and a third to the German Ambassador in Buenos Aires. He made his feelings perfectly clear in the last:

'Rather than expose my ship to danger, after her fight, of falling... into enemy hands, I decided not to fight but to destroy the equipment and sink the ship. It was clear to me that this decision might be misinterpreted, intentionally or unwittingly, by persons ignorant of my motives as being attributable partially or entirely to personal considerations. I therefore decided, from the beginning, to bear the consequences involved in this decision. A captain with a sense of honour cannot separate his own fate from that of his ship... [and]... I can only prove by my death that the fighting services of the Third Reich were ready to die for the honour of the flag.'

Then, sealing the letters inside their envelopes, Langsdorff unwrapped a German naval ensign and took out the Luger pistol which he had obtained from the embassy armoury. His Flag Lieutenant, Hans Dietrich, found his body at 0830 the following morning. *Kapitan zur See* Hans Langsdorff had done his duty and, true to the tradition of the sea, he had died with his ship.

CHAPTER FOUR

'We Come As Friends'

ALTHOUGH CHURCHILL WAS QUITE PREPARED to flout Norwegian neutrality by ordering the Royal Navy to lay minefields inside that country's territorial waters in an attempt to block the shipment of Swedish iron ore to Germany, it was Grand Admiral Erich Raeder who first seriously considered a military occupation of Norway.

Raeder later claimed in his memoirs that his interest in Norway was prompted by a justified fear that Britain was contemplating an invasion of the Narvik area. But in the time-frame of the relevant events this is transparent rubbish for the Grand Admiral first asked his Staff to consider the question on 3 October, 1939, only five days after Churchill had presented his proposals to the British War Cabinet on 29 September. Churchill's scheme, at that moment, only envisaged a minelaying operation which, although strictly illegal, offered no threat to Norway's territorial integrity. His subsequent plan to land troops in Norway as part of a larger operation to provide military aid to the Finns in their war with Soviet Russia, the pretext to which Raeder was referring, was not, in fact, formulated until December, 1939, at the earliest.

The Grand Admiral explained in his memoirs that when he met Hitler on 10 October he did no more than present the Führer with the facts. 'I did not express myself as being in favour of our establishing bases in Norway ... my only aim was to inform Hitler of the situation and draw his attention to its great dangers and, at the same time, to make it clear to him that, in certain circumstances, we could be forced in self-defence to take preventative action.'* But the Führer was too engrossed in his plans for the invasion of France and the Low Countries to give the matter serious consideration.

Soviet Russia's attack on Finland on 30 November brought the whole Scandinavian question to the fore again and, after a meeting with the Norwegian traitor Major Vidkun Quisling on 14 December Hitler ordered the *Oberkommando der Wehrmacht*, the Supreme Command or *OKW*, to

---

* *Struggle for the Sea*, p 160.

prepare a feasibility study for an attack on Norway which was duly delivered to him in late December and which he passed to the three services on 10 January, 1940. *Studie Nord* was apparently only taken seriously by Raeder's OKM and after a further and detailed examination of the problems involved the Grand Admiral felt unable to recommend a military occupation of Norway unless it was forced upon Germany by the actions of the Allies. But, now that he had the bit between his teeth, Hitler was not deterred by Raeder's chronic pessimism and he ordered the *OKW* to prepare a full-scale operational plan. The army, however, showed only lukewarm interest in the project, while Goering's *Luftwaffe* could not even be bothered to send a representative to the initial planning conference. As a result the final plan for Operation *Weserübung* was almost entirely naval in its conception, execution and command structure.

The seizure of the *Altmark* on 14 February and the subsequent release of 299 British merchant seamen which the *Graf Spee*'s former supply ship was bringing back to Germany provided further evidence, so far as Hitler was concerned, of Britain's complete disregard for Norwegian neutrality for the *Altmark* was inside territorial waters when the Royal Navy intervened and not even the presence or protection of Norwegian warships proved sufficient to deter Captain Philip Vian from putting the destroyer *Cossack* alongside the Nazi prison ship and boarding her.

Finland's armistice with Soviet Russia, signed on 12 March, put a stop to Allied plans for sending troops to the aid of the gallant Finns, plans which included landing three brigades for the occupation of Narvik. In Churchill's view, however, Norway remained a potentially significant theatre of operations, a view somewhat strangely shared by Hitler at a later stage of the war. Although the Allied occupation force was immediately stood down, Churchill continued to press the War Cabinet to support his original September plan to mine the iron-ore route inside Norwegian territorial waters. His argument that Germany would bring pressure to bear on Norway if the minefield was laid and that this, in turn, would force the Norwegians to turn to the Allies for military assistance, a typical example of Winston's aptitude for wishful thinking, won his colleagues over and gained Cabinet approval for the scheme.

The minelaying sortie, code-named Operation Wilfred, was scheduled for 8 April and the ships taking part sailed three days earlier on the 5th. In the meanwhile British troops embarked on cruisers and transports at Rosyth and various other Scottish bases ready to be rushed to Norway's aid as soon as the Oslo government requested assistance − a triumph of optimism over reality that bordered on lunacy.

The German plan for the peaceful occupation of both Norway and Denmark, code-named *Fall Weserübung*, was completed at the beginning of

April with W-day set for the 9th. As was only to be expected, Hitler's battleships were selected to spearhead the invasion. For, although Hitler entertained hopes that there would be no serious resistance, Raeder, a pessimistic realist, had little doubt that the Royal Navy would counter-attack swiftly.

'The operation is in itself contrary to all principles in the theory of naval warfare,' he told the Führer. 'According to this theory it could only be carried out by us if we had naval supremacy. We do not have this. On the contrary, we are carrying out the operation in the face of a vastly superior British fleet. In spite of this the C-in-C Navy believes that, providing surprise is complete, our troops can and will be successfully transported to Norway.' Raeder, it seemed, had forgotten his earlier warning to Hitler in October that if the *Kriegsmarine* became embroiled in a campaign to seize Norway 'it was possible that Germany might lose her entire fleet'.

With the *Bismarck* and *Tirpitz* still incomplete and the *Admiral Scheer* undergoing a major refit that would keep her out of service until October, 1940, Germany had only three battleships, plus the First World War veterans *Schleswig-Holstein* and *Schlesien*, available. Of these the *Scharnhorst* and *Gneisenau*, which had both been equipped with *Seetakt* 80cm radar in December, had spent most of the winter at Kiel frozen in for long periods by unusually severe weather conditions. They had steamed north as far as Bergen in the course of a three-day combat sortie, Operation *Nordmark*, in mid-February but had seen no action and were now lying at Wilhelmshaven waiting orders.

The third and last of the *Kriegsmarine*'s heavy ships was the *Lützow*, formerly the *Deutschland*. Raeder originally intended to employ her as a surface raider − the *raison d'etre* of the pocket-battleship − and had already briefed her new captain, August Thiele, for a nine-month operational mission that would take his ship into the South Atlantic for an attack on the Antarctic whaling fleets. Such a sortie accorded exactly with Raeder's concept of strategic dispersion. For, like the *Graf Spee*, the *Lützow* would draw a disproportionate number of British and French heavy ships into the southern oceans to hunt her down, which meant that the Allied naval strength available to counter a German assault on Norway would be seriously weakened.

In the circumstances the strategy was sound, but Hitler failed to match the Grand Admiral's global vision of sea warfare. In early March he vetoed Raeder's orders and insisted that the *Lützow* must take part in the Norwegian campaign with the rest of the fleet. Against his better judgement Raeder acquiesced and assigned the battleship to Group Five − the task force designated to carry out the troop landings at Oslo. But he refused to give up his plan for a foray into the southern hemisphere and Thiele was told that, having completed his mission with the Oslo force, he was to break out into the Atlantic.

At the end of March the Grand Admiral withdrew the *Lützow* from Group Five and replaced her with the newly commissioned heavy-cruiser *Blücher*, a vessel much more suited to the task ahead than the pocket-battleship. But on learning of the changes Hitler again intervened and insisted that the *Lützow* must play a role in the Norwegian operation before being detached for her planned raiding mission to the South Atlantic. Raeder gave in once more and on 2 April, only five days before he was due to sail with Group Five for Oslo, Thiele received orders to join Group Two, the Trondheim force, at Wilhelmshaven.

Vice-Admiral Günther Lütjens, who had been appointed in overall command of Groups One and Two when Marschall had fallen ill, showed little enthusiasm for his new recruit. All the ships in both groups were capable of at least 30 knots. The *Lützow* had a maximum speed of 24 knots. And Lütjens, a coldly taciturn personality, made it quite clear to Thiele that he regarded the slow-moving *Lützow* as an expendable liability. On being asked what he would do if the force encountered the British Home Fleet he merely shrugged and told the *Lützow*'s captain that he would increase speed to 30 knots. He did not add, 'And devil take the hindermost,' but there was no doubting the implication.

Thiele's worst fears were never realized, however, for on 6 April, with only ten hours left until zero hour, serious cracks were discovered in the pocket-battleship's engine mountings during a routine inspection, a major fault that meant the raiding sortie into the South Atlantic would have to be cancelled. Raeder was informed by telephone and, at the very last minute, the *Lützow* was switched back to Group Five, the Oslo landing force under the command of Rear-Admiral Oskar Kummetz. Late that evening she left Wilhelmshaven to join the *Blücher* and the *Emden* at Kiel.

The main fleet, led by the *Scharnhorst* and *Gneisenau*, assembled off the mouth of the River Weser in the early hours of 7 April. In addition to the two battleships it included the cruiser *Hipper* and fourteen destroyers, ten of the latter acting as transports with each carrying 200 mountain troops complete with equipment, weapons and light vehicles. With surprise the key element for success Lütjens needed bad weather to cover his movements, but his hopes were dashed when dawn revealed smooth seas and clear skies. There was worse to come; as the ships passed through the Skagerrak they came under attack by RAF Blenheim bombers. Although the machines were driven off without inflicting any damage Lütjens knew that the vital element of surprise had been lost, and to a certain extent his pessimism was justified for the returning bombers reported the presence of the ships, although they incorrectly identified them as 'One battle-cruiser, two cruisers, and ten destroyers'.

Despite intelligence reports confirming that an attack on Norway was imminent, the British Admiralty decided in its wisdom that Lutjens' ships intended to break out into the Atlantic. Later that evening Admiral Sir Charles Forbes and the Home Fleet left Scapa to block the probable route of the enemy ships as they headed north. Other cruisers and destroyers were either despatched to sea or instructed to join up with the Home Fleet and, further to the south, Vice-Admiral Whitworth with the battle-cruiser *Renown* and nine destroyers was ordered to cover any attempt by the enemy to break westwards. Not one of the vessels involved was directed towards the defence of Norway and, indeed, Vice-Admiral John Cunningham's cruisers, lying at Rosyth, actually disembarked the troops which they had on board in anticipation of defensive landings in Norway before they left the Forth to join the search for Lütjens' ships.

By evening the weather had worsened, much to the satisfaction of the German Admiral, although his elation was not shared by the wretched soldiers crammed below decks on the destroyers, many of whom had never been to sea before. As darkness closed over the storm-tossed waters the winds veered and increased to Force 7. But Lütjens, single-minded as ever, had a timetable to maintain. With a callous indifference to the sufferings of the troops on board the destroyers, the Vice-Admiral refused to permit any slackening of the 26-knot fleet speed he had set. The destroyers, however, were unable to keep up with the big ships in the appalling weather conditions and within hours all semblance of formation had been lost; by dawn Lütjens' fleet was reduced to a scattered rabble of single vessels. To make matters worse, the *B-Dienst* monitors in Berlin had warned him at 22.28 the previous night that the British Home Fleet was at sea.

During the morning of the 8th Captain Hellmuth Heye led the *Hipper* and the destroyers of Group Two away from the main force and set course for Trondheim. The weather was still atrocious and some hours later, in raging seas, the *Hipper* was rammed by the British destroyer *Glowworm* in a suicidal attack that won her captain, Gerard Roope, a posthumous Victoria Cross. Despite heavy damage and serious flooding Captain Heye succeeded in nursing his stricken flagship into the sheltered waters of Trondheim fjord where, in the early hours of the 9th and in accordance with the operational timetable, Group Two's destroyers disgorged their troops who occupied the town in the face of little resistance.

After Heye's departure the two battleships and the destroyers of Group One had continued northwards towards their own objective of Narvik, a busy port some two hundred miles inside the Arctic Circle. By the time they reached the approaches to Vestfjord the gales had increased in fury to Force

10, the destroyers suffering fearful punishment as heavy seas smashed their boats, damaged fittings and equipment, and even washed some of the army vehicles that had been lashed down on deck overboard. At 21.00 Lütjens ordered the destroyers to enter Vestfjord and early on the morning of the 9th the troops, now recovered from their ordeal, went ashore, the first contingent disembarking from the *Wilhelm Heidekamp* at 04.15. The Norwegian Navy attempted to defend its homeland but the two old coast-defence ships *Eidsvooll* and *Norge* stood no chance against the *Kriegsmarine*'s more modern and powerful vessels and both were sunk by torpedoes. As the mountain troops were setting up machine-gun posts on the pier General Dietl told a Norwegian officer who had been roused from his bed by the unseemly commotion: 'I greet the Royal Norwegian Army. The German Army has come to protect Norway and her neutrality. We come as friends.' At 06.15 the local commander, Colonel Sundlo, anxious to avoid unnecessary bloodshed, handed the town over to General Dietl. Raeder's gamble had succeeded — for the moment.

Although Lütjens had fulfilled his orders and delivered the destroyers and troops on schedule, his task of covering the landings in northern Norway was by no means complete and the vital role of his battleships was highlighted at 03.30, nearly an hour before the first German soldiers had landed in Narvik, when the battlecruiser *Renown*, alerted by warning signals transmitted by the *Glowworm* shortly before she sank, was sighted fleetingly at a range of nine miles during a momentary pause in the arctic storms that had been raging continuously for nearly two days.

Snow squalls prevented an immediate engagement developing and more than an hour was to pass before Vice-Admiral Whitworth's 32,000-ton flagship was able to open fire with her 15-inch guns. The odds were remarkably even. The *Renown* had the bigger weapons but the *Scharnhorst* and *Gneisenau* were faster and better armoured. Lost in the arctic murk, however, and struggling to regain contact with the battle-cruiser in the heavy seas and tempestuous gales, were nine Home Fleet destroyers. If they succeeded in joining battle the scales would swiftly tilt in favour of the Royal Navy.

Gneisenau certainly had the worst of the engagement. Although she hit the *Renown*'s foremast and destroyed the flagship's transmitting aerials she suffered the misfortune of seeing a shell from one of her 11-inch guns pass clean through her massive target without exploding. In return, despite the appalling weather conditions which made accurate shooting almost impossible, the *Renown* straddled the *Scharnhorst* and scored three hits on the *Gneisenau*, one knocking out her fire-control system and a second silencing her rear turret. Fortunately casualties were light, with only two men killed and a further eight wounded.

Lutjens decided to break off the action when the *Scharnhorst*'s temperamental starboard engine began to give trouble and, at 04.40, the two German battleships drew ahead and vanished into the snow. Some hours later the Admiral brought them to shelter under the lee of Jan Mayen Island. Although he had achieved his purpose by keeping a British capital ship away from the lightly protected landing forces his job was not yet complete for he now needed to inform Raeder of the *Renown*'s presence in Arctic waters – without breaking radio silence. He solved the problem by despatching the *Gneisenau*'s Arado seaplane to Trondheim with a report which the *Hipper*'s wireless room would be able to pass on to Navy Group West.

Although desperately short of fuel the seaplane's pilot succeeded in reaching his destination and the contents of Lütjens' report were relayed to Admiral Alfred Saalwachter by the *Hipper*'s senior radio operator. Several hundreds of miles to the west the Fleet Commander, having licked his wounds, emerged from the desolate shelter of snow-covered Jan Mayen Island and, after joining up with Captain Hellmuth Heye's Trondheim force, finally reached Wilhelmshaven on the 12th where the three largest vessels, the *Gneisenau*, *Scharnhorst* and *Hipper*, were immediately berthed for urgent repairs to the battle damage they had sustained off northern Norway. Indeed they had been lucky to survive at all, for of the ten destroyers from Group One that had gone into Narvik on 9 April none was destined to return to the Fatherland, every single ship being either sunk by the Royal Navy or scuttled during and after the first and second battles of Narvik.

Their loss was a grievous blow to the *Kriegsmarine*. They had been built soon after the Nazis first came to power and two of the class, the *Maas* and *Schultz*, had already been sunk in error by *Luftwaffe* aircraft during Operation Viking in February, 1940. Now, as a result of the Norwegian campaign, a further ten ships from the surviving twenty vessels had been lost, more than 50% of the navy's modern destroyer strength in just eight months of war. In addition the cruiser *Karlsruhe* had been torpedoed by the submarine *Truant* and later sunk by her own escort forces south of Kristiansand while the *Königsberg* was sent to the bottom by Fleet Air Arm Skua dive-bombers at Bergen, and, as will be detailed later in this chapter, the *Blücher*, Germany's most modern cruiser, was sunk during the occupation of Oslo on the first day of the invasion. Raeder's prophecy of doom was certainly not misplaced. But the accuracy of his forecast brought him little comfort.

The task of capturing the Norwegian capital of Oslo was given to Rear-Admiral Oskar Kummetz and Group Five, the force commander flying his flag in the *Blücher*. Germany's first post-war cruiser, *Emden*, also formed part of the Group together with the battleship *Lützow* which arrived in Kiel with only hours to spare as a last-minute addition. The *Albatros*, *Kondor* and

Möwe, veterans of the Weimar Republic's first destroyer programme of 1923 now reclassified as torpedo boats, provided the escort screen and they were supported by the eight-strong 1st Motor Minesweeping Flotilla under Lt-Cdr Gustav Forstmann. Two small whalers, *Rau-7* and *Rau-8*, completed Kummetz's task force.

In accordance with the movements laid down in Operation *Weserübung* Group Five left Kiel during the early hours of 8 April and passed safely through the Great Belt and the Kattegat. Although, so far, everything had gone according to plan any danger of complacency was shattered when, during the evening as the Oslo force was approaching Skagan, a British submarine sighted the squadron and fired a full spread of torpedoes at the *Lützow*. But something went inexplicably wrong with the attack and every torpedo of the *Trident*'s ten-weapon salvo missed by a substantial margin. After her earlier run of misfortune it seemed that Lady Luck was smiling upon the *Lützow* again.

There were no further untoward incidents as Group Five closed the Norwegian coast and *Lützow*'s Captain Thiele, anxious to maintain the element of surprise, suggested to Kummetz that, on arriving off the fjord, the ships 'should dash in at once at high speed'. The Admiral, conscious that the Oslo attack was only one segment of a vast interlocking plan, and aware of the importance of adhering rigidly to the operational timetable, which required him to pass through the Dröback Narrows at 05.00 on the morning of the 9th, responded coldly to Thiele's exuberant enthusiasm. But the critical timetable suffered a rude shock when, at 00.25, the *Blücher* was exposed by searchlights as she approached the entrance to the fjord and came under fire from the island fortresses of Rauöy and Bolärne. Kummetz responded calmly to the emergency by ordering the German ships to switch on their navigation lights. The bluff worked splendidly. Assuming that the vessels, still only vague shapes moving in the darkness, were friendly the Norwegian gunners ceased fire. Nevertheless when the patrol boat *Pol III* came out to investigate the strangers she was promptly engaged by the torpedo boat *Albatros* and sunk.

Although all hopes of surprise had been dashed, Kummetz made no effort to exploit the enemy's confusion. According to the operational plan two spar-breakers were to move into the Narrows ahead of the main force to clear mines and other defensive obstacles and the Rear-Admiral decided that he must await their arrival. In the meanwhile the assault troops were transferred from the cruisers into the R-boats of the 1st Minesweeping Flotilla and then, moving forward at nine knots, the three big ships crawled slowly up the fjord towards the Narrows, the *Blücher* leading followed by the *Lützow* with the *Emden* bringing up the rear. But even this funereal speed proved to be too fast for Kummetz's pre-set timetable and he was forced to reduce the rate of advance to seven knots, an incredible risk to take in hostile waters. Soon, at 04.00, two more Norwegian gunboats sallied to meet the oncoming German warships. Kummetz, aware that the Führer wanted a peaceful occupation of Oslo, ignored the challenge and, treating his tiny adversaries with the disdain of an elephant brushing off a flea, swept past as if they did not exist. By 05.15 it was becoming clear that the two *sperrbrechers* were not going to arrive on time and Kummetz decided, reluctantly, that he must depart from the strict details of the master plan. Five minutes later, the German warships by now faintly discernible as grey ghosts sliding silently through the dawn mists shrouding the waters of the fjord, increased to half-speed and headed towards the Narrows.

The element of surprise, as Raeder had pointed out to Hitler during the initial planning stages of Operation *Weserübung*, was essential for success. As events were to prove in the course of the next few minutes, the Grand Admiral's assessment was correct. There was only one problem. It was the Germans who were caught by surprise. It was the enemy who gained the success!

As the *Blücher* nosed her bows into the Narrows the shore-defence searchlights suddenly dazzled out of the darkness and moments later, pin-pointing their target with deadly accuracy, the coastal batteries opened fire. The flagship was hit almost immediately with two 11-inch shells that destroyed the foretop observation post and started a fierce fire in the aircraft hangar, but although the Nazi cruiser retaliated with her secondary flak-armament it was impossible to identify the precise location of the guns and her main 8-inch weapons remained impotently silent.

Disaster struck within the first minute of the Norwegian's spirited defence when a shell exploded in the stern section of the ship jamming the rudder and disabling the steering gear. But the *Blücher*'s agony was not yet complete. As she veered out of control two torpedoes, launched from submerged tubes on the island of Kaholm, detonated in the engine room. Without power the cruiser was doomed and with fires raging below decks, her port side torn open like a sardine can, and ready-use ammunition exploding in various parts of the ship, she drifted towards the rocks that edged the steep-sided fjord. At 06.30 the *Blücher* shuddered as a magazine exploded and, half an hour later, as her list to port worsened, Captain Woldag gave the order to abandon ship. At 07.32 the flagship slipped quietly beneath the surface of the fjord, the raging flames only quenched as the sea closed over the blackened carcass of Germany's most modern warship.

Lützow, following next astern of the *Blücher*, did not escape the opening blast of fire from the Norwegian shore batteries. She, too, was hit by the devastatingly accurate fire from the guns mounted on the island fortress of Kaholm. One 11-inch shell struck her forward main turret and immobilized it, a lucky shot which rendered the battleship virtually powerless for, in the confined waters of the fjord, Thiele was unable to turn and bring his after turret to bear and the *Lützow*'s firepower was now effectively reduced to eight 5.9-inch guns and her six 3.9-inch flak weapons. Unable to assist the *Blücher*, and anxious to save his own ship, Thiele ordered full speed astern and hurriedly backed away from the holocaust in the Narrows, only bringing the retreating battleship to a halt some distance below Dröbak where she was safely beyond range of the shore batteries.

Thiele, who now found himself in command of Group Five, decided to land the assault troops at Sons-Bukten, a small village with a direct rail-link to Oslo. It was not strictly in accordance to plan, but with the blazing *Blücher* blocking the seaward approach to the Norwegian capital it was a realistic alternative. The Norwegians, however, were putting up a fiercer resistance than anticipated and *Lützow*'s captain soon received the disquieting news that the soldiers transferred from the *Blücher* to the R-boats earlier that morning had been repulsed in their attempts to land on the islands of Rauöy and Bolärne and that only a small number of infantrymen had got ashore at Horten. In addition the minesweeper *R-17* had been sunk and her flotilla-mate, *R-21*, damaged.

During the morning the *Luftwaffe*'s dive-bombers joined in the assault on the shore batteries, but, despite the weight of explosives dropped on the Norwegian fortresses, it was impossible to guarantee a safe passage through the Narrows. To add to Captain Thiele's problems, he was still unsure about the ultimate fate of the *Blücher*, for, although the *Luftwaffe* pilots must have been aware that the cruiser had gone down, no attempt was made to contact the *Lützow* and inform Thiele of the situation.

Some time later the motor-ship *Norden* volunteered to enter the Narrows in search of the *Blücher*. While recognizing the hazards of a reconnaissance operation under fire, Thiele was desperate for hard information. Having put a *Kriegsmarine* wireless operator and a portable radio on board the coaster, he moved the *Lützow* up the fjord so that her 11-inch guns could provide cover for the attempt. Smothered by a barrage of exploding shells the Norwegian defenders on Kaholm were unable to offer any serious resistance and the *Norden* passed through the Narrows unscathed. Fifteen minutes later the radio operator confirmed that the *Blücher* had been sunk but that, happily, a number of survivors had managed to get ashore, among them, although Thiele was unaware of the fact for several hours, the commander of Group Five, Rear-Admiral Kummetz.

There was more good news a short while later when the *Albatros* reported that the Horten naval base had surrendered. But Dröbak was still in Norwegian hands and until its defences had been reduced it remained too dangerous to pass through the Narrows, especially as the torpedo battery at

Kaholm was known to be still operational. During the early evening dive-bombers again pounded the Norwegian defences, without much material effect, and, convinced that enemy morale must be declining, Thiele sent a landing-party to Dröbak and offered the commanding officer of the Kaholm fortress the opportunity of an honourable surrender. The ploy proved to be effective and, following a brief parley, Colonel Erichsen accepted the German terms. With the passage through the Narrows now open Thiele prepared to move on the Norwegian capital. Better late, he told himself, than never.

Much to Goering's satisfaction, however, the *Luftwaffe* had beaten the *Kriegsmarine* to the target, and when the *Lützow* and the other ships of Group Five reached Oslo shortly before noon on the 10th they found the city already occupied by *Wehrmacht* troops who had been brought in by air the previous day. The *Blücher*, it seemed, had been sacrificed for nothing. It was a bitter blow.

Now that her part in Operation *Weserübung* had been completed, Thiele's next priority was to get the damaged *Lützow* back to Germany so that she could be repaired and made ready for her projected sortie into the Atlantic. So, less than twelve hours after her arrival in Oslo, the battleship was at sea again heading south for the Kattegat. Thiele kept prudently close to the Danish coast after receiving reports of enemy submarines lurking to the east but in the early hours of the following morning the *Lützow*'s radar detected a suspicious object some 15 kilometres to starboard. With his narrow escape from the *Trident* still fresh in mind, Thiele took immediate avoiding action and at 01.26 he ordered a sharp turn to port. Three minutes later a violent shock reverberated through the ship as at least one, and probably two, torpedoes from the British submarine *Spearfish* exploded under the battleship's stern, blowing off both of her propellers and disabling her steering.

Lützow was in a bad way. Her stern was literally hanging off and the sea was surging into the battleship. Although her engines were still turning she had lost her propellers and, listing to port and sinking slowly by the stern, she drifted helplessly towards the Danish coast. While damage control teams hurriedly manned the pumps and attempted to shore up the shattered bulkheads, the remainder of the crew assembled on deck in disciplined groups and waited for the inevitable order to abandon ship. One more torpedo from the submarine would spell the end of the *Lützow* for she was too badly damaged to withstand any further injuries. But, as ever, the *Lützow*'s luck remained with her, for, unaware that the battleship was on her knees, the *Spearfish* was already speeding away from the scene before her victim's escorts counter-attacked with depthcharges. Disregarding instructions to maintain radio silence, Thiele transmitted an urgent distress signal to Kiel and within the hour the first tugs and salvage ships were hurrying to the scene. By a miracle the pocket-battleship was still afloat when they arrived and, thanks to the expertise of the salvage teams, not to mention the seamanship of the *Lützow*'s captain and officers, the crippled vessel was towed safely back to Kiel.

Perhaps the last word on the disastrous Oslo expedition should rest with the German Admiralty. In an appraisal prepared on the same day that the *Lützow* was torpedoed it was admitted that 'their [*Blücher* and *Lützow*] dispatch to Oslo has proved to be an unequivocal mistake'. Raeder, for his part, made no mention of the Oslo fiasco, nor indeed any of the other landings carried out by the navy in Norway, in his memoirs. No doubt he had understandable reasons for wishing to draw a veil over a plan that had cost the *Kriegsmarine* a major part of its battle fleet.

The battleships *Scharnhorst* and *Gneisenau* had returned to Wilhelmshaven shortly before midnight on 12 April at the conclusion of their initial sortie in support of the Norway landings. By the time they were fit for combat operations again six weeks later a great deal of water had passed under the bridge. To begin with the Fleet Commander, Navy Group West, Vice-Admiral Wilhelm Marschall, had recovered from his illness and Lütjens had to stand down. *Scharnhorst*, too, was still plagued by problems with her high-pressure boilers and had spent virtually the entire time in dockyard hands while the *Gneisenau*, exercising at sea after repairs to her fire-control system, had the misfortune to encounter a mine, the underwater damage sustained leading to a further spell in dry-dock.

The entire war situation had also changed dramatically for, during the intervening six weeks, the German army and air force had overrun Holland and Belgium in a lightning blitzkrieg campaign that had brought France to her knees and driven the British Expeditionary Force back to Dunkirk. In Norway, however, the position was not quite so clear-cut. Although the *Wehrmacht*, with the not inconsiderable assistance of the *Luftwaffe*, was now in occupation of southern and central Norway, the situation in the north of the country was still very fluid. The fighting around Narvik was particularly bitter with first one side and then the other gaining the advantage.

Although the Allies had the upper hand during May, the pressures caused by Hitler's attack on the Low Countries and France forced the British government to reconsider its position in Scandinavia and on 24 May it was decided to abandon Norway. Trondheim had already been evacuated with heavy naval losses between 30 April and 2 May, most ships falling victim to the *Luftwaffe* in a chilling demonstration of what aircraft could achieve when they dominated the skies. But the destruction of the iron-ore trade remained the prime military objective and, taking advantage of their superior numbers, the Allies launched an attack which forced Dietl's forces to withdraw from the town and, on the 28th, Narvik was once again in friendly hands — the phrase 'liberated' had not yet been coined by the propagandists.

The enemy's success was greeted with dismay in Germany and, in momentary panic, the Führer suggested sending the transatlantic liners *Europa* and *Bremen* to northern Norway with troops, guns and tanks to retrieve the situation. It was a lunatic idea, for the Royal Navy was in total control of the seas around Narvik and a wholesale massacre would have ensued. There was, however, an alternative plan, which, although as hazardous as the *Europa* and *Bremen* idea, at least offered a faint chance of success. Code-named Operation Juno it was Raeder's own brainchild and typified his unshakeable confidence in the *Kriegsmarine's* battleships. In outline the Grand Admiral's plan was, in his own words, 'to relieve Force Dietl by effective engagement of British naval forces and transport in the Narvik-Halstad area'. It was an open-ended directive that was intended to allow Marschall full discretion and freedom of action. Unfortunately, due to the strange structure of Germany's higher naval command, Navy Group West and Admiral Alfred Saalwächter was interposed between Raeder's directive and its detailed execution by Marschall. Saalwächter added his own icing to Raeder's somewhat plain cake by ordering the Fleet Commander to penetrate the fjords at Harstad and attack the Allied beachhead.

Having been robbed of his initial freedom of action by the intervention of his immediate superior, Marschall now received a phone call from Berlin informing him that it was Hitler's wish that the battleships should act primarily to protect the German ground forces which, hindered by British naval bombardment, were trying to move north through central Norway to reinforce and relieve the hard-pressed Dietl. The unhappy Admiral turned to Raeder for clarification of his priorities but received an ambiguous reply which left him with the impression that the attack on the Harstad beachhead was a matter for his personal discretion.

It was in this atmosphere of confused orders and muddled command that the *Scharnhorst* and *Gneisenau* sailed from Kiel on 4 June with an escort of four destroyers. Joined en route by the cruiser *Hipper* and a support tanker, the squadron reached a position several hundred miles to the west of Harstad on the 7th and, that evening, Marschall called a conference of his senior officers on board the flagship *Gneisenau*. Reports of wireless traffic intercepted by the *B-Dienst* had confirmed the presence of numerous Allied ships in the area, but their exact location could only be determined by air reconnaissance and, at this crucial moment, the *Luftwaffe* failed to co-operate. An hour before the conference opened Marschall was informed that all flying had been suspended 'owing to bad weather'. Yet, so far as the Fleet was concerned, weather conditions seemed perfect and visibility was good to 25 miles.

Later that evening reports came in from U-boats operating in the area that three large groups of vessels, including transports, had been observed off both Harstad and Tromsö. Surprisingly, the signals indicated that the enemy ships were steaming westwards *away* from Norway. Could it be, a junior staff officer ventured uncertainly, that the Allies were withdrawing? Lacking confirmation from *B-Dienst* the suggestion was dismissed out of hand. But, as the evening lengthened and further evidence began to accumulate, Lieutenant Heinz Kohler's suggestion looked increasingly probable.

A single *Luftwaffe* aircraft that had overflown Harstad earlier in the day reported that it had been fired on by one warship and that no others could be seen, while the battleships' own Arado floatplanes, scouting to the north-east, confirmed that one of the three convoys was heavily escorted. With a certain amount of relief Marschall cancelled the attack on the beachhead and ordered his ships to hunt down the most important of the three convoys. However, he delayed informing Navy Group West of the change of plan until 05.00 the next morning and was promptly rewarded with a curt reprimand ordering him to proceed with his primary operational objective – the attack on Harstad.

By the time Marschall had received Saalwächter's signal his ships were already in action, not with the troop concentrations on the beachhead as Navy Group West intended but with a Norwegian tanker and its armed trawler escort. A few well-aimed salvoes from the *Hipper* left the tanker in flames, while the *Gneisenau* accounted for the trawler in double-quick time. The squadron swept on and, a short while later, encountered the liner *Orama*. The P&O vessel was in service as a transport but, mercifully, she was carrying no troops at the time and the *Hipper*'s 8-inch guns took only bare minutes to send her to the bottom. The cruiser next ran upon the hospital ship *Atlantis*, but, observing the strict requirements of the Geneva Convention, she was allowed to pass unharmed.

Saalwächter, sitting in the relative comfort of his command-post in Wilhelmshaven, was unaware of the Allied withdrawal and, ignorant of the new situation, saw no reason to change his original plans. Another signal beamed its way to *Gneisenau*: 'Convoy attack to be delegated to *Hipper* and destroyers. Further target Trondheim. Main objective remains Harstad'.

Marschall was furious at this latest interference. As the 'man-on-the-spot' he considered that decisions should be made by himself. And he was convinced that Raeder had given him *carte-blanche* to act on his own initiative. He therefore took the extreme step of ignoring Saalwächter's orders and, although he compromised by sending the *Hipper* and the destroyers towards Trondheim, he took the battleships in search of a British aircraft carrier whose signals had been intercepted and identified by the civilian *B-Dienst* experts in the flagship's radio room.

Marschall's gamble reaped its reward late that same afternoon when, at 16.45, Midshipman Goos, high up in the spotting-top of the *Scharnhorst*'s foremast, sighted a thin stream of smoke on the horizon at a range of some 28 miles. Moments later a mast was confirmed by the battleship's powerful rangefinder. Tension mounted on the flagship as Marschall and his officers waited for the vessel to emerge above the distant horizon. 'What do we do if it's a battleship and not a carrier?' his Chief of Staff, Backenkohler, asked. 'We shall attack regardless.' Marschall snapped without hesitation.

The crews of both battleships came to action stations at 17.02 and, with the *Scharnhorst* leading, they altered course to close the enemy vessel which was identified, at 17.10, as an aircraft carrier. A few minutes later the presence of two escorting destroyers was confirmed by the *Scharnhorst*'s Chief Gunnery Officer. At 17.21 Marschall ordered an alteration of course to 150° as the chase developed and, eleven minutes later, the *Scharnhorst* opened fire with her two forward turrets. The 11-inch shells fell short of the target and, having corrected for range and elevation, a second salvo was on its way 55 seconds later.

Just why the carrier *Glorious* and her two destroyers, *Ardent* and *Acasta*, were sailing independently of the main force further to the north has never been adequately explained. Churchill did not accept the official story that the carrier was short of fuel and other writers have suggested that her captain, Guy d'Oyly Hughes, a somewhat eccentric character, was returning to Scapa in order to convene a court martial following a dispute with one of his senior officers. Available evidence certainly suggests that, at wardroom level, the *Glorious* was not a happy ship, although Hughes was adored by the men of the lower deck. But more puzzling is the fact that she had no machines airborne at the time of the German attack despite her presence in a war zone and, apparently, none ranged on her flight-deck ready for immediate action if the enemy was encountered. By the same token not a single signal was despatched by the carrier throughout the 23-minute chase to the south.

The first serious damage was inflicted on the *Glorious* by the *Scharnhorst* at 17.38, the *Gneisenau*, which had been kept busy warding off the destroyers with her secondary armament, not joining the main action until eight minutes later. By 17.52 several fierce fires were raging in the hangar deck and, at long last, the carrier tried to transmit a radio signal, but the message was so broken and distorted that it made little sense. A second signal, sent at 18.19, was jammed by the *B-Dienst* experts on board the flagship. Ten minutes later the vessel was listing so severely that her flight-deck was trailing in the water and aircraft were sliding over the side into the sea. Half an hour later, her agony mercifully at an end, she went to the bottom. 1,474 members of her crew died with their ship together with 41 RAF personnel, the latter figure including all but two of the fighter pilots who, without experience of deck-landings, had flown their Hurricane and Gladiator machines onto the carrier after evacuating their extemporized base on a frozen lake at Bardufoss.

It had been a stunning success for Marschall and he was no doubt relieved that his defiance of orders had been blessed with victory. But the battleships had not escaped scot-free from the engagement. Although the destroyer *Ardent* had been sunk by the *Gneisenau* at an early stage of the action, her flotilla-mate *Acasta* remained afloat and, soon after 18.30, she emerged from behind the burning carrier and steered at high speed towards the German ships. Despite being hit time and time again by heavy shells she continued to close the battleships and, as she swept across the *Scharnhorst*'s bows, she was observed to fire three of four torpedoes at a seemingly impossible angle. Captain Hoffmann was not a man to take unnecessary chances and, although the chances of a hit appeared to be highly unlikely, he swung his ship to starboard while the *Scharnhorst*'s secondary armament continued to hammer the burning destroyer with relentless precision. Nine minutes later, after the battleship had resumed her original course, one of the torpedoes, supposedly fired from too long a range even to reach its intended target, struck the *Scharnhorst* and exploded beneath *Caesar* turret.

The battleship's speed fell to 20 knots and, before the damage control teams could stem the flood, she shipped 2,500 tons of water. In addition the explosion had killed 48 members of the crew. In a matter of seconds the *Scharnhorst* had been transformed from an asset to a liability and Marschall decided to make for Trondheim where temporary repairs could be carried out and where, as a bonus, he would be relatively safe from the ships of the Royal Navy which would by now certainly be seeking vengeance for the loss of the *Glorious*. His deliberate flouting of Saalwächter's orders were beginning to take on a new and somewhat worrying perspective.

But while Trondheim may have offered sanctuary from the British Navy it provided no protection from the Royal Air Force and, on 11 June, twelve Hudson aircraft carried out a high-level attack using 500-pound armour-piercing bombs, all thirty-six of which providentially missed their targets. Marschall received another rude shock when he discovered that, although he was safe from the *ships* of the Royal Navy, he was still vulnerable to the Fleet Air Arm. On the 15th, two days after the RAF's abortive attack, fifteen Skua dive-bombers from 800 and 803 Squadrons took off from the *Ark Royal* and headed for Trondheim. The sortie ended in tragedy. Eight machines, more than 50% of the strike force, were destroyed by *Luftwaffe* fighters and flak. In return the navy pilots succeeded in landing only one bomb on the *Scharnhorst*, and that failed to explode.

The battleship spent some ten days completing temporary repairs and left Trondheim for her return passage to Kiel on 20 June, a journey that was certainly to lack nothing by way of excitement. It opened with Captain Hoffmann seeking enforced refuge in Stavangar to escape the unwelcome attentions of the Home Fleet. This was followed with an attack by six Fleet Air Arm torpedo bombers, another failure which cost the British two more machines. Later the same day she came under threat again, this time by nine Bristol Beaufort bombers from Coastal Command's Wick-based No 42 Squadron.

The *Scharnhorst* had, by now, become the nucleus of a small but powerful squadron consisting of six destroyers and a motor torpedo boat. The *Luftwaffe*, too, was present in force and a combat air patrol made up of nine Me-109 fighters circled above the ships as they moved southwards down the Norwegian coast. It was a rare example of inter-service co-operation and, on this occasion, it was to pay handsome dividends. The Beauforts, taking part in the machine's first offensive operation of the war, dived valiantly through the shot and shell of the flak defences to release their bombs from an altitude of 1500 feet, as their target, twisting and turning like a trapped rabbit, churned the sea to white foam with its threshing propellers and sharp movements of the helm. But again the British pilots obtained no hits and the Beauforts suffered heavily at the hands of both the *Luftwaffe* and the anti-aircraft guns of the ships. The ferocity of the flak defences during these two attacks can be gauged by the ammunition returns: 900 rounds of 4.1-inch being expended by the *Scharnhorst* alone plus a further 1,200 rounds of 37mm by her light anti-aircraft batteries. But the Beaufort raid proved to be the end of their three-day ordeal and the battleship finally entered Kiel harbour safely on the 23rd, home at last from what had been, in the final analysis, a remarkably successful mission.

Marschall, in the meanwhile, had not allowed the grass to grow under his feet and, even while the *Scharnhorst* was lying at Trondheim licking her wounds, he had taken the *Gneisenau* and *Hipper* to sea in search of fresh targets. But, alarmed by the loss of the *Glorious* and her two destroyers and aware that Hitler's two most powerful battleships were at large north of the Arctic Circle, the Royal Navy took the sensible precaution of adding capital ships, cruisers, and even carriers, to their escort forces. Although Marschall found two convoys, he decided, on both occasions, that their defences were too strong to challenge and withdrew before being sighted by the enemy.

On 20 June, the day on which the *Scharnhorst* began her journey back to

Kiel, Marschall again sortied from Trondheim in the hope of finding a lightly defended convoy off Iceland. But, while still inside Norwegian waters, the ships were sighted by the submarine *Clyde*, which, having skilfully penetrated the protective destroyer screen, hit the *Gneisenau* with a well-placed torpedo that blew a large hole through her bows. It was a bitter blow for the unfortunate Marschall who was forced to return to Trondheim for the second time in ten days with a crippled battleship.

Despite the skilled help of the shipwrights from the repair ship *Huaskaren*, it was 25 July before the flagship was in a fit state to leave Trondheim and head for home and the *Gneisenau* enjoyed a lucky escape the following day when one of her escorts, the torpedo boat *Luchs*, was sunk by a submarine. Ironically, on this particular occasion, the attack was carried out in error by a German U-boat which only served to make the loss even more tragic.

The *Gneisenau* limped into Kiel on 27 July and Marschall knew that he must now face the wrath of both Raeder and Saalwächter for disobeying orders during the execution of Operation Juno. He solved the problem in the time-honoured manner. He reported sick — although sick of what he failed to make clear — and, resigning as Fleet Commander, Navy Group West, on health grounds he was replaced by Gunther Lutjens who had been waiting impatiently on the sidelines ever since the Vice-Admiral's return to the fleet in May.

Marschall nevertheless came under bitter criticism from Raeder who seemed to find fault even with the Admiral's successes. Why, he asked, were the tanker and trawler not seized as prizes rather than sunk? And why had a valuable ship like the *Orama* been sunk when the Reich was in urgent need of large transports? He even refused to acknowledge any merit in the destruction of the *Glorious* and her attendant destroyers. 'Mere target practice,' he observed dismissively. Of course he returned over and over again to Marschall's failure to attack the Harstad beachhead, conveniently overlooking his own part in the confusion of orders that had precipitated the Admiral's disobedience.

Although the Grand Admiral refused to retract his accusations against Marschall the latter was reinstated to favour in the summer of 1942 when he was appointed to succeed his former chief, Saalwächter, as C-in-C Navy Group West. It was the nearest thing to an apology that Raeder was capable of making.

CHAPTER FIVE

'Beyond Reproach'

With NOT ONE OF ITS BATTLESHIPS operational, the fleet which Vice-Admiral Lütjens took over from Marschall existed in little more than name only. The *Scharnhorst* and *Gneisenau* were both under repair following the torpedo damage they had sustained during the closing stages of the Norwegian campaign; the *Lützow* had lost her stern and would need many months of reconstruction in dry-dock; the *Admiral Scheer* was at Wilhelmshaven undergoing a prolonged facelift which, on paper, would reduce her to the status of a heavy cruiser; while both the *Bismarck* and the *Tirpitz* were still fitting-out, although, admittedly, the former was due to be commissioned into the fleet within a few weeks. Even so she would need many more months of trials, exercises and training before she and her crew were battleworthy.

Work on the aircraft-carrier *Graf Zeppelin* had been suspended on 10 April and by the end of May, 1940, the *Kriegsmarine* found itself down to just four 5.9-inch gunned light cruisers: *Emden, Köln, Leipzig* and *Nürnberg*, and a single 8-inch gunned heavy cruiser, the *Hipper*. Finally, the heavy losses suffered by Bonte's flotilla at Narvik had left the navy with only ten modern destroyers, although more were nearing completion. In the space of two months Hitler's Norwegian gamble had slashed the strength of Germany's surface fleet to a level inferior to that allowed to the Weimar Republic's *Reichsmarine* by the Treaty of Versailles. Raeder's prophecy, made in October, 1939, that an attack on Norway 'might lose us the whole of our fleet' had proved to be uncomfortably close to the truth.

But if the battleships had suffered severe damage at the hands of the Royal Navy at sea, they were soon revealed to be equally at risk even in harbour. On 1 July five Whitley bombers made an abortive daylight attack on the *Scharnhorst* at Kiel and that night the first 2,000-pound bomb of the war was aimed at the battleship during a raid on the naval base by Hampden aircraft from 83 Squadron. The weapon, which missed its intended target, exploded in a residential part of the city killing at least ten civilians. In another night attack on 8/9 July the *Lützow* enjoyed a lucky escape when she was hit by a bomb which failed to detonate. Although the RAF's efforts had so far been in vain it was becoming abundantly clear that Germany's big ships now faced as much danger from the skies as they did from the guns and torpedoes of the British fleet. Indeed, by the end of the war the bomber was to pose by far the greater threat to Hitler's battleships.

With the commissioning of the *Bismarck* on 24 August, 1940, the prospects for Germany's surface fleet began to look a little brighter, although Captain Ernst Lindemann had many months of hard work ahead of him before the battleship could be regarded as fully operational. Her sea trials began on 15 September and, passing through the Kiel Canal the following day, she proceeded to Gdynia for crew training and working-up. Her first full-power engine tests were delayed for various technical reasons until 23 October but her performance during speed trials the following month when she achieved a creditable 30.8 knots over the measured mile boosted confidence in her ability to give the Royal Navy a hard time when she finally became operational.

Unfortunately, her sister-ship *Tirpitz* did not enjoy such a happy start to her career. On the night of 8/9 October, some three months before she was formally commissioned into the fleet, she came under attack by seventeen Bomber Command Hudson aircraft while berthed in the fitting-out basin at the Wilhelmshaven dockyard. As it happened she suffered no serious damage, but the incident was an uncomfortable omen of things to come.

With the *Bismarck* about to join the fleet and the *Scharnhorst* and *Gneisenau* likely to be operational again before the end of the year, Raeder felt that the time was ripe for another commerce-raiding sortie. On 14 October he obtained Hitler's permission to despatch the *Admiral Scheer* into the Atlantic to wage war against Britain's oceanic trade routes. The Führer was initially somewhat reluctant to risk one of his precious battleships in such a venture, but he finally approved Raeder's proposals and the *Seekriegsleitung* in Berlin began to prepare detailed operational instructions for the *Scheer*'s commanding officer Captain Theodore Krancke, a former Commandant of the *Kriegsmarine*'s Naval College and, during the Norwegian campaign, a staff officer serving on Raeder's *Oberkommando der Kriegsmarine*.

The *Scheer* left Gdynia on 23 October, 1940, and, after a brief visit to Brunsbuttle, arrived at Stavangar on the 28th. Three days later the pocket-battleship was fighting her way south through the heavy seas and Arctic gales of the Denmark Strait, the *Kriegsmarine*'s favourite surface-ship route into the North Atlantic. Despite losing two men overboard, Krancke was more than satisfied with his progress. Having made good use of his newly-fitted radar to avoid visual contact with enemy patrols, he was confident that the Royal Navy was, at this stage, unaware that a German battleship was once again prowling the Atlantic for victims.

Thanks to the *B-Dienst* monitoring service Krancke knew that a large British convoy, HX-84, had left the Canadian port of Halifax on 27 October and, on the basis of information received from Berlin, he carefully plotted its probable route on his charts. By 5 November the *Scheer* was in position to intercept the enemy and at 09.40 that morning the battleship's Arado floatplane was catapulted off to search for prey. The machine returned some hours later and its *Luftwaffe* pilot, Lieutenant Pietsch, was able to confirm the presence of the convoy. It was good news. But, even better, despite flying a considerable distance in all directions, he had seen no sign of any escort ships in the vicinity.

Krancke decided to strike at once and, as the alarm gongs sent the crew hurrying to their battle stations, the *Scheer* turned towards her still invisible target. There was an unexpected hitch at 14.30 when a solitary unescorted ship suddenly loomed over the horizon. It was a worrying moment for *Scheer*'s captain. If the merchantman identified the approaching warship as an enemy raider she might transmit an R-R-R distress call. And if she did so there was little doubt that the convoy would scatter in all directions. It was a chance that Krancke did not dare risk taking and, throwing discretion to the wind, he closed the steamer, the 5,389-ton banana boat *Mopan*, and ordered her to stop. To his undisguised relief she obeyed instantly. Her crew took to the boats and, most importantly, her radio remained silent. Unable to spare the time to put a prize-crew on board Krancke opened fire with the *Scheer*'s 4.1-inch flak guns and, holed along her waterline, the banana boat began to settle deeper in the water, finally sinking at 16.05, just ninety minutes after being first sighted.

But Krancke had already lost interest in his unfortunate victim even before she took her last plunge to the bottom. For the long-awaited convoy had meanwhile emerged over the southern horizon, thirty-seven hapless ships huddled together for mutual protection and, so far as Krancke could make out, without a warship escort. As *Scheer*'s captain examined the target through his binoculars he saw a large single-funnel vessel with the towering superstructure of a passenger liner steaming at the head of the convoy suddenly break away from the main body of ships and alter course towards the *Scheer*. A signal lamp flickered from her bridge.

What ship?

Krancke made no attempt to answer. He suspected that the challenger was a British armed merchant cruiser and he wanted to entice her within range of his main armament before revealing his true identity. While the enemy captain remained uncertain he would probably hold his fire. Krancke knew he was gambling with fate, but it seemed to be a chance worth taking.

Standing on the bridge of the *Jervis Bay* Captain Edward Fegen peered at the approaching stranger through his glasses. No one had warned him that a pocket-battleship was at large in the North Atlantic and in the first instance he had to assume that the warship — for such she appeared to be — was friendly. And, if she proved to be hostile, Fegen knew that he must sacrifice his own vessel to save the merchant ships that were sailing under his protection. His uncertainty was soon resolved. The *Scheer* altered course to open the A-arcs of her two main turrets and Fegen recognized his opponent for what she was, a Nazi battleship. Six 11-inch and eight 5.9-inch guns versus the *Jervis Bay*'s seven antiquated 6-inch weapons. The captain of the British armed merchant cruiser realized that he was about to embark on a battle he could not win, but like Kennedy of the *Rawalpindi*, Fegen did not flinch from his duty.

The two vessels were still 17,000 yards apart when the *Scheer*'s 11-inch guns opened fire and the battleship's very first salvo straddled the auxiliary cruiser with alarming accuracy. Disregarding the danger, Fegen placed the *Jervis Bay* squarely between the Nazi sea wolf and the convoy and, in accordance with Admiralty instructions, ordered the merchantmen to scatter. Krancke watched the ships break formation and run for safety with thick black smoke billowing from their funnels as they built up speed. But, despite a growing feeling of frustration, he realized that there was nothing he could do to stop them until he had disposed of the armed merchant cruiser.

Salvo after salvo smashed into the unarmoured superstructure of the *Jervis Bay*, cutting men down as they stood at their posts, splintering steel, shattering wood and starting numerous fires that were soon blazing out of control. One shell demolished the charthouse, knocked out the steering and killed or wounded every person on the bridge. Fegen himself was wounded severely, but, despite horrific injuries to one of his arms, he made his way through the flames and wreckage to the emergency steering position in the after part of the ship.

Although her forward guns had been destroyed and those in the stern could not be brought to bear on the enemy, the *Jervis Bay* continued to close the *Scheer* and Krancke was forced to concentrate his main 11-inch guns on the auxiliary cruiser instead of using them to sink the escaping merchantman from the convoy. But the *Scheer* still had her secondary armament of 5.9-inch weapons and Krancke employed them to good effect against the fleeing steamers. The tanker *San Demetrio* and the cargo-liner *Rangitiki* were both badly damaged before they finally gave Krancke the slip and vanished over the horizon.

Fegen, however, fought to the bitter end and the order to abandon ship was only given when it was physically impossible to resist any longer. Battered and burning, with her decks literally running with blood, the *Jervis Bay* rolled over on her beam ends and sank beneath the waves soon after 20.00. Her captain, Edward Stephen Fogarty Fegen, who was later awarded

1. Grand Admiral Erich Raeder—the man who created Hitler's war fleet.

2. Grand Admiral Karl Doenitz, who succeeded Raeder as C-in-C of the *Kriegsmarine* in January, 1943, won a last-minute reprieve for the battleships following Hitler's decision to scrap them.

3. Vice-Admiral Wilhelm Marschall whose battleships sank the armed merchant cruiser *Rawalpindi* during their first combat sortie in November, 1939.

4. Admiral Boehm, Hitler's first fleet commander, resigned in October, 1939, following a dispute with Raeder.

5. Vice-Admiral Otto Ciliax implemented Hitler's plan to bring the *Scharnhorst*, *Gneisenau* and *Prinz Eugen* through the Channel.

6. Vice-Admiral Günther Lütjens was probably Hitler's best fighting admiral. He was lost when the *Bismarck* was sunk by the Royal Navy in May, 1941.

7. Vice-Admiral Otto Schniewind succeeded Ciliax as fleet commander. He later became C-in-C Navy Group North.

8. Described as 'a man of great humanity', the *Graf Spee's* captain, Hans Langsdorff.

9. Germany's first post-war battleship, *Deutschland*, was laid down in February, 1929—four years before Hitler came to power.

10. Her sister-ship *Admiral Scheer* helped to support Franco's forces during the Spanish Civil War.

11. *Admiral Graf Spee*, the third and last of Hitler's pocket-battleships, steams down-Channel to represent Germany at the 1937 Spithead Coronation Review.

12. *Scharnhorst*—Hitler's most successful battleship. Launched in October, 1936, she was sunk in action by the Royal Navy off the North Cape on Boxing Day, 1943.

the posthumous Victoria Cross for valour, was sadly not numbered among the sixty-five survivors who were scooped out of the sea by a Swedish freighter after the battle.

Having disposed of the convoy's only armed escort Krancke was now free to give chase, but with dusk closing in he had only a short period of daylight left in which to accomplish his task. A slaughter of the innocents followed, a massacre that would have been even worse had the *Jervis Bay*'s gallant sacrifice not delayed the battleship from getting to grips with the convoy an hour or so earlier. Nevertheless five ships, *Maidan*, *Trewellard*, *Kanbane Head*, *Beaverford* and *Fresno City*, were sunk by gunfire, while a sixth was damaged. With the *Mopan* and the *Jervis Bay* also to his credit, Krancke had sent a total of 52,884 tons of British shipping to the bottom in the space of six hours, as well as inflicting damage on three other vessels. It was a dramatic demonstration of what a battleship could achieve given a modicum of luck.

The fate of the convoy sent a cold wind shivering through the corridors of Whitehall. Two other Liverpool-bound convoys which had already left Halifax were hurriedly ordered to return to Canada and, at the same time, steps were taken to seal off the main exits from the North Atlantic in an attempt to trap the raider. The Home Fleet battleships *Nelson* and *Rodney* were deployed to block the Iceland-Faeroes passage while the battle-cruisers *Hood*, *Renown*, and *Repulse*, together with the cruisers *Dido*, *Naiad* and *Phoebe*, were despatched to cover the approaches to the Bay of Biscay – five powerful capital ships to hunt down a single pocket-battleship with the displacement of a large cruiser and an armament of just six 11-inch guns!

In a major shift of policy it was also decided that, in future, no convoy would cross the Atlantic without at least one battleship among its escort. Indeed the *Scheer*'s sortie against HX-84 caused the Admiralty such grave concern that, until the *Tirpitz* was crippled in 1944, modern capital ships of the *King George V*-class were held back for service with the Home Fleet for the sole task of countering a raiding foray by one or more of Hitler's battleships, a strategic decision that was to cost Britain its Asiatic empire in 1941 and 1942.

Krancke, of course, had no intention of running into the trap which the Royal Navy was so carefully organizing. Signals from the *B-Dienst* interception service in Berlin kept him informed of British movements and, mindful of the instructions he had received from Raeder, he took his ship southwards away from the hornet's nest which his presence in the North Atlantic had stirred up.

Like Langsdorff and the *Graf Spee*, Krancke needed to refuel the *Scheer* at regular intervals. But before rendezvousing with his supply ship, *Nordmark*, he first met up with the *Eurofeld*, a German freighter which had been holed up in Tenerife ever since the outbreak of war. The *Eurofeld* was suffering from endemic engine trouble and, somewhat incredibly, she was ordered to make contact with the *Scheer* so that the battleship's Chief Engineer could investigate the problem and offer his expert advice on how to solve it.

The two ships duly met on 12 November and the *Scheer*'s engineering staff went aboard the steamer to carry out temporary repairs to the *Eurofeld*'s leaking boilers pending the arrival of the *Nordmark*, the latter having the necessary spares in her stores to allow a more permanent repair to be executed. The supply-ship arrived four days later on the 16th and, as she came alongside, she was welcomed by the *Scheer*'s band which was playing appropriately cheerful music on the battleship's quarterdeck. To the casual observer it was difficult to believe that Germany was at war or that the world's oceans were dominated and controlled by the Royal Navy.

The three ships remained in company for four days during which time the *Scheer* embarked some 1,327 tons of diesel oil and transferred many tons of food and other provisions from the *Nordmark* to her capacious storerooms. Then, after arranging his next meeting with the supply ship, Krancke took the *Scheer* south towards the Equator while the now rejuvenated *Eurofeld* set off to rendezvous with another raider, the auxiliary cruiser *Thor*.

On Sunday 24 November the battleship returned to the fray by attacking the 7,500-ton refrigeration ship *Port Hobart*, Krancke thoughtfully allowing his victim to transmit a raider distress signal in the certain knowledge that it would bring the Royal Navy hotfoot to the scene, by which time, of course, he would have departed for pastures new. The Prize Law rules, however, were strictly observed and, before sinking the steamer, her passengers and crew, the former somewhat disconcertingly including seven women, were brought off to the *Scheer* by motorboat. The arrival of his guests posed no problems for the ever-resourceful Krancke who placed the men under guard in one of the seamen's messes while gallantly making cabins available for the ladies.

Exactly a week later the battleship's Arado floatplane sighted the steamer *Tribesman* some 900 miles off the coast of Gambia and the *Scheer* stealthily closed her victim in readiness for a night attack. The British ship attempted to transmit a distress call but this time Krancke wanted to keep his presence secret and shot away the *Tribesman*'s aerials to ensure her silence. Her crew, comprising eight European officers and 69 lascar seamen, were brought on board the battleship and, having taken the Europeans to join their compatriots on the forward mess deck, the Indians were segregated and confined under guard in another part of the ship. Then, having disposed of the unfortunate *Tribesman*, Krancke made his way back to the relative safety of the central Atlantic.

While the *Scheer* was roaming an empty ocean in a fruitless search for further victims, Germany's newest battleship, the *Bismarck*, was still undergoing her long-drawn-out period of gestation. The Baltic trials had revealed numerous, if minor, faults and on 5 December the battleship left Rügen with *Sperrbrecher 6* and, after a two-day passage through the Kiel Canal, arrived at Hamburg on the 9th where she was warped into her berth at the Blohm & Voss shipyard so that the necessary work could be carried out. There were no complaints from her crew who, as a result, were given a welcome spell of Christmas leave. But frustration set in with the New Year when the officers and men returned from furlough. For although the battleship was ready for further trials on 24 January, 1941, a return passage to the Baltic via the Kiel Canal had to be postponed until a sunken ore-carrier, which was blocking the waterway, had been cleared.

Severe weather conditions prevented salvage operations, however, and the extreme cold also caused damage to some of the *Bismarck*'s instruments and electrical systems. But, after several postponements, the obstacle was ultimately raised and towed away and, on 7 March, the battleship entered the waterway en route to Kiel. Thick ice made conditions hazardous and the veteran *Schlesien*, acting as an extemporized icebreaker, led her newly-built sister out into the Baltic for another period of gunnery exercises and calibration shoots before she finally berthed in Gdynia on 17 March. The pride of the *Kriegsmarine* and, by common consent, one of the world's most handsome and powerful battleships, was at last ready to make her contribution to the war at sea.

Raeder's plan to step up surface attacks on Britain's trade routes was taken one step further at the beginning of December, 1940, when the cruiser *Hipper* was despatched through the Denmark Strait with orders to attack the vulnerable HX convoys and, having completed her task, to return to the French port of Brest which the *SKL* considered to be a more suitable base than Kiel or Wilhelmshaven for a ship of *Hipper*'s limited capabilities. The sortie proved to be a dismal failure. Bad weather hampered operations and no Halifax-Liverpool convoys were sighted. But on Christmas Eve, while returning despondently to Brest, the cruiser's radar picked up the echoes of a large convoy, WS-5A, a glittering prize comprising no fewer than twenty transports carrying troop reinforcements, tanks, guns and other vital military equipment to the 8th Army in North Africa. Not surprisingly, it was strongly protected.

Hipper shadowed the ships throughout the night, but, as Captain Wilhelm Meisel prepared to attack on the morning of Christmas Day, the heavy cruiser *Berwick* and two light cruisers emerged from the dawn mists. Obeying Raeder's instructions not to take any unnecessary risks nor to seek action with superior forces, the German captain turned away and, although a brief exchange of salvoes resulted in damage to the *Berwick* and one of the transports, *Empire Trooper*, the *Hipper* herself escaped unscathed. The cruiser's precipitate flight only served to reinforce Raeder's preference for employing only heavily armed battleships for raiding operations. The *Hipper* simply did not have the power to take on the *Berwick*, but the *Scharnhorst* and *Gneisenau* were immeasurably superior, and on 28 December, the day after the *Hipper* arrived at Brest, the two battleships left Germany for a sortie against the Atlantic convoy routes which promised to be the most devastating so far launched.

Promises, however, are notoriously fickle, and late December was scarcely the most opportune time to venture into the wild Arctic waters through which the ships would have to pass in order to reach the Denmark Strait. On the 29th mounting gales forced the escorting destroyers to turn back and, instead of improving, the weather only deteriorated further. The mountainous seas crashing over the bows of the two battleships caused considerable damage to their delicate fire-control systems, a chronically weak spot in their design, while the *Gneisenau* suffered the additional misfortune of fracturing several deck beams. Lütjens, a realist as well as a practical seaman, recognized the futility of proceeding any further, especially as faults had also developed in the ships' anti-aircraft defence equipment and, giving best to the weather, he reversed course and brought the two battleships back to Kiel for structural repairs.

Krancke, many thousands of miles to the south, had been suffering similar frustrations and the fortnight that had followed his destruction of the *Tribesman* had found the central Atlantic disappointingly empty of shipping, even though he had enjoyed better weather than Lütjens. The *Scheer* had refuelled from the *Nordmark* on 14 December and, the following morning, Krancke had taken the opportunity to transfer his prisoners to the supply ship before moving south in search of fresh prey. Two days later his patience was rewarded when the *Scheer* intercepted the 8,650-ton refrigeration ship *Duquesa* whose holds were crammed full of eggs, frozen meat, and crate upon crate of tinned provisions, enough, as one of the battleship's crew observed, to feed an army. Aware that the *Hipper* was operating in the North Atlantic, Krancke made no attempt to block his victim's R-R-R distress call, reasoning that the presence of a German raider on the equator would draw off some of the British units currently engaged in hunting the *Hipper*, thus relieving the pressure on Meisel's cruiser.

Examination of the *Duquesa*'s manifest revealed that she was far too valuable to be sunk out of hand, although, unfortunately her antiquated coal-burning engines and depleted bunkers meant that she had insufficient endurance to be returned to Germany as a prize. Nevertheless there was plenty of plunder for the taking and Krancke had not overlooked the fact that Christmas was coming. Almost licking his lips in anticipation, he put an armed party of seamen aboard the *Duquesa* and, with his now captive victim sailing in company, he set off to meet the *Nordmark*.

In a scene reminiscent of the Spanish Main in the 17th Century the crews of the *Scheer* and the *Nordmark* stripped the hapless merchantman bare when the three ships came together soon after dawn on the 22nd − or, at least, they would have done so had there been sufficient room to stow their loot. Nevertheless they managed to remove no less than 604 cases of eggs, 503 crates of tinned meat, a quantity of bacon, and 177 sides of frozen beef and mutton. But, unlike the pirates of yesteryear, Captain Krancke exhibited a chivalrous regard for his prisoners and, aware of the unsuitable conditions on board the *Nordmark*, he transferred the seven women taken from the *Port Hobart* to the more civilized and commodious accommodation available on the *Duquesa*, a gesture much appreciated by the ladies.

Krancke, meanwhile, remained hopeful that he would be able to replenish the *Duquesa*'s coal stocks so that she could be sailed back to Germany and, with this in mind, he decided to retain the refrigeration ship as a floating store-cupboard at least for the time being. Having decided upon a new rendezvous, 25S 14W, with Captain Grau of the *Nordmark*, the *Scheer* went her separate way.

The battleship's crew celebrated Christmas in traditional style with beef, beer, walnuts and a plentiful supply of cigarettes, by courtesy of the unfortunate *Duquesa*. Coloured paper decorations hung gaily from the armoured steel deckheads in the messes and, in a poignant reminder of home, a fir tree was lashed to the foremast. The prisoners aboard the *Nordmark* fared less well and had to be content with bread, jam and sausages for their festive repast, although, on Christmas Eve, the masters and officers from the merchant ships, who were accommodated in the after part of the ship, received a visit from Captain Grau who brought them a bottle of champagne to mark the occasion.

German movements in the South Atlantic in the immediate post-Christmas period were complicated by the arrival of the captured Norwegian tanker *Storstad*, whose cargo was utilized to restock the *Nordmark*'s tanks; the supply ship *Eurofeld*; and the *Thor*, a former merchant ship which had been converted into an auxiliary cruiser for long-range commerce raiding operations. All five ships came together on 29 December when the *Scheer* took on 656 tons of oil from the *Nordmark* before steaming to the south-east in company with the *Thor*. But New Year's Eve saw the two warships and the *Nordmark* together again with the *Eurofeld* close at hand, the squadron being watched over by the battleship's Arado floatplane which maintained a standing patrol to provide early warning of an unexpected enemy approach. It is impossible not to admire the *Kriegsmarine*'s self-confidence. Despite being more than 6,000 miles from home, and with the world's oceans dominated and controlled by the Royal Navy, Raeder had had the nerve, or perhaps the impudence, to concentrate no fewer than six vessels, one of which was an 11,700-ton battleship, with apparent impunity. As the *Scheer*'s radio room was taking down an encoded signal from *SKL* in Berlin congratulating her captain and crew on the success of the sortie so far, the assembled ships were flashing New Year greetings to each other with typical peacetime abandon. For the young sailors serving on the battleship it was a heartening and morale-boosting experience.

The South Atlantic was destined to become the focal point for German anti-commerce operations during the opening months of 1941 and the *Scheer* was soon joined by three other vessels, the *Pinguin*, the *Kormoran* and the *Atlantis*, former merchant ships which, like the *Thor*, had been converted into auxiliary cruisers. The *Nordmark* and the captured prizes also played a pivotal role in the deadly game of hide-and-seek between the *Kriegsmarine* and the Royal Navy, for without the support of their oil fuel and stores the entire operation would have collapsed within a fortnight. The *Nordmark*, for this reason, was restricted to an isolated area of ocean some 600 miles to the north of Tristan da Cunha, identified by the codename *Andalusia*, where she made her services available not only to the surface raiders but also to three Italian submarines which were operating in the South Atlantic.

The *Scheer*, of course, took the lion's share of the *Nordmark*'s oil and provisions, but the *Duquesa* continued to act as a bottomless pit of stores, an Aladdin's cave of treasure of which Captain Grau made good use. During one three-day period in the middle of January a further 3,240 cases of eggs, 1,371 crates of corned beef and 235 sacks of frozen lamb, mutton and beef were transhipped to the supply vessel, while the majority of the prisoners held on board the *Nordmark* were transferred to the *Eurofeld*, the latter reaching Occupied France with her human cargo in March. The *Storstad* too, having been bled dry of her consignment of high-quality fuel oil, also returned to Europe with a further batch of prisoners some while later.

After nearly a month of relative inactivity, the *Scheer* struck again on 18 January when the battleship seized the Norwegian tanker *Sandefjord* which Krancke sent back to the *Nordmark* with a prize crew on board. The next day two ships were sighted simultaneously, a situation that posed Krancke with an unexpected dilemma. He selected the Dutch freighter *Barneveld* as his first victim and, having bluffed her crew into supposing that the *Scheer* was a British warship, boarded her without firing a single shot. He then turned his attention to the other vessel, the British-registered *Stanpark*. His initial bluff now paid a double dividend. For the *Stanpark*'s officers, having watched the battleship approach the Dutch vessel without opening fire, assumed not unnaturally that she must be a Royal Navy cruiser and no resistance was offered when a boarding-party came across in a motorboat and clambered up the side. By the time they realized that their visitors were wearing *Kriegsmarine* uniforms it was too late. Armed seamen seized the radio office before a distress signal could be transmitted while the bewildered crew of the freighter found themselves being bundled into the motorboat and taken back to the *Scheer*.

Having disposed of the crew, the boarding-party proceeded to place demolition charges in vital parts of the *Stanpark* and, completing their task of destruction by opening the sea-cocks, they left the freighter to die, but she failed to sink quickly enough for Krancke's liking and she was finally helped on her way to the bottom of the Atlantic with two of the *Scheer*'s torpedoes. He then set off in pursuit of the *Barneveld* and, catching up with her the following morning, took off her crew, recovered the boarding-party, and sent her to join the *Stanpark* on the ocean floor with the help of strategically placed explosive charges.

The feverish activity in the South Atlantic was mirrored in Germany where the *Scharnhorst* and *Gneisenau* were preparing for another sortie. But the optimism of their crews as they readied themselves for glory was not shared by their more inexperienced comrades in the *Tirpitz*, the last of Hitler's battleships to be completed. Her first commanding officer, Captain Karl Topp, was due to commission her into the fleet on 25 January, 1941, and, having finished fitting-out in the naval dockyard at Wilhelmshaven, she was busy loading stores and equipment when the RAF struck on the night of 8/9 January. A mixed force of thirty-two Hampden, Whitley and Wellington bombers carried out a heavy raid on the dockyard area during which their crews reported that their bombs had straddled the *Tirpitz* and started a number of fires. But despite the weight of high explosives dropped by the British bombers the battleship emerged from the raid virtually unscathed. Nevertheless it was a nerve-wracking experience for her newly-joined crew, many of whom had never seen a gun fired in anger or heard a bomb explode at close range. Mercifully none of them could foresee what horrors the Royal Air Force had in store for them in the months that lay ahead.

On 22 January, three days before the *Tirpitz* officially joined the fleet, Vice-Admiral Lütjens took the *Scharnhorst* and *Gneisenau* to sea again in a renewed attempt to break out into the Atlantic. The dyspeptic cigar-loving Kurt Hoffmann was still in command of the *Scharnhorst* but the *Gneisenau* had a new captain, Otto Fein, who had joined the ship following Harold Netzbandt's promotion to the post of Lütjen's Chief of Staff. The enterprise, codenamed Operation Berlin, got off to a bad start when the two ships were observed steaming through the Great Belt by a British agent who promptly alerted London. The warning brought an immediate response. The Home Fleet, a formidable force of three battleships and eight cruisers, together with numerous escorting destroyers, put to sea immediately, while the Air Ministry, working in close co-operation with the Admiralty, ordered Coastal Command to strengthen its patrols over the Skagerrak and the waters off the Norwegian coast through which the German ships must pass if an Atlantic sortie was planned.

Lütjens originally intended to break out through the Iceland-Faeroes channel, but when a lookout on the *Gneisenau* glimpsed two British cruisers, a sighting confirmed moments later by the flagship's radar plot, he altered course northwards and made for the Denmark Strait with the intention of exploiting its notorious fogs and bad visibility to escape detection. On this occasion, however, the Strait failed to live up to its awesome reputation and, after refuelling from the tanker *Thorn* off Jan Mayen island, the skies were clear and the ships bathed in bright sunshine as Lütjens steamed south-westwards.

Unbeknown to the Admiral, the cruiser *Naiad* had caught a momentary glimpse of the battleships some time earlier when the *Gneisenau* had first detected enemy warships north of the Faeroes. But she had made no serious attempt to investigate or confirm the contact and the vague shadows vanished into the mists before the lookouts realized the reality of what they had seen. On receiving the *Naiad*'s report, however, Sir John Tovey, the C-in-C Home Fleet, concluded that the lookouts had been misled by a trick of the light. Without more ado he took the fleet back to Scapa.

As the two battleships cleared the Denmark Strait and entered the Atlantic Lütjens told his men triumphantly if somewhat untruthfully: 'For the first time in our history German surface warships have today succeeded in breaking through the British blockade' — a claim that conveniently overlooked the achievements of both the *Scheer* and the cruiser *Hipper*, although, admittedly, the *Scharnhorst* and *Gneisenau* themselves had failed to break out while under Marschall's command in November, 1939, following the sinking of the *Rawalpindi*.

The operational directive which Lütjens had received from Raeder was brief but ambitious. The Grand Admiral was no longer content with the mere disruption of convoy schedules. He wanted blood. Lütjens was told in blunt terms that his primary task was to seek the 'destruction of merchant shipping bound for Britain' or, as Lütjens himself put it: 'Our job is to put as many [enemy merchant ships] as possible under the water'. Nevertheless, despite the brave words, the 'no risks' policy had not been rescinded and Lütjens remained under strict orders to avoid combat on equal terms, the latter being somewhat curiously defined as a single enemy heavy ship. It was a policy which, although tacitly approved by Hitler, was to lead to high-level recriminations in the future and which was ultimately destined to turn the Führer against both his trusted adviser, Erich Raeder, and the *Kriegsmarine*'s battleships. Indeed the first signs of Hitler's paranoia were already beginning to manifest themselves at this time. Reliable witnesses have attested that the Führer, fascinated yet alarmed by the *Scheer*'s record-breaking sortie, made the lives of officials at the Admiralty in Berlin a nightmare by continually demanding news of the battleship at every conceivable opportunity, often in the early hours of the morning.

The Atlantic weather, capricious as ever, had begun to deteriorate again and the heavy seas and gale-force winds compelled Lütjens to heave to as vicious snow squalls swept across the spray-crested waves and reduced visibility to zero. Fortunately the storm finally abated and hopes were raised when the *B-Dienst* reported that convoy HX-106 had left Nova Scotia on 31 January and was confirmed as heading in the direction of the waiting battleships. Lütjens' plan of campaign was simple. The *Gneisenau* would attack the convoy from the south while the *Scharnhorst*, executing an encircling pincer movement, would strike from the north.

At 08.30 on 8 February an officer on lookout in the foretop of the flagship sighted the masts of the convoy on the horizon and, in accordance with Lütjens' tactical plan, the *Scharnhorst* increased speed to 32 knots and steered north. But Lütjens' high hopes were quickly dashed. As the two German vessels were closing the convoy the *Scharnhorst* discerned the vague outline of what looked suspiciously like a battleship amongst the escorts. Some ten minutes later the mystery ship was identified as the *Ramillies*, a First World War veteran who, despite her slow speed of 21½ knots, was heavily armoured and boasted a main armament of eight 15-inch guns.

Hoffmann was in favour of enticing the British capital ship away from the convoy by offering battle and then using the *Scharnhorst*'s superior speed to draw the enemy into a chase which would leave the merchant ships exposed to the *Gneisenau*'s ravenous guns. It would have been a risky venture, for the *Ramillies*' broadside was almost three times as heavy as that of the *Scharnhorst* and the thickness of her armour would have offered considerable protection from the latter's 11-inch shells. But Hoffmann's tactics were not put to the test. Faced by a British battleship Lütjens, hamstrung by his orders to avoid battle with a superior force, broke off the action and beat a hurried retreat. It was a disappointing conclusion to what had promised to be a stunning success. Even worse, the abortive brush with the convoy meant that the British Admiralty now had positive confirmation that there were two German battleships at large in the Atlantic again. The *Naiad*'s earlier report that she had seen enemy warships off the Faeroes had not been an optical aberration after all.

But for once the Admiral's luck was in. The unexpected appearance of the *Scharnhorst* on the northern horizon had distracted the attention of the *Ramillies*' lookouts and they failed to see the *Gneisenau* away to the south.

As a result the battleship reported the sighting of only *one* raider. And, to compound their error, the British were confused yet again by the similarity in appearance of Germany's big ships and the 11-inch gunned *Scharnhorst* was mistakenly identified as the smaller 8-inch gunned cruiser *Hipper*, a ship which the Admiralty knew was already at sea.

Raeder was always eager to exploit the *Kriegsmarine*'s ability to read the Royal Navy's radio traffic and, as soon as the *B-Dienst* monitors discovered the enemy's error, he seized the opportunity to increase British confusion by ordering the *Hipper* to attack the homeward-bound Gibraltar convoy HG-53. Meisel, who had been at sea in the cruiser since 1 February, her second Atlantic sortie in the space of less than three months, obeyed with alacrity. Guided by shadowing reports from the *U-37*, he intercepted the convoy without difficulty on the 11th, only to discover that it had already been savaged so severely by Doenitz's U-boats and *FW-200* aircraft from the *Luftwaffe*'s 2/KG- 40 that his success was limited to the scalp of a solitary straggler. But at nightfall Meisel caught up with SLS-64, an unescorted convoy of nineteen ships. By the time the *Hipper* left the scene the next morning seven of the vessels had gone to the bottom and two more had been badly damaged. Satisfied with his haul, and having achieved all that Raeder had demanded of his ship, Meisel returned to Brest on the 15th, leaving the *Scharnhorst* and *Gneisenau* with a clear field.

But bad weather was continuing to hamper the movements of the two battleships and although a relatively quiet spell had enabled the vessels to top up their bunkers from waiting tankers on the 16th conditions worsened rapidly later in the day and Lütjens was forced to call off his search for the convoy HX-111 which the *B-Dienst* had reported earlier. The raiders were some 500 miles east of Newfoundland when the gales finally blew themselves out on 22 February and with the change in the weather came a change in their fortunes. During the early morning lookouts detected smoke on the horizon and the battleships increased speed to investigate. But expectations were dashed yet again when the convoy was found to be a disappointingly lean and hungry group of empty ships on their way back to Canada in ballast.

Lütjens would have preferred to save his ammunition for more worthwhile targets but he realized that it was foolish to look a gift horse in the mouth. In a commendable attempt to reduce casualties he opened the action by firing warning shots into the air. But the British masters ignored his forbearance and fled as fast as they could in all directions. The battleships opened fire in earnest at 11.00 and over the course of the next two hours their weapons inflicted grievous execution among the fleeing and helpless merchant ships. The *Gneisenau* accounted for three vessels of 14,126 tons, while the *Scharnhorst* claimed a large tanker. Ten hours later the raiders caught up with the 5,500-ton freighter *Harlesden* which had been located earlier by one of the *Gneisenau*'s floatplanes following an alert from the *B-Dienst* that she was in the vicinity. The 5.9-inch guns of the flagship's secondary armament carried out their task with merciless efficiency and it was all over in a matter of minutes.

The attack on the convoy could have been a bloody massacre, but Lütjens had show considerable restraint. The merchant ships were defenceless and, recognizing the fact, the Admiral had tempered duty with mercy. In all, 180 British officers and seamen were rescued from the water or saved from lifeboats and rafts and, almost incredibly, there had been only eleven casualties. Lütjens had good cause to feel satisfied with the day's work.

After this flurry of activity the battleships moved south into the central Atlantic and, as the weather improved, the crews were able to enjoy their periods of off-duty recreation in the clean fresh air for the first time since they had left Germany. There were cinema shows every evening and, during the day, they were able to participate in organized deck sports and inter-mess competitions. Relaxation, however, was far from Lütjens' mind and by 3 March his battleships were in the vicinity of the Cape Verde Islands, having steamed some 11,000 miles since their departure from Kiel. But to his chagrin the seas were empty, and any hope of another easy victory were dashed when, on 7 March, the *Scharnhorst* sighted the masts of the British battleship *Malaya*.

Hoffmann prudently turned away and rejoined the *Gneisenau* which was some 40 miles away to the north-east. Scenting the approach of a convoy, Lütjens took his flagship to investigate and a short while later he found a group of twelve ships steaming south for Freetown. It was a tempting prize, but with the *Malaya* lurking close-by Raeder's directive vetoing combat with superior forces meant that an attack on the convoy was ruled out and the Admiral turned away with a heavy heart.

Although forbidden to launch a surface attack, Lütjens was determined to see the convoy destroyed and, informing Navy Group West of its course and speed, he suggested that the information should be passed to U-boat headquarters at Kernevel in occupied France. The intelligence was duly relayed to Doenitz and in the early hours of the following morning (8th) the *U-124* and *U-105* closed the unsuspecting convoy and in the space of just fifteen minutes sank five ships totalling 28,488 tons between them, a success due entirely to Lütjens' timely and accurate shadowing reports.

Despite the losses it had suffered, Convoy SL-67 held together and shortly before nightfall the Vice-Admiral closed the huddled mass of ships again in the hope of easy pickings. But disappointment awaited him once more. The *Malaya* was now sailing in company with the convoy and the *Gneisenau* suddenly found herself confronted by the British battleship at a range of 26,000 yards. Lütjens turned away sharply and, thanks to the flagship's six-knot speed advantage, she had soon run out of danger. Nevertheless it had been a nasty moment while it lasted. The *Scharnhorst*, too, enjoyed a similarly narrow escape when she was sighted by a Walrus amphibian aircraft from the same ship. It was becoming increasingly clear that the African coast was now unhealthy and, with characteristic boldness, Lütjens decided to renew his offensive against the HX convoys in the North Atlantic. En route to the new area of operations the *Scharnhorst* chanced upon and snapped up the 7,926-ton Greek collier *Marathon*. Small fry, perhaps, but still better than nothing.

Lütjens, however, was not the master of his own destiny, for, like his predecessor, Marschall, he remained under the direct control of Saalwächter and Navy Group West. On 11 March he received a signal from the Group's Paris headquarters directing him to cease all operations against the HX convoys in seven days' time. The *Scheer*, it seemed, was about to return to Germany at the conclusion of her record-breaking cruise in the South Atlantic and Indian Oceans, while the *Hipper* was to shift her berth from Brest to Kiel. Saalwächter explained that the *Scharnhorst* and *Gneisenau* would be required to create a suitable diversion to cover the movements of both ships. But that was not all. To his surprise Lütjens was additionally ordered to bring his two battleships into Brest instead of returning, as originally planned, to Kiel.

In his final week of freedom the Admiral struck swiftly and effectively. Making use of the supply ships *Uckerman* and *Ermland* to help in the search for targets, he spread his quartet of ships thirty miles apart in a broad sweep that covered a swathe of ocean some 120 miles wide. His new tactic gained a swift reward when the *Uckerman* sighted the advanced elements of convoy HX-114 some two hundred miles to the south of Cape Race. This time the merchant ships had no battleship to protect them and Lütjens struck like a bolt from the blue. The *Gneisenau* captured the tankers *Bianca* (5,688 tons), *San Casimiro* (8,100 tons), and *Polykarb* (6,400 tons), and, placing prize crews aboard each vessel, sent them back to France. In fact only the latter ship reached Bordeaux; the other two were found by aircraft from the *Ark Royal* and intercepted by the battle-cruiser *Renown* to the chagrin of the prize crews, who, in an unexpected reversal of roles, found themselves seized as prisoners-of-war and the 46 British seamen they had been holding captive below decks released.

In addition to making prizes of the three tankers, the *Gneisenau* sank a fourth ship, while the *Scharnhorst* sent two other vessels to the bottom. It was the squadron's first major success since the assault on the outward-bound convoy on 22 February and Lütjens was understandably pleased, especially as survivors which had been picked up by the *Gneisenau* indicated that the second and slower section of the convoy was following only a short distance behind. Their information proved to be correct, for at 01.00 the next morning the two supply vessels reported contact with two further merchant ships and the onset of daylight revealed that the German squadron was literally in the middle of the convoy. The startled merchantmen attempted to scatter, but, like chickens trapped in a cage with two hungry foxes, they stood no chance of escape. *Empire Industry*, *Mangkai*, *Demerton*, *Grandi*, *Silberfix*, *Royal Crown*, *Sardinian Prince* and *Myson* all went down under the guns of the two battleships. But one ship, the smallest of the bunch, the 1,800-ton *Chilean Reefer*, stood her ground and made a fight of it, even to the extent of using the ludicrous pop-gun mounted on her poop-deck against the armoured might of the Nazi battleships.

Both Lütjens and the *Gneisenau*'s Captain Fein suspected a trap. Perhaps the vessel was a decoy Q-ship sailing with the convoy hoping to entice an enemy surface raider within range of her concealed torpedo tubes. Or perhaps she was acting as a scout for heavier ships still invisible beyond the horizon. Unwilling to risk his ship, Fein opened the range and began to pound his tiny adversary with the massive 11-inch guns of the *Gneisenau*'s main armament. Even then it took an amazing 73 full-calibre shells to despatch the little ship to the bottom, her sacrifice emulating the example set by Sir Richard Grenville's *Revenge* in her lone battle with the Spanish Fleet in 1591.

Lütjens worst fears were realized some fifteen minutes later when the ungainly bulk of the British battleship *Rodney* waddled over the horizon; her nine 16-inch guns posed a threat that not even he was prepared to challenge. It was an occasion when discretion was the better part of valour and, with his Admiral's approval, Captain Fein turned the *Gneisenau* away and rang down for flank speed as the *Rodney* flashed an interrogative: *What ship?* Lütjens, an old hand at the game of blind man's bluff, replied with the identification letters of the British cruiser *Emerald*. Although clearly incorrect, the reply was sufficient to persuade *Rodney*'s captain to hold his fire and the brief interval of understandable indecision allowed the *Gneisenau*, which was now moving at 32 knots, to get away. For, despite her overwhelming firepower, the British warship's maximum speed was too slow to allow her to give chase.

Although he had escaped retribution yet again, Lütjens could be by no means certain that his two battleships would now enjoy an unopposed passage back to their new base in France. The *B-Dienst* monitors had already warned him that the *Malaya* was still prowling off the Cape Verde Islands and that the Gibraltar-based Force H, which included the battle-cruiser *Renown* and the carrier *Ark Royal*, was also at sea, although precisely where no one seemed to know. Fortunately for the German commander, the Royal Navy was equally in the dark about the whereabouts of the elusive

Scharnhorst and *Gneisenau*. Nevertheless the British were agreed on one thing. Lütjens' force intended to make its way back to the Third Reich via either the Denmark Strait or the Iceland-Faeroes passage.

Quite by chance a Fulmar aircraft from the *Ark Royal* found the enemy ships during the late afternoon of the 20th. But at the crucial moment of sighting the machine's radio developed a fault and forty-five minutes were lost before the information could be reported back to the *Ark Royal*. In the meanwhile Lütjens, realizing that he had been seen by the aircraft, altered course from north-east to north in an attempt to mislead his pursuers.

By the time the news reached Admiral Sir James Somerville on the *Renown* it was too late in the day for the *Ark Royal*'s Swordfish to launch a torpedo attack. Only an hour of daylight remained and, with weather conditions deteriorating, success was uncertain, even supposing the strike aircraft could find their target, and Somerville was not a man to risk the lives of his air-crew on a wild goose chase. Furthermore, Lütjens' new northerly course convinced him that the Admiralty's assessment of his intentions was correct and that the two battleships were heading for Iceland – a scenario that would give the Royal Navy ample time to locate and attack the raiders before they reached the Norwegian coast and returned to Germany. Unfortunately both Somerville and the Admiralty's strategists were wrong in their assumptions. Raeder's bold decision to base the ships at Brest had already paid its first dividend even before it had been fully implemented.

Having eluded their pursuers the battleships arrived off the French coast at around noon on the 22nd, but, due to bad weather, their destroyer escort did not arrive to greet them until 03.00 the next morning. They did not finally enter Brest harbour until 07.00. The *Kriegsmarine*'s ambitious Operation Berlin was over and both ships had returned undamaged after a voyage of 17,800 miles lasting some sixty days. They had sunk 21 ships and seized another, the *Polykarb*, as a prize. Raeder was delighted by the success of his strategy, especially as he could now look forward to a renewal of his surface offensive on even better terms in a month's time when the *Bismarck* and the cruiser *Prinz Eugen* would be joining the fleet, for he could then stage a simultaneous two-pronged attack with the *Bismarck* entering the Atlantic from the north and the *Scharnhorst* and *Gneisenau* operating on the Royal Navy's eastern flank from their base in France. But in his euphoria the Grand Admiral had overlooked one highly significant fact: between 10 April, 1940, and 17 March, 1941, a period of approximately one year, Doenitz's submarines had destroyed a total of 2,314,000 tons of British, Allied and neutral shipping – statistics which would have given a less arrogant man pause for thought.

But, like his leader Adolf Hitler, Raeder was concerned only with his precious battleships, and their successes had so far surpassed his most ambitious dreams. Not only had they sunk and captured enemy ships and scattered British convoys, they had disrupted the enemy's shipping schedules and created chaos and panic on both sides of the Atlantic. The fact that they had been forced to run away each time they encountered a British battleship was shrugged off as of no importance.

In the first flush of victory, before the senior officers of the *Seekriegsleitung* had had time to analyse and criticize Lütjens' handling of the operation or, indeed, find fault with the Grand Admiral's own strategy, Raeder expressed the view that Lütjens' actions throughout Operation Berlin had been 'beyond reproach' and that 'he invariably judged the situation accurately and met with deserved success'. But the recipient of Raeder's fulsome accolade was tragically given little time in which to enjoy his moment of glory. By the end of May, 1941, Vice-Admiral Gunther Lütjens was dead, killed in action aboard the *Bismarck* in vain pursuit of Raeder's flawed strategy that battleships could destroy Britain's sea trade more efficiently than U-boats.

CHAPTER SIX

'We Wish You Success In Your Hard Fight'

FEBRUARY 20, 1941, marked the *Scheer*'s 123rd day at sea. And her tally of twelve merchant ships sunk or captured plus her destruction of the British armed merchant cruiser *Jervis Bay* already comfortably exceeded the nine victims claimed by Langsdorff and the *Graf Spee* in 1939. Even more remarkably, she was now cruising off the Seychelles, some 500 miles below the equator and more than 2,000 miles farther north than the furthermost point reached by the *Graf Spee* during her tentative foray into the Indian Ocean fourteen months earlier.

That morning the *Scheer*'s Arado floatplane sighted another likely victim and, as Krancke stalked his prey, he adopted his favourite ploy of disguising the battleship's tell-tale triple turrets by elevating two of the guns and depressing the third so that, in the distance, they resembled the twin-barrel gunhouses of a typical British cruiser. On approaching the freighter *Scheer*'s captain could see a large American flag painted on the side of its hull and concluded that he was not the only one trying to conceal his true identity. Refusing the bluff, he swung the battleship broadside-on to the merchantman and a signal lamp high up on the *Scheer*'s control tower began to blink rapidly: *Stop at once. Do not force me to open fire. You are behaving very suspiciously.*

The reply from the 6,994-ton *British Advocate* — for such was the identity and indeed the nationality of the freighter despite the Stars and Stripes daubed on her side — was equally forthright. *So are you*, a hand-held Aldis lamp flashed from her bridge-wing. *You are acting like a German.* Moments later her radio began transmitting the by now familiar R-R-R distress call which the *Scheer*'s wireless operators promptly jammed. But despite this single gesture of bravado the *British Advocate* sensibly offered no resistance when the launch carrying an armed boarding-party from the *Scheer* came alongside and the steamer's crew even lowered rope ladders over the side to help the enemy sailors climb on deck — a process which, to their undisguised amusement, left the white tropical uniforms of their uninvited guests liberally smeared with red and blue paint from the recently executed United

States ensign. They did not find it quite so funny, however, when they were taken back to the battleship under guard while the boarding-party prepared to scuttle their ship with explosive charges.

The next day the *Scheer* intercepted the Greek steamer *Grigorious* whose Master claimed that she was carrying Red Cross supplies to New York under the protection of the neutral flag. But an examination of the cargo revealed that the crates in the hold contained military weapons and Krancke had no compunction about ordering her destruction after first removing her crew to safety. Some hours later the battleship encountered another medium-sized freighter, the 7,178-ton *Canadian Cruiser*, which tried to make a run for it. She was easily caught thanks to the *Scheer*'s superior speed, but not before she, too, had transmitted a distress signal which the battleship's radio-room confirmed had been acknowledged by a British naval shore station.

Once again the crew was taken off as prisoners while a boarding-party placed scuttling charges in the bilges, a procedure repeated two days later when the *Scheer* intercepted the Dutch steamer *Rantau Pandjang*. But this satisfying run of success posed Krancke with a dilemma. Thanks to the *B Dienst* monitoring service he was aware that a major troop convoy, WS-5B, made up of twenty large transports, had left Durban on 15 February escorted by the cruisers *Australia* and *Emerald*. The most recent report from Berlin indicated that it had arrived off Mombasa on the 21st.

It was a tempting and valuable target. But the *Scheer*'s four-day foray against shipping south of the Seychelles had alerted the Royal Navy to her presence in the Indian Ocean and time was running out. The cruisers *Capetown*, *Canberra*, *Shropshire*, *Emerald* and *Hawkins*, together with the carrier *Hermes*, had already been ordered to hunt down the pocket-battleship before she could do any more damage, and, some 400 miles to the east, the 6-inch gunned cruiser *Glasgow*, responding to the *Canadian Cruiser*'s distress call, altered course south-eastwards to cut off the *Scheer*'s probable escape route should Krancke decide to move away from the West African coast into more open waters. It was this latter vessel that was to pose the greatest threat to the raider.

The sinking of the *Rantau Pandjang* two days later enabled Captain Harold Hickling to pinpoint the battleship's position and during the forenoon of 22 February the *Glasgow*'s Walrus amphibious aircraft sighted its prey. Wisely, however, the pilot maintained radio silence and, banking away before he could be positively identified, he returned to the cruiser and made a verbal report to his commanding officer. The absence of wireless traffic from the aircraft gave Krancke a false sense of security for he assumed, not unreasonably, that the *Scheer* had not been seen. Nevertheless, with Raeder's 'no risks' policy firmly in mind, he decided that, convoy or no convoy, it was clearly time to leave the Indian Ocean and to lie low for a few weeks in the lonely but relatively secure wastes of the South Atlantic while he reviewed his options. Having made his decision, he altered course westwards – unaware that the *Glasgow* was already hot on his trail and was now only 80 miles astern.

The Walrus was catapulted off from the British cruiser again shortly before 14.00 and this time the pilot was given orders to shadow the Nazi raider while Hickling took the opportunity to inform Vice-Admiral Sir Ralph Leatham, the C-in-C of the East Indies station who was in overall control of the search operation, of the situation. But, unfortunately for the British, worsening weather conditions which frequently reduced visibility to less than three miles, made a mockery of Hickling's plans to shadow the *Scheer*. The final blow to his hopes came some hours later when a shortage of fuel forced the *Glasgow* to abandon the pursuit and return to Mauritius to replenish her empty bunkers. It had been a gallant effort and success had only eluded Hickling by a hairsbreadth. As the *Glasgow*'s captain ruefully admitted in his memoirs, the battleship's escape had been '*Scheer* bad luck'.*

But although Krancke had successfully, if unintentionally, eluded the *Glasgow*, he was not yet out of danger, for the heavy cruiser *Cornwall*, which was to sink the raider *Pinguin* off Mombasa two months later, had left Cape Town on 2 March and while en route to the island of St Helena crossed the *Scheer*'s track on two separate occasions without either ship realizing how close they were to an encounter. Indeed, had the *Cornwall* not been delayed by her interception of the Vichy French transport *Ville de Majunga*, which was on her way to Madagascar with troops, it is possible that the *Scheer* might have suffered the same fate as the *Graf Spee*. But it was not to be, and Krancke was able to escape into the South Atlantic undetected.

The battleship rendezvoused with her supply ship *Nordmark* on 8 March for refuelling. It was the first time the two vessels had met in more than three months and, two days later, they were joined by the *Alsterufer* with mail and a consignment of spares which Krancke urgently needed for the repair of his *Seetakt* radar apparatus, a vital piece of equipment if the *Scheer* was to negotiate the fog-bound waters of the Arctic Sea safely on her return passage to Germany.

The homeward run began on 11 March and by the 25th the battleship was already in the vicinity of the Denmark Strait where Krancke was forced to quarter the empty ocean with growing impatience as he waited for the weather to deteriorate. Poor visibility was essential if the *Scheer* was to evade the cruiser patrols which the Royal Navy maintained east and west of Iceland to catch enemy blockade runners. Taking advantage of the new moon Krancke entered the Strait on 27 March and, using his recently repaired

---

* *Sailor at Sea*, Vice-Admiral Harold Hickling, Kimber, 1965

radar to evade the cruisers *Fiji* and *Nigeria* which were standing guard at the northern end of the passage, he arrived off German-occupied Bergen three days later and anchored in Grimstadfjord where he remained for the next 24 hours so that his men could get the *Scheer* shipshape for her homecoming. The battleship finally reached Kiel on 1 April, her arrival being greeted by Grand Admiral Raeder who celebrated the historic moment by inspecting the crew and shaking hands with each individual officer before he mounted a flag-bedecked rostrum and launched into a rousing speech of welcome. On this occasion Raeder's eulogy was justified for, by any standard, the *Scheer* had achieved a remarkable success. Her 161-day cruise had taken her from the ice-floes of the Arctic to the balmy waters of the Indian Ocean. More importantly she had sunk or captured seventeen merchant ships totalling 113,233 tons and sent the auxiliary cruiser *Jervis Bay* to the bottom. Despite the strenuous efforts of the Royal Navy to catch her, she had returned to the Fatherland unscathed.

On the night of 7/8 April, as a direct consequence of Churchill's demand for a concentrated air offensive against Germany's U-boat bases and submarine building facilities, a force of 229 bombers attacked Kiel in a five-hour raid on the naval dockyard and the industrial areas of the city which left 88 persons dead and a further 184 injured. Although the *Scheer* was fortunately not damaged it was a rude awakening after the relative tranquillity of the previous five months. Apart from the brief one-sided engagement with the *Jervis Bay* in November, 1940, the battleship's crew had never found themselves under fire from hostile guns. It came as something of a shock to discover that they were at greater risk from the enemy in their home port than they had been in the Atlantic and Indian Oceans.

Bomber Command was back again the following night with 160 aircraft but this time, by mischance, most of the bombs fell on the residential areas of the city killing 125 civilians and injuring many hundreds more. There were four more attacks during April and a 70-bomber raid on the night of 17/18 May. But the *Scheer* continued to enjoy a charmed life and she emerged from this series of aerial assaults without a scratch. She also escaped undamaged from a night attack by 14 Whitley bombers at the end of May in which the RAF concentrated its venom against the *Tirpitz*, the last of Hitler's battleships, which had been commissioned into the fleet by Captain Karl Topp on 25 January and which was berthed at Kiel following a prolonged period of training exercises in the Baltic.

Despite the violence of their homecoming, the *Scheer*'s crewmen were more fortunate than their comrades in the *Scharnhorst* and *Gneisenau*. Their new haven at Brest was another of the RAF's designated priority targets and the *Kriegsmarine* was soon to discover that Bomber Command posed a far greater threat to its battleships than the Royal Navy. For while it was possible to evade and out-run enemy ships if they were encountered at sea, it was virtually impossible to escape the growing menace from the skies.

The two vessels had separated shortly after their arrival at Brest. The *Scharnhorst*, whose high-pressure boilers were still giving trouble, tied up alongside the Quai de la Ninon, the berth originally reserved for France's answer to Germany's pocket-battleships, the battle-cruiser *Dunkerque*, while the *Gneisenau* was warped into Dry Dock No 8 to undergo some minor hull repairs. Although specialist personnel and the flak crews remained on board, a large proportion of the men from both ships were driven to a rest camp at Landernau, some 15 miles from Brest, which to the delight of the sailors proved to be situated on the main railway line to the French capital, giving them a tempting opportunity to enjoy the fleshpots of Paris in their off-duty hours.

The future at this stage remained shrouded in uncertainty. Lütjens himself had been recalled to Berlin so that Raeder could brief him personally on the forthcoming Operation *Rheinübung*, a sortie into the North Atlantic by the *Bismarck* and the cruiser *Prinz Eugen*, the date of departure being provisionally set for the period of the new moon at the end of April. The Grand Admiral also planned to despatch the *Gneisenau* from Brest a few days later with the intention of concentrating the three ships for an assault on Britain's North Atlantic convoys. Having discussed the details with Raeder in Berlin, Lütjens left for Paris where he was to meet Doenitz, the co-operation of the latter's U-boats being of vital importance if the surface operation was to succeed. There was, however, one unresolved problem. Would the enemy be content to sit back and allow Raeder's plan to go ahead unchallenged? And, with Brest within range of British bombers, what part would the RAF play in Raeder's Grand Strategy?

Bomber Command's answer came on the night of 30/31 March, just a week after the *Scharnhorst* and *Gneisenau*'s arrival in France, when a force of 109 aircraft launched a concerted attack on Brest, although, despite this daunting show of strength, no hits were obtained on the two battleships. A spell of bad weather kept the bombers grounded for the next few days but the RAF was back again on the night of 4/5 April with 54 machines and this time they did not return empty-handed. The German naval staff, together with a number of junior and middle-ranking officers from both the *Scharnhorst* and the *Gneisenau*, were staying at Brest's Continental Hotel whose four-star accommodation was infinitely preferable to the starkness of the battleships' wardrooms. They were about to sit down for their evening meal, a welcome luxury after the plain fare served up by the navy's cooks, when the sirens began wailing. Encouraged by the failure of the previous raid, they made no attempt to seek shelter in the hotel's cellars and remained in their seats as the waiters appeared with the soup. The dinner, however, never progressed beyond the first course. Before the dishes had been cleared from the tables the dining-room had been reduced to rubble by a direct hit. The precise number of casualties was never revealed but French sources put the total of dead at over two hundred.

The bomb which was to cause the greatest chaos on that night of terror was the one which, ironically, failed to explode. It fell into Dry Dock No 8 and ended up on the floor of the basin in some twelve feet of water dangerously close to the *Gneisenau*'s keel. Captain Fein, who had fortunately taken his evening meal on board instead of joining his comrades at the Continental Hotel, at first favoured using a crane to lift it clear, but, after considering the risks of accidentally detonating the bomb, he decided to leave it where it was and, instead, to move the *Gneisenau* out of dock at daylight so that the UXB experts could render it safe without endangering the battleship.

It took most of the next morning to flood the dock but finally, just after noon, the flagship was eased clear and shepherded to her new berth in the inner harbour. Fein gave a sigh of relief as the ship was brought safely to her mooring buoys some 500 yards inside the mole and, as the bomb disposal team set to work, he returned to his quarters to continue the preparation of his operational orders for the forthcoming sortie with the *Bismarck*. He took little notice of a lone Spitfire which was, at that moment, passing overhead at some 20,000 feet. A single fighter could scarcely endanger the armoured might of the *Gneisenau*, but on this occasion Fein was wrong. The Spitfire was equipped with a remote-control camera and the photographs it was taking proved to be of considerable interest to Bomber Command's intelligence officers. After detailed analysis they were rushed by despatch rider to the Command's headquarters at High Wycombe.

The pictures showed that the *Gneisenau* − wrongly identified by the British as the *Scharnhorst* − was now moored in open water and no longer protected by the concrete walls of the dock. This meant that it would be possible to launch a torpedo strike on the battleship, a mode of attack which the RAF's experts now favoured following the apparent failure of conventional bombing tactics. Their recommendation was accordingly passed to the AOC, Coastal Command, and within hours the project had landed on the desk of Wing-Commander Braithwaite, the Commanding Officer of No 22 Squadron, a unit equipped with Bristol Beaufort torpedo-bombers. It presented a daunting task, for Brest, even at this early stage, was protected by more than a thousand guns plus, of course, the flak batteries of the two battleships themselves. In addition the *Gneisenau* was lying at right-angles to the quay of the inner harbour and was moored only 500 yards from the enveloping arm of the mole.

This meant that the attacking machines would have to fly over the outer harbour in the face of heavy crossfire and release their torpedoes *before* they reached the mole so that the weapons would pass over the breakwater and enter the water of the inner harbour on the far side of the stone-built pier. It called for cool judgement and strong nerves, for during the crucial seconds when the weapons were being aimed and released each aircraft would become the focus for every weapon that the Germans could muster. Finally, the anti-torpedo nets protecting the *Gneisenau* would have to be destroyed if the Beauforts' weapons were to succeed in reaching the target.

With only a limited number of aircraft available Braithwaite selected three machines to carry out the preliminary bombing attack on the nets, with a further three, each armed with a 21-inch RNTF torpedo, to carry out the main strike. No 22 Squadron, like many other RAF units, had no reserve machines, and that meant that everything had to be right first time. Unfortunately, and inevitably, it wasn't. Two of the bomb-carrying aircraft failed to take off from the mud-covered airfield at St Eval and the only pilot to succeed in getting airborne lost his way en route and never reached the target area.

The first two aircraft of the torpedo-strike component arrived over Brest at around 06.30, the third following some thirty minutes later, but was met by such a murderous hail of fire that it was forced to return home. The pilot of the second Beaufort, whose orders required him to attack after the net defences had been bombed, realized that this part of the plan had failed, so he also broke off and flew back to St Eval with his mission unaccomplished.

Flying Officer Kenneth Campbell, the skipper of the remaining aircraft, also waited in vain for the sound of exploding bombs and, with the dawn sky slowly brightening in the east, decided to strike while he still had a chance of success. Opening the throttles, he roared over the outer harbour at 300 feet and aimed his machine at the stern of the stationary *Gneisenau*. The mole was coming up fast and the Beaufort was now down to 50 feet. Yet, amazingly, not a single one of the thousand-gun defence system opened fire. Campbell's attack had been so sudden and unexpected that the flak batteries had been caught completely by surprise, an unexpected bonus, for had the bombing attack taken place as planned every anti-aircraft weapon in Brest would have been alert and waiting when Campbell made his approach run over the roadstead and outer harbour.

The hiatus did not last long. As the torpedo dropped away from the belly of the Beaufort and Campbell hurled his machine into a steep climb to avoid the *Gneisenau*'s towering mast, all hell was let loose with seemingly every weapon opening fire at the same time, a barrage in which the battleship's flak batteries joined with enthusiastic determination. The torpedo-bomber staggered as cannon shells ripped its fuselage and splintered steel shredded its wings. Then, with its engines still screaming at full throttle, the Beaufort dived into the harbour.

Flying Officer Campbell was awarded a posthumous Victoria Cross for his gallantry in the face of impossible odds. The *Kriegsmarine* also saluted the bravery of its foes: the bodies of the Beaufort's crew were removed from the water and taken back to the battleship where they were laid on the quarter-deck and draped with flags while an honour-guard stood vigil with reversed arms. The remains of the four airmen were subsequently buried in the military cemetery in Brest with appropriate ceremony.

The Beaufort's torpedo had struck the *Gneisenau* on the starboard side towards the stern and an inspection in dry dock the next morning revealed that the starboard propeller and shaft tunnel had been completely wrecked – damage which would take many weeks to repair and which would effectively prevent the battleship from taking part in Operation *Rheinübung*. Raeder may have been wiser to have cancelled, or at least postponed, the *Bismarck* sortie at this stage of the proceedings, for the absence of the *Gneisenau* seriously weakened the tactical reasoning behind the operation, but with arrogant obstinacy the Grand Admiral refused to back down and ordered the raiding mission to go ahead with just a single battleship supported by a heavy cruiser.

Although both the *Scharnhorst* and the *Gneisenau* were now out of service and undergoing prolonged repairs at Brest, the German Admiralty decided to make the best of a bad job by sending a hundred newly appointed midshipmen to join the vessels in harbour for onboard training, their main duties being to take charge of the battleships' numerous batteries of light anti-aircraft guns. For many of them, however, their training was brutally short. Only four days after Campbell's attack a force of 53 aircraft arrived over Brest in what was to prove Bomber Command's most effective raid to date. The *Gneisenau* was hit four times and, in addition to severe structural damage, she suffered a heavy toll of human casualties with at least fifty dead and a further ninety wounded, a total that sadly included most of the young midshipmen who had just arrived on board and whose exposed flak batteries had borne the brunt of the attack. The injuries which the *Gneisenau* sustained on this occasion dashed any remaining hopes of carrying out rapid repairs to the starboard propeller and the experts told Fein that it would probably be six months before his ship was seaworthy again, a verdict that ruled out any chance of the battleship taking part in Operation *Rheinübung*.

Pictures taken on photo-reconnaissance sorties supplemented by reports from the highly efficient network of agents which the French resistance maintained in Brest confirmed the serious nature of the damage which the *Gneisenau* had sustained, but Churchill was determined to encompass the complete destruction of the two vessels before they could threaten Britain's vital Atlantic and Middle Eastern convoys again, so the RAF was ordered to step up its attacks.

But the task by no means as easy as was at first supposed and the successes of 4 and 5 April and the night of 10/11 April were not repeated for many months. There were five more raids in April involving a total of 278 aircraft and a further three in May in which 219 took part, but although a number of hits were claimed subsequent investigation proved them to be no more than wishful thinking. There was, however, a credit side to the balance sheet, for in the course of the first sixteen raids only three aircraft had been lost. Nevertheless, the senior officers of Bomber Command were unhappy at being forced to divert scarce resources away from their strategic bombing campaign against industrial targets in Germany to what they considered to be the sideshow at Brest. Indeed, on 15 April Air Chief Marshal Sir Richard Peirse, the AOC Bomber Command, complained to the Chief of Air Staff that since the attacks began on 10 January he had been 'compelled to throw some 750 tons of high explosives into Brest harbour for the benefit... of the *Scharnhorst* and *Gneisenau*'. According to the Official History* he did not consider that his aircraft could destroy the ships and was convinced that the bombs dropped on Brest would have been more effectively employed against Bremen or Mannheim. 'We can do more [to win] the Battle of the Atlantic,' he said, 'by attacking targets in Germany.' Peirse was, of course, unaware of the chaos which the air attacks on the *Scharnhorst* and *Gneisenau* were causing to the *Kriegsmarine*'s strategic plans. Had he known the truth he might well have modified his views.

Operation *Rheinübung* was originally scheduled for the period of the new moon at the end of April and the *Bismarck* completed her final preparations in the peaceful surroundings of the Baltic where she was safely beyond the range of the RAF's bombers. But the forthcoming mission continued to be dogged by misfortune and had to be postponed at the very last minute when the *Prinz Eugen* accidentally triggered a 'friendly' magnetic mine on 24 April and had to be placed in dry-dock. Repairs were estimated to require two weeks for completion and this meant putting the departure date back to 18 May when the next new moon was due. Raeder, however, wanted to go ahead without the *Prinz Eugen* and called Lütjens to Berlin for another conference.

The fleet commander was not impressed by Raeder's impatience. At an earlier meeting he had favoured delaying the sortie until the *Scharnhorst* was operational again or, even better, until the new and more powerful *Tirpitz* could sail in company with the *Bismarck*. On that occasion the Grand

---

* *Strategic Air Offensive Against Germany*, Webster & Frankland, HMSO, 1961, Vol 1, p 168

Admiral had succeeded in persuading his more realistically-minded fleet commander to accept his views and noted in his memoirs that 'although Lütjens was perhaps not entirely convinced... our discussion ended in complete understanding'. This time Lütjens stood his ground and refused to countenance a lone mission by the *Bismarck*. Raeder, albeit reluctantly, agreed to postpone the sortie until the *Prinz Eugen* was fully seaworthy again.

Nevertheless the background disagreements and disputes continued. And when Hitler visited the two battleships at Gdynia in the middle of May Lütjens had a long and private talk with him during which he gave him 'his views on the tactical use of the *Bismarck*... [and warned of] the dangers which might arise from enemy aircraft carriers.'* He was also rumoured to have used the opportunity to try and persuade the Führer to override Raeder's authority and postpone the sortie until such time as the *Bismarck* could be joined by either the *Scharnhorst* or the *Tirpitz*. Hitler did not respond to Lütjens' suggestions but Raeder admitted after the war that, although the Führer had not opposed his plans for Operation *Rheinübung*, 'it was easy to see that he was not particularly enthusiastic'. The *Kriegsmarine*'s archives, however, make it clear that Hitler did not personally order the execution of Operation *Rheinübung* and Raeder certainly accepted that 'the responsibility [for the sortie] was mine'. More significantly, the Grand Admiral did not bother to inform the Führer of the *Bismarck*'s departure until 22 May — *four days after the battleship had sailed.*

The two warships finally left Gdynia on 18 May and, with a heavy escort of destroyers, minesweepers, R-boats and aircraft, steamed through the Great Belt and the Skagerrak into the North Sea. They reached Bergen on the 20th and made their way into Korsfjord, the *Bismarck* anchoring in Grimstadfjord while the *Prinz Eugen* and the destroyers continued into Kalvanes Bay for refuelling. Conditions were good with bright sunshine and clear skies and the first stage of Navy Group North's plan had been successfully completed although Lütjens had decided to gain access to the Atlantic via the Denmark Strait rather than through the Iceland-Faeroes passage as originally intended by Group North's staff.

Despite the secrecy surrounding their movements the two German vessels had, in fact, already been sighted in the Skagerrak by the Swedish cruiser *Gotland*. Word of the encounter reached the British Naval Attaché in Stockholm who promptly warned London. The Admiralty's response was swift and comprehensive. Indeed some preliminary dispositions were already underway in anticipation of an enemy break-out into the Atlantic following reports of unusual activity at Gdynia from agents based in the port and the

* *Struggle for the Sea*, p 212.

heavy cruisers *Norfolk* and *Suffolk* were at that moment moving into position to close the entrance to the Denmark Strait. The Home Fleet, too, was brought to short notice; two cruisers supported by a number of trawlers were hurried to the Iceland-Faeroes passage and the Air Ministry was requested to increase the RAF's reconnaissance flights over Norwegian and Arctic waters. Suspecting that the fjords around Bergen were the most likely places for the enemy ships to hide, an RAF Coastal Command photo-reconnaissance Spitfire was despatched to overfly the coast while a second unit carried out a similar sweep south from Oslo into the Skagerrak. The pilot of the first machine located the two vessels in Korsfjord shortly after 13.00 and, after examination by Coastal Command's experts, the photographs were rushed to the Admiralty. From that moment the drama of the *Bismarck* began to unfold with the relentless inevitability of a Shakespearian tragedy.

Admiral Sir John Tovey, the C-in-C Home Fleet, had meanwhile already pre-empted his instructions from the Admiralty and at 21.00 that evening the *Hood* and the *Prince of Wales*, together with six escorting destroyers, were given orders to make for Iceland where they would be well placed to cover both of Lütjens' probable routes into the North Atlantic. An hour earlier, and unbeknown to Tovey, the *Bismarck*, with the *Prinz Eugen* and accompanying destroyers, had left Korsfjord and, having skirted the Skerries, were already hurrying northwards at 25 knots towards the Arctic Sea. Lütjens felt certain that his ships had been seen at anchor in the fjord but there was little he could do about it and he was now too committed to return to Germany.

Nevertheless nearly 24 hours were to pass before the British received confirmation that the *Bismarck* and her consort had left Norway, the news coming from an obsolete Fleet Air Arm Martin Maryland which overflew the fjord and reported it empty. Although no one knew where the battleship had gone Tovey decided to take the remainder of the Home Fleet – the 14-inch gunned *King George V*, the carrier *Victorious*, four cruisers and six destroyers – to sea and at 07.10 the next morning, having been joined by the battle-cruiser *Repulse* and her three attendant destroyers off the Butt of Lewis, the force steamed north-westwards to cover the Iceland-Faeroes gap.

But Sir John Tovey was not the only person to receive confirmation of the *Bismarck*'s departure on 22 May. For, as already noted, Raeder did not inform the Führer that the sortie was in progress until the two men met for their routine weekly conference on the same day. The Grand Admiral recalled that Hitler 'expressed lively misgivings' when he heard of the venture, an euphemistic choice of words that suggests he was more than a little angered by Raeder's conspiracy of silence. Indeed the Admiral's next sentence sheds considerable light on Hitler's reaction: 'I did my best to soothe his anxiety and explained that the Naval Operations Command had the highest expectations of the operation, whereupon he agreed that it should continue.' It was, however, the last occasion on which Raeder was able to present the Führer with a *fait accompli*. For the disastrous outcome of Operation *Rheinübung* was to lead ultimately to Hitler imposing a series of rigid restrictions on the activities of his independently-minded Navy chief.

Admiral Tovey was, of course, unaware of the friction and bad feelings which the *Bismarck*'s sortie had engendered at the Führer's headquarters at the *Wolfsschanze* in East Prussia. The main problem facing him as the *King George V* punched her way through heavy seas towards Iceland was the *Bismarck*'s precise location. Since leaving Korsfjord she and the *Prinz Eugen* had seemingly vanished off the face of the earth. Despite the speed with which he had responded to the first news of the *Bismarck*'s departure, there was still much to worry about, especially the eleven convoys which were at that moment scattered across the ocean and which would be at the raider's mercy if she broke out into the Atlantic. The most important of these was the troop convoy WS-8B whose escort had been reduced to only two cruisers and eight destroyers following the withdrawal of the *Repulse* and *Victorious* to join the forces searching for the Nazi battleship. In an attempt to restore the convoy's escort to full strength the Admiralty ordered Vice-Admiral Somerville to bring his Force H* northwards from Gibraltar to provide additional cover for the vulnerable and valuable transports.

Lütjens, whose ships were now well inside the Arctic Circle, intended to enter the Denmark Strait at 07.00 on 23 May and, with a forecast of fog, he was optimistic of passing through without interference from British ships, especially as he had been assured by his experts that the enemy was not equipped with shipboard radar. But at 19.22 on the 22nd his carefully calculated plans were shattered when the cruiser *Suffolk* sighted the enemy ships at a range of seven miles. Having confirmed the contact, Captain R.M. Ellis of the *Suffolk* increased speed and, concealing his ship in the mists and fogs to seaward of the Greenland ice-edge, transmitted an urgent report to Rear-Admiral Wake-Walker who relayed it in turn to Tovey. The search for the *Bismarck* was over. But, in view, of the poor visibility conditions, could the *Suffolk* – now joined by Wake-Walker's flagship *Norfolk* – maintain contact until the big ships of the Home Fleet could arrive on the scene?

When the *Bismarck*'s electronic detection equipment picked up the pulses from the *Suffolk*'s Type-284 radar Lütjens realized that, not only had he been found by the Royal Navy, but also that his information concerning the enemy's lack of radar had been over-optimistic, and for the first time since leaving Gdynia he began to entertain serious doubts as to the outcome of the

* The battle-cruiser *Renown*, the carrier *Ark Royal*, the cruiser *Sheffield* and six destroyers.

sortie, although, at this stage, he was convinced that he could deal with a single cruiser that lacked both the armour and the firepower of the *Bismarck* and was, indeed, inferior even to the *Prinz Eugen*. And when, at 20.30 a second cruiser, Wake-Walker's *Norfolk*, unexpectedly loomed out of the murk the battleship responded to this new threat with five salvoes from her massive 15-inch guns, three of which straddled the newcomer forcing her to turn away and seek safety in the rolling banks of fog to port. With two shadowers to contend with Lütjens' initial optimism quickly faded and he ordered his ships to increase speed to 28 knots in an attempt to out-run his shadowers. But, to his dismay, the two cruisers clung on with the tenacity of limpets and it proved impossible to shake them off. It was during this particular period that the *Bismarck*'s forward radar was disabled by excessive hull vibration, a phenomenon attributed to the structural stresses of repeated full-salvo firing. Like a blind man in need of a white stick, Lütjens moved the *Prinz Eugen* into the van so that the cruiser's radar could search ahead and provide him with early warning of an enemy ambush.

Admiral Tovey was unaware of the dramatic events developing in the Denmark Strait until he received *Norfolk*'s sighting report which Wake-Walker relayed at 20.32. But Vice-Admiral Holland, further to the north, had intercepted the *Suffolk*'s original signal and, at 20.54, he ordered the *Hood* and *Prince of Wales* to increase speed to 27 knots and steer towards the Denmark Strait. Although the two German ships were some 300 miles to the north-west both groups were on roughly converging courses and he calculated that he could intercept Lütjens' squadron during the early hours of the 24th.

To achieve his object he was reliant on the shadowing reports which the two shadowing cruisers were transmitting at regular intervals despite Lütjens' attempts to silence them. But his hopes of battle were dashed when, at around midnight during a fierce snow squall, the *Suffolk* lost radar contact with her prey. The *Norfolk*, too, no longer had the enemy in sight and the sudden cessation of signals posed Holland with a dilemma. Had the *Bismarck* succeeded in sinking the two shadowers and, if so, was she still proceeding through the Strait? Or had Lütjens managed to shake off his pursuers and then reversed course back in the direction of Jan Mayen Island? Whichever conclusion Holland decided upon – and the evidence suggests that he favoured the first – he reduced speed to 25 knots at exactly one minute to midnight and altered course northwards. He also transmitted a radio signal that action was imminent. Nevertheless he apparently still had reservations for thirty minutes later he indicated his intention to alter course southwards if contact had not been established by 02.10. If this proved necessary he would wait for the cruisers to find the enemy again. In other words he was now beginning to favour the alternative proposition that Lütjens had escaped from his shadowers and was already making his way northwards into the Arctic.

The frustrating uncertainty was, at least for the British, resolved when the *Suffolk* suddenly regained contact with the battleship and resumed her reports of the enemy's position, speed and course. These signals, amplified by radio direction-finding bearings on the cruiser, pin-pointed the exact position of the *Bismarck* and the *Prinz Eugen* and Holland was able to lay his plans accordingly. At 03.40 he altered course to 240° and, thirteen minutes later, increased speed to 28 knots. By 04.30 visibility had improved to 12 miles and the two opposing groups were now hurtling towards each other on converging courses at a combined speed of some sixty miles per hour. The clash of the giants could not be long delayed and at 05.37 the *Prince of Wales* flashed a signal to the flagship: *Enemy in sight. Distance 17 miles*.

Holland's response to this electrifying news was an alteration of course towards the enemy and just before 05.52 he ordered his ships to open fire and to concentrate their salvoes on the leading, lefthand, vessel which he mistakenly thought was the *Bismarck*. The gunnery officer of the *Prince of Wales* fortunately recognized the Admiral's mistake and, acting entirely on his own initiative, shifted his 14-inch guns onto the *Bismarck* shortly before the first salvo was fired. Although Holland quickly realized his error and ordered both ships to 'Shift target right' there is reason to suppose that the *Hood*'s fire control officer did not receive the order and that her guns remained targeted on the *Prinz Eugen*.

The *Hood* opened the action at a range of 25,000 yards and she was followed, half a minute later, by the *Prince of Wales*. The flagship's main armament of eight 15-inch guns was exactly equal in strength to that of the *Bismarck*, but the ten 14-inch weapons of the *Prince of Wales* were overwhelmingly more powerful than the battery of eight 8-inch guns mounted by the *Prinz Eugen*. In theory the Royal Navy's superiority in firepower made victory inevitable. In practice, however, Holland's angle of approach had reduced the gunnery potential of the two British ships to four 15-inch and six 14-inch guns, while, by contrast, the *Bismarck*'s full broadside could be brought to bear. In addition both German ships concentrated their fire on the *Hood* whereas the British vessels, as noted earlier, divided their salvoes between the *Bismarck* and the *Prinz Eugen*, At 05.55, however, Holland altered course again to open his A-arcs and this enabled the two capital ships to employ all their guns against the enemy.

Although the *Prince of Wales* straddled the *Bismarck* with her sixth salvo the German battleship quickly demonstrated her superior fire control. Her first salvo exploded in the water ahead of the *Hood*; her second fell astern;

and her third straddled its target. At the same time an 8-inch shell from the *Prinz Eugen* hit Holland's flagship and ignited some ready-use anti-aircraft rocket ammunition, causing a fire that was observed to spread rapidly forward along the boat-deck, while another exploded on the upper deck killing a number of men sheltering in the battle-cruiser's aircraft hangar. But Holland shrugged off the punishment and, determined to carry the fight to the enemy, he ordered another 20° turn in a renewed effort to close the range. The brightly coloured signal flags were still fluttering from the halyards when the *Bismarck* fired her fifth salvo. One shell was seen to strike the *Hood* amidships and penetrate the inadequately armoured deck. It detonated in one of the 4-inch magazines and the resultant flash touched off the aft 15-inch magazine. There was an appalling explosion. A pillar of fire 'four times the height of the mainmast' leapt into the air and wreckage fell out of the sky as a mushroom column of smoke welled up in the wake of the flame. 'It was like a huge Chinese cracker blowing up,' one eye-witness recalled as the world's largest warship* disintegrated into a million white-hot pieces of splintered steel.

Admiral Holland and all but three of the *Hood*'s crew went to the bottom with their ship. As Germany had proved at Jutland in 1916 her battleships were the equal of anything the enemy possessed, and no one was more pleased with the *Bismarck*'s success than the Führer whose support for his battleships had always been more paternal than enthusiastic. Raeder recalled that when Hitler received the news he 'congratulated me delightedly and in person on the achievement'.

In fact Lütjens had come close to scoring a double triumph. Now that the German guns had only one target on which to concentrate they seemed to reach new heights of ferocity. Shell splashes rose on all sides of the *Prince of Wales* and in the twelve minutes that followed the destruction of the *Hood* the battleship was hit by four 15-inch projectiles, one of which struck the bridge and killed everyone save Captain Leach, his Chief Yeoman of Signals, and the navigating officer; three 8-inch shells also found their target. Two of the latter had penetrated below the waterline allowing 400 tons of sea-water to flood into the ship before the section was sealed off by damage control teams. Another shell had smashed through the plating further forward but had fortunately failed to explode. The damage, although heavy, was not fatal. Captain Leach, however, had other equally pressing problems. The battleship was not yet fully worked-up. In fact she still had civilian shipyard workers on board, and her guns were

* Although the *Hood*'s displacement of 41,200 tons was less than the *Bismarck*'s 41,700 tons, her overall length of 860 feet 6 inches exceeded that of the German battleship by a margin of more than 37 feet.

achieving neither their maximum rate of fire nor their full potential. Indeed on several occasions she had only three weapons operational.

After twelve minutes Leach decided that discretion was preferable to valour, a judgement fully supported by Admiral Wake-Walker who was now in overall command following the death of Holland, and at 06.13 the *Prince of Wales* turned away under cover of smoke and, as the *Suffolk* and *Norfolk* resumed their shadowing roles, the battleship fell back to act as a support for the two cruisers if occasion demanded.

Unaware that his erstwhile victim was neither fully combat-worthy nor manned by an experienced crew, Lütjens allowed the *Prince of Wales* to withdraw from the battle without challenge. He was content enough with the victory he had won so far. And he had problems of his own to contend with. For the *Bismarck* had not emerged unscathed from the encounter. One of her dynamos had been disabled, five men had been wounded, and a minor leakage of oil in No 2 boiler room which was contaminating the fuel in adjacent tanks had reduced the *Bismarck*'s speed to 28 knots. The leak seemed to be no more than a minor inconvenience at this stage, but it was destined to be the Achilles Heel of the battleship in due course.

Having rejected the option of turning back through the Denmark Strait, Lütjens decided to throw off his shadowers and head for St Nazaire in Occupied France which possessed the only dry-dock large enough to accommodate the battleship and at 09.01 he sent a signal reporting his intentions to Navy Group West in Paris. But the shadowing cruisers proved to be more difficult to elude than anticipated, and as the *Bismarck* weaved and twisted its way to the south-west the British Admiralty began to close its net.

During the evening of the 24th Lütjens ordered Captain Brinkmann to take the *Prinz Eugen* to Brest to join the *Scharnhorst* and *Gneisenau* and, to cover the cruiser's escape, he reversed the *Bismarck*'s course when a convenient rain squall reduced visibility to near-zero. *Suffolk* had followed the manoeuvre by radar and she swung her helm hard over to mirror the battleship's movement. As the *Bismarck* emerged from the squall she opened fire on the cruiser but Captain Ellis held his ground and, making smoke, returned fire despite the huge disparity in their respective armaments. A few minutes later he was given long-range support by the *Norfolk* and the *Prince of Wales*, and Lütjens, unwilling to risk damage to his ship, turned away westwards, only resuming his southerly course some time later. Wake-Walker had achieved his primary aim of preventing the *Bismarck* from escaping to the north, and now, like a team of beaters on a country estate, his ships were driving their prey towards the guns.

Nine Swordfish aircraft from the *Victorious*, which Tovey had detached from the Home Fleet some time earlier, located the *Bismarck* on radar at

23.27 that night and three minutes later made visual contact. Their attack was delivered at 23.50 in the face of a heavy flak barrage but the only torpedo to strike home caused little damage. Nevertheless the attack achieved an unexpected success for the vibration of the guns had opened up the leak in No 2 boiler room and Lütjens was forced temporarily to reduce speed to 16 knots.

But Tovey's hopes of intercepting the *Bismarck* with superior forces were dashed when, at around four o'clock in the morning of the 25th, the *Suffolk* lost radar contact with her target and, so far as Tovey was concerned, the battleship had vanished off the face of the Atlantic. It was a golden opportunity for Lütjens to make his escape, but because the *Bismarck*'s detection equipment was still picking up the search pulses from the *Suffolk* he assumed that the British cruiser had the battleship's echo on her radar screen and, unaware that the Royal Navy had lost touch, he saw no reason to maintain radio silence. He therefore proceeded to transmit a long report which detailed his successful action with the *Hood*. The signal lasted more than thirty minutes and it afforded the British ample time in which to use their wireless direction-finding apparatus to pinpoint the *Bismarck*'s exact position. It is difficult to understand why the *B-Dienst* service, which must by now have been aware that the Royal Navy had lost the battleship, did not intervene and warn Lütjens to keep quiet, but the Berlin monitors remained mute while Lütjens prepared the noose for his own execution.

Even so, luck remained on the *Bismarck*'s side, for the bearings supplied by the Admiralty were confused by Tovey's staff and, following a false scent, the flagship and the rest of the Home Fleet reversed course *away* from their quarry and set off on a wild goose chase to the north-east. Fortunately the Admiralty warned the *Rodney* to assume that the *Bismarck* was making for Brest, a logical inference form the direction-finding bearings which the Home Fleet had misinterpreted, and Somerville, coming northwards from Gibraltar with Force H, was given a similar unambiguous warning.

It was early in the evening of the 25th before Tovey, having finally realized his error, reversed course east-south-east to resume his pursuit of the enemy. He no doubt experienced a sense of relief when the Admiralty confirmed an hour later its opinion that the *Bismarck* was heading for Brest for it at least meant he was heading in the right direction. Nevertheless the battleship had not been seen since the *Suffolk* had lost contact and her location and intended destination were by now little more than wild guesses.

While uncertainty bedevilled the British an atmosphere of unreality bemused Lütjens as he stood drinking a cup of coffee on the *Bismarck*'s bridge. The next day, 26 May, was the Vice-Admiral's birthday and at 23.52, on the eve of the anniversary, Raeder sent him greetings by radio from Berlin, expressing the hope that he would 'continue to be equally successful

13. *Gneisenau's* two forward 11-inch gun turrets. Raeder would have preferred 15-inch weapons but Hitler overruled him for diplomatic reasons.

14. This dummy second turret formed part of the *Graf Spee's* disguise during raiding operations in the South Atlantic.

15. RAF bombers over Brest in 1941. Smoke from the burning *Gneisenau* is visible in the bottom left of the picture.

16. A dramatic photograph of the *Bismarck* salvo-firing at HMS *Hood*. Only three men survived when the British battlecruiser—the world's largest warship—blew up.

17. Adolf Hitler on board one of his battleships during a wartime visit to the fleet.

18. *Tirpitz* in Kaafjord following an attack by Fleet Air Arm aircraft on 3 April, 1944.

19. The RAF's six-ton Tallboy bomb. These weapons, designed to destroy the Ruhr dams, sank the *Tirpitz* and crippled the *Lützow*.

20. Stripped of her guns, the once-proud *Gneisenau* was scuttled as a block-ship at Gdynia. Her sacrifice failed to stem the Russian advance, however, and the naval base fell to the Red Army 24 hours later.

in the coming year'. Hitler's personal good wishes followed a short while later. It was sometimes difficult to believe that there was a war going on.

Meanwhile Tovey's situation was deteriorating by the hour. The *Prince of Wales* and her destroyers had long since withdrawn to Iceland for refuelling and they had been followed some time later by the *Victorious* and four cruisers. His own flagship, *King George V*, was beginning to get short of fuel and it was on the cards that her speed would soon have to be reduced to conserve her dwindling oil supplies. To make matters worse there was considerable uncertainty concerning the whereabouts of both the *Rodney* and the *Ramillies*. All hopes now centred on Force H which was rapidly closing the flagship from the south, but not even Somerville could save the situation unless the *Bismarck* could be found, and no one had seen her for 31 hours.

The miracle which the Royal Navy needed came at 10.30 on the morning of the 26th when a Coastal Command Catalina flying-boat sighted the fugitive battleship steaming steadily south-eastwards at 21 knots and making for the French coast which was by now only some 690 miles distant. Any doubts which the pilot may have had about the vessel's identity were resolved when the *Bismarck*'s flak defences opened up and, as the Catalina sought shelter amongst the clouds, her radio began transmitting details of the battleship's course, speed and present position.

It was welcome news but, so far as Tovey was concerned, it was not necessarily good news, for both the *King George V* and the *Rodney* were too far away to intercept unless the *Bismarck* could be slowed down, and the only way in which that could be achieved was by means of a torpedo attack from Somerville's *Ark Royal*. Was it expecting too much to ask for another miracle?

The first strike took off from the carrier at 14.50 in appalling weather conditions that would, in ordinary circumstances, have shut down all flying operations. By mischance the aircraft launched their attack on the British cruiser *Sheffield* instead of the *Bismarck*, a mistake that could have resulted in a terrible tragedy, but, fortunately, most of the torpedoes exploded prematurely on hitting the sea while the remainder were skilfully evaded by Captain Larcom who, recognizing the aircraft as friendly, made no attempt to open fire, despite the threat to his ship.

Still unaware that his machines had attacked a British cruiser, the Squadron Commander reported the failure of the sortie to Somerville who passed the news on to Tovey. With fuel running low, there was now a real possibility of the *Bismarck* making her escape and so when, at 17.40, the *Sheffield* established visual contact with the enemy, Somerville decided to launch a second strike of fifteen Swordfish which took off from the *Ark Royal* at 19.10. The machines attacked in the face of a tremendous anti-aircraft barrage. Thirteen torpedoes splashed into the water — the remaining two had been jettisoned earlier — and two struck home.

The first hit the battleship amidships and did little damage, but the second exploded astern and jammed the port rudder as well as causing structural damage and flooding. In the space of a few minutes Lütjens' high hopes of returning home triumphant had been shattered. The *Bismarck* swung out of control and, realizing that nothing could now save his ship, the Vice-Admiral sent a brief signal to Navy group West at 21.40: *To the Führer of the German Reich, Adolf Hitler. We fight to the last in our belief in you, my Führer, and in the firm faith in Germany's victory.* Two hours later Hitler replied from his headquarters in Rastenberg: *I thank you in the name of the German people. The whole of Germany is with you. What can still be done will be done. The performance of your duty will strengthen our people in the struggle for their existence.*

Raeder, too, sent a signal: *Our thoughts are with you and your ship. We wish you success in your hard fight.* Admiral Carls, not to be outdone, added: *We are all thinking of you with faith and pride*, while Saalwächter, C-in-C Navy Group West and Lütjens' immediate superior, sent: *Best wishes. Our thoughts are with our victorious comrades.* Once again there was a macabre air of unreality about the signals which were phrased like messages of sympathy to the bereaved at a funeral. But the corpse was not yet dead, let alone ready for burial, and it is questionable whether the sentiments expressed by the senior officers ashore did much to raise morale. Few people enjoy reading their own epitaphs while they are still alive.

Death, however, was not far away. As the *Bismarck* circled helplessly the Royal Navy began to move in on its quarry. But the battleship was still capable of fighting back and when the *Sheffield* ventured too close she was greeted with a fierce cannonade that killed three men and forced Captain Larcom to turn away under cover of smoke. Captain Vian's 4th Destroyer Flotilla arrived on the scene at virtually the same moment and, turning its guns on the newcomers, the *Bismarck* snarled her defiance by straddling the Polish *Piorun* with three salvoes of 15-inch shells.

Nevertheless, the destroyers remained in position as darkness closed over the sea and the little ships were subjected to heavy fire each time they tried to close the crippled giant. The *Zulu* launched an abortive attack at 01.00. The *Maori* followed and secured a single hit with a four-torpedo salvo and, three minutes later, Vian's own ship, the *Cossack*, claimed another. The *Bismarck* was now seen to be stopped in the water and at 02.18 the last ship of the flotilla, the *Sikh*, struck her again. The battleship, having licked its wounds, finally got under way at 02.40 and began to limp north-westwards, *away* from the French coast, at slow speed. But Lütjens refused to give best to his enemy and, making use of poor visibility and frequent rain squalls, he again gave his tormentors the slip until the *Maori* finally ran him to ground at 05.50.

Dawn on 27 May found the *King George V*, the *Rodney* and the cruiser *Norfolk* close at hand. The hounds had finally brought the fox to bay. Now it was the turn of the huntsmen to achieve the kill. The *Rodney* opened fire with her 16-inch guns at 08.47 and was joined a minute later by the 14-inch weapons of Tovey's flagship the *King George V*. The *Bismarck*, now crawling through the water at a funereal 10 knots, replied at 08.50 and quickly straddled the *Rodney*. But, like a punch-drunk boxer reeling on the ropes, there was little she could do to defend herself. Shell after shell crashed into her superstructure and hull and at 09.02 *Rodney*'s massive 16-inch guns knocked out her two forward turrets.

The range was by now almost point-blank with the *Rodney* shooting from 8,600 yards and the flagship from 12,000. Nothing could withstand such a devastating hail of high explosive and armour-piercing shells. Nevertheless, the *Bismarck* gallantly continued to work her two after-turrets, but by 10.10 even these had been silenced. Conditions on board the German battleship were horrific. Fires were burning out of control, the heat so fierce that the armour plating was glowing white hot. Shell splinters hissed and whined across the decks. The dead and dying lay in heaps, their white uniforms red with blood, while the living did their best to place the wounded behind cover. A torpedo attack by the *Norfolk* failed to achieve any hits but it was clear that the end could not now be long delayed and at 10.10 orders were given to prepare scuttling charges.

At 10.20 the *Dorsetshire* hit the enemy with two torpedoes on the starboard side and at 10.36, having passed ahead of the battleship, put another into her port quarter. Aided by the sea which was now flooding in through the opened sea-cocks the *Bismarck* listed to port and began to sink by the stern as the British guns finally fell silent. She vanished from sight at 10.40 leaving a handful of survivors swimming for their lives in the oil-scummed water. Only 119 were saved from her total complement of 2,065 officers and men, 114 being rescued by the *Maori* and *Dorsetshire* and a further five, some hours later, by a German weather ship and the submarine *U-75*. Among those who died were Lütjens together with his entire staff, Captain Ernst Lindemann, and all but two of the battleship's officers.

'The *Bismarck* had put up a most gallant fight against impossible odds, worthy of the old days of the Imperial German Navy,' Admiral Sir John Tovey wrote in his official report, 'and she went down with her colours flying.'

The *Hood* had been bloodily avenged. Now only five of Hitler's battleships remained. Could they achieve the victory that had so far eluded the *Kriegsmarine*?

CHAPTER SEVEN

Cerberus — The Dog That Twisted The Lion's Tail

Relations between Hitler and Raeder had already been soured by the Admiral's lack of frankness over the departure of the *Bismarck* and *Prinz Eugen*, and the disastrous conclusion of Operation *Rheinübung* proved to be a watershed in the politics of the naval high command. From May, 1941, onwards Hitler became the dominant voice in all decisions relating to the *Kriegsmarine*'s five surviving battleships. And, inevitably, his views on naval affairs were contrary to those held by the Commander-in-Chief.

In dealing with the aftermath of the *Bismarck* episode in his memoirs Raeder made no effort to conceal this significant new emphasis. 'Hitler's attitude towards my proposals now changed too,' he recalled. 'Up to then he had left me more or less a free hand... but now he became much more critical and more inclined to insist on his own views than before. He had always been worried about our heavy ships and he had been quite satisfied when I delayed reporting [the despatch] of our heavy units, as this saved him restless nights and days. His [new] instructions to me considerably circumscribed my use of such heavy units [ie battleships].'

The *Kriegsmarine* suffered another dissipation of its battleship strength on the evening of 12 June when the *Lützow*, attempting to break out into the Atlantic on a raiding sortie, was located off Lindesnes and attacked by a Coastal Command Beaufort torpedo-bomber. The machine was wrongly identified by the anti-aircraft lookouts as a friendly Ju-88 and the battleship's guns remained silent throughout Flight Sergeant Ray Loveitt's three-mile approach run. By the time they recognized the bomber's hostile intent it was too late. Loveitt, who had come in at wavetop height, suddenly pulled the Beaufort up into a steep climb and, as the target came into his cross-sights, he released his torpedo. The weapon performed faultlessly, ran straight and true and exploded against the *Lützow*'s port quarter. The effect was devastating. The battleship shuddered, her engines stopped, and she developed a sharp list to port. In addition to suffering serious underwater hull damage, her port propeller shaft was badly distorted and, within minutes, the upper part of her main deck was level with the sea, despite the efforts of the damage-control teams struggling to stem the inrush of water.

The escorting destroyers closed the crippled vessel with tow-lines and an hour later they began the long slow haul to Stavanger, their task made no easier by two more, fortunately unsuccessful, torpedo attacks by Coastal Command Beauforts. By 04.00, however, the engineering staff had restored the starboard diesel motor to life. Spirits were raised further when a fourth British bomber was driven off by the battleship's flak defences and then shot down by a *Luftwaffe* fighter.

But by this time Captain Kreisch had had enough. Giving up his attempt to reach Norway, he reversed course and headed back to Germany. Nearly twelve more hours were to pass before the British found the battleship again and, when they did, she was already off the Skaw and safely beyond reach of the RAF's deadly torpedo bombers. The *Lützow* finally limped into Kiel during the afternoon of 14 June and was in such a parlous state that she had to be dry-docked immediately. Indeed, she had been so badly crippled that she was to remain out of service until January, 1942.

Meanwhile the Admiralty, prompted by Churchill, continued to view the presence at Brest of the *Scharnhorst* and *Gneisenau* as a major threat to the Empire's vital sea communications. For given suitable weather – and now reinforced by the arrival of the cruiser *Prinz Eugen* whose full-load displacement of 18,500 tons was considerably greater than that of the original pocket-battleships – they could sortie into the Atlantic whenever they chose, without first having to face the rigours of a hazardous passage through Arctic waters and the fog-bound Denmark Strait.

The Royal Navy did all it could, short of a close blockade, to contain them. Minefields were laid in the channels leading in and out of Brest and a standing patrol of submarines kept watch off the French coast to give early-warning of an enemy sortie, while, in the background, the Home Fleet waited to pounce as soon as news of a breakout was confirmed. It was a terrible waste of resources, especially later in the year when Japan overran South-East Asia and every available ship was needed in the Far East. If evidence is needed, the disruption caused by the presence of the *Scharnhorst* and *Gneisenau* in Brest provides a more than adequate justification for Raeder's commerce raiding strategy.

But although the Royal Navy could take little positive action unless the enemy actually went to sea, the Royal Air Force, as it had already demonstrated, could certainly fill the vacuum, although its task was not easy. Indeed, due to the German Navy's increasing use of smoke generators to shroud the docks in an impenetrable pall of black smog, none of the four raids on Brest in June achieved results. An attack on the *Tirpitz* at Kiel on the night of 20/21 June met with a similar lack of success, the aircraft dropping their bombs on the unfortunate town when they failed to locate their primary target.

June also saw the opening of Operation Barbarossa, the invasion of Soviet Russia. This, however, did not involve the *Kriegsmarine*'s battleships and, in fact, Hitler issued a specific order that 'large scale naval operations in the Baltic are to be avoided until [Leningrad is taken]'. But the attack on the USSR led, at a later date, to the Allies making use of the northern shipping route to Murmansk to sail supply convoys to their new comrades-in-arms. This, in turn, forced the German Navy to transfer its heavy units, including its battleships, into Arctic waters where, operating from bases in Norway, they could wreak havoc on British and American shipping en route to the Bering Sea and Kola inlet. All of this, however, still lay in the future, but the change in emphasis of the *Kriegsmarine*'s strategy was to have far-reaching effects on the future careers of both the *Scharnhorst* and the *Gneisenau*.

The RAF's tenacity reaped its reward on the night of 1/2 July when, in the course of a 52-aircraft attack on Brest, a British bomber crashed into the quay alongside the *Prinz Eugen* and a bomb, released in the final moments, burst in the forward transmitting station killing some sixty men including the cruiser's executive officer, Otto Stooss. Two further raids followed on the nights of 4/5 and 6/7 July, but, although a total of 197 aircraft took part in the attacks, the German smokescreen defences kept the bombers at bay and no damage was inflicted.

The *Scharnhorst*, which had so far emerged from the raids unscathed, had now completed her engine repairs and, after two days of trials in Brest roadstead, she was moved to a new berth at La Pallice on 23 July where, so it was fondly hoped, she would escape the attentions of the RAF. The resistance network immediately warned London of the battleship's movements and Bomber Command, switching tactics, decided to carry out its next attack in daylight. To the surprise and dismay of the Germans, it was launched within 24 hours of the *Scharnhorst*'s arrival at her new home.

The raid was divided into two parts. A force of one hundred bombers escorted by three squadrons of Spitfires was allocated to targets in Brest, while a smaller group consisting of fifteen Halifax bombers, flying without fighter cover, was to strike at the *Scharnhorst* which had now been promoted to the status of flagship by the new fleet commander, Otto Ciliax, who had been the battleship's first captain when she commissioned in May, 1938.

The force scheduled to attack Brest was spearheaded by three American-built B-17 Flying Fortresses which were ordered to overfly the target at 30,000 feet in an attempt to draw off the *Luftwaffe*'s fighters. They were followed by eighteen obsolescent Hampden bombers with their Spitfire escorts, while the main group of seventy-nine Wellingtons was to attack only after the fighters were safely out of the way. The plan, however, proved to be a dismal failure. The *Gneisenau* escaped without damage while the bombers paid a heavy price for operating in daylight, twelve machines falling victim to German flak guns and fighters.

By contrast the unescorted attack against *Scharnhorst* was relatively successful. Five bombs struck the battleship although three merely pierced her deck and went out through the keel without exploding. The remaining two, however, damaged a dynamo room and the starboard propeller shaft tunnel. Although no casualties were reported, underwater damage caused serious flooding and it took a considerable time to bring her back onto an even keel. But, as at Brest, the German flak defences proved to be highly efficient and five of the Halifax bombers were shot down while, according to RAF records, 'all the remainder [of the machines] suffered damage'.

Ciliax quickly concluded that La Pallice was not the place for his flagship and at 19.00 that evening the *Scharnhorst* weighed anchor and made her way back to the relative security of Brest. Observers noted that Captain Hoffmann looked decidedly gloomy as the battleship nudged her way into dry-dock for examination. His pessimism was not without reason, for when the dock was pumped out and the experts had completed their inspection of the damage they informed him that the flagship would need at least four months' work before she was seaworthy again. It was scarcely a promising start for Admiral Ciliax's new command.

Britain's Air Staff, however, remained unhappy about the dissipation of their limited resources on the warships at Brest at a time when every bomb and every machine was required for the strategic air offensive against Germany's industry and communications; indeed, official statistics revealed that more than 10% of Bomber Command's strike capacity was being absorbed by the attacks on the *Scharnhorst*, *Gneisenau* and *Prinz Eugen*. And when French underground sources reported that all three ships were under repair and likely to remain out of commission for many months there was a collective sigh of relief at Adastral House. Now, at least for the time being, the RAF could withdraw the bulk of forces earmarked for Brest and use them more gainfully against targets in the German heartland.

Nevertheless a 24-hour reconnaissance vigil was to be maintained over the Brittany and Cherbourg peninsulas by machines equipped with surface surveillance radar and plans were also prepared to counter a possible break-out from Brest by the ships. The latter, code-named Operation Fuller, were allocated a force of 108 assorted bombers, with fighter support, which were given the specific task of preventing any attempts by the battleships and the *Prinz Eugen* to return to Germany or to embark on the Atlantic sortie. Periodic air attacks continued. There was one in September and a further two in November. They caused no damage and a full aerial offensive against the three warships was not resumed until December, 1941, when intelligence sources confirmed that repairs had been completed and the vessels were again ready for sea.

The focus of attention was transferred to northern waters on 4 September when the *Admiral Scheer*, rested and refreshed after a major refit, left Swinemünde under the command of her new captain, Meendsen-Bohlken, for a shakedown cruise in the Kattegat, followed by a brief visit to Oslo. The RAF soon learned of the battleship's departure and on 8 September four B-17 Flying Fortress bombers were despatched to hunt her down. From a British point of view the operation was a disaster. The aircraft were intercepted by the *Luftwaffe* before they even came within sight of the *Scheer* and two of the bombers were shot down by *Luftwaffe* fighters, while a third, having safely returned to base, crashed on landing. While the Royal Air Force ruefully licked its wounds and swore yet again to abandon daylight attacks, Meendsen-Bohlken brought the battleship back to Swinemünde where it was to be prepared for another raiding sortie into the Atlantic.

Raeder travelled to the Führer's East Prussian headquarters at Rastenberg on 17 September for his routine monthly conference with Hitler. Such meetings normally consisted of a report from the Grand Admiral outlining the current naval situation, followed by his proposals for future operations and major fleet movements. The Führer would put questions to his senior naval adviser on particular points and the conference usually concluded with his rubber-stamp approval of Raeder's various submissions after which the two men retired for a modest meal in the dictator's bunker. But this particular meeting marked a change in direction and heralded the clash of wills that was to lead ultimately to the Grand Admiral's downfall.

The initial decision was entirely negative. Still shaken by the loss of the *Bismarck* and alarmed by the attacks on the *Lützow* and *Scheer*, the Führer vetoed any further raiding sorties into the Atlantic, a policy reversal that was, as Raeder observed, to change the character of the war at sea. Nor was this all, for by this stage of the conflict Hitler had convinced himself that Britain intended to invade Norway. 'The Atlantic can be left to the U-boats,' he told Raeder bluntly. 'Your battleships... must be stationed along the Norwegian coast. They can be of some use in guarding Norway against invasion and they will be safer from air attack there than they would be at Brest.' In a moment of impassioned rhetoric he referred to Norway as Germany's 'zone of destiny'. Savouring Raeder's discomfiture, the Führer then proceeded to reveal his true sentiments: 'Battleships are not good for anything. Their big guns would be of more use, and certainly less vulnerable, in emplacements ashore. I have plans for disarming these steel monsters and using them for the defence of the Norwegian coast.'

The Grand Admiral could scarcely believe what he was hearing, but, wisely, he remained silent. He was familiar with Hitler's moods and no doubt felt that he would emerge from his brooding pessimism and see things in a more rational light in due course. But his hopes were quickly dashed, for Hitler returned again and again to the charge that the battleships were doing nothing to help the war effort and the relationship between the two men, both equally determined to win the battle for the control of German naval strategy, continued to degenerate as one crisis succeeded another.

Hitler's failure to maintain a consistent policy was highlighted on 23 September when his earlier order of 22 June that 'large-scale naval operations in the Baltic are to be avoided until [Leningrad is taken]' was overturned and the newly formed Baltic Fleet, which included the battleships *Tirpitz* and *Admiral Scheer*, was transferred to the Aaland Sea with orders to prevent a breakout by the Soviet Navy. Vice-Admiral Ciliax was recalled from Brest to command the fleet and the heavy ships, who with the cruisers *Köln* and *Nürnberg* formed the Northern Group, steamed out of Swinemünde on the 23rd to take station in the Aaland Sea. On this occasion, however, the *Luftwaffe* came to the rescue of the *Kriegsmarine* and, in sustained air attacks on Kronstadt, they crippled or sank the battleships *Marat* and *Oktyahrskaya Revolutsiya*, the cruisers *Kirov* and *Gorki*, and a total of six destroyers. With the power of the Soviet Baltic fleet broken the battleships were no longer required and, under growing threat from Russian submarines, Ciliax brought his heavy units back to Swinemünde without having to fire a single shot. Hitler regarded the episode as further proof that the *Luftwaffe* could achieve success where the battleships had failed. It was an unjustified conclusion, for Ciliax had been provided with no opportunity to give battle, but the Führer was not best known for rational thinking.

Although Britain's first convoy of war materials to Russia, codenamed PQ-1, had sailed from Iceland in late September with a second, PQ-2, leaving Scapa Flow on 17 October, Raeder's eyes remained firmly fixed on the North Atlantic and tentative plans were evolved to send both the *Tirpitz* and the cruiser *Hipper* to join the *Scharnhorst*, *Gneisenau* and *Prinz Eugen* at Brest in readiness for a massive raiding sortie which, if successful, would have had a decisive effect on the war at sea, but, not surprisingly, it was vetoed by Hitler the moment he heard about it. Raeder, too, was beginning to entertain second thoughts about the *Tirpitz*'s role as a commerce raider. For shortages of oil fuel were beginning to make prolonged operations impractical, and, following the *Bismarck* débâcle, he wisely accepted that Britain's growing superiority in radar technology would make such sorties too hazardous.

The naval conference on 13 November, 1941, brought a further clash of opinion between the Führer and the *Kriegsmarine*'s Commander-in-Chief. Raeder first reported that repairs to both the *Scharnhorst* and *Gneisenau* would be completed in December and that, following a period of exercises and gunnery practice, the two battleships would be ready for sea by

February. Sticking to his guns, he proposed that they should then operate from Brest in a series of short-range hit-and-run raids on Britain's Gibraltar convoys. Hitler, however, flatly refused to consider using the ships for commerce raiding, and he also curtly vetoed Raeder's further proposal to send the *Admiral Scheer* through the Denmark Strait for another sortie into the Indian Ocean.

Faced by the Führer's determination to reverse the *Kriegsmarine*'s previous strategic policy, Raeder reluctantly accepted that, sooner or later, the two battleships would have to return to Germany, and he suggested that their best escape route would be via the Denmark Strait, although he conceded that the smaller *Prinz Eugen* might succeed in breaking for home through the Channel.

Hitler showed an unwelcome interest in this latter suggestion and asked whether it would be possible to bring all three ships back to Germany by the Channel route. Raeder, a conservative by nature, was aghast at the idea.

'Such an attempt would create many problems,' he explained. 'It would involve very great dangers and I would most urgently warn you, *mein Führer*, against attempting anything of the sort.'

Hitler made no comment and the conference closed without further discussion. But as he left the *Wolfsschanze* that evening Raeder must have been hoping that, by the time of their next meeting in December, the Führer would have forgotten all about such a madcap plan. Nevertheless the Grand Admiral's long experience of Hitler's methods had taught him not to be too optimistic, for once the Nazi leader had been inspired by an idea he clung to it like a terrier with a rat, despite every effort by his professional advisers to dissuade him. On his return to Berlin he instructed his staff to examine the problems which could arise if an attempt was made to bring the three warships back to Germany through the Channel.

America's entry into the war sidetracked the agenda of the next naval conference. Raeder, however, in a ploy to divert Hitler's attention away from the battleships at Brest, suggested that the *Tirpitz* could be sent to Trondheim to help defend the Norwegian coast from British landings. The Führer, pleased to see that the *Kriegsmarine* chief was finally coming round to his way of thinking, gave his approval to the move but then added ominously, 'Every ship that is not in Norway is in the wrong place.' It was an unsubtle hint that Raeder, despite his misgivings, could not afford to ignore.

With repairs to the *Scharnhorst* and *Gneisenau* now completed, and after a lull of some four months, Bomber Command's offensive against Brest was resumed on the night of 7/8 December when a force of thirty Wellington and Stirling aircraft, the latter equipped with the newly developed Oboe blind-bombing device, carried out an unsuccessful attack on the battleships.

There were seven further raids on Brest during December involving 302 individual sorties, but, although several hits were claimed, the ships were undamaged and the attacks cost the RAF eleven aircraft.

The air offensive continued into January, 1942, with a total of eleven raids in the course of a month and, on the night of 6/7th, the *Gneisenau* was holed by a near-miss which left two compartments flooded. It was, however, a poor return for the number of aircraft involved; statistics show that 719 sorties were flown against Brest during the month. But the RAF could take consolation from the fact that only eight aircraft were lost, an extremely low casualty rate by comparison with the losses incurred by Bomber Command in its operations over Germany.

Meanwhile the wrangle over the return of the battleships from Brest continued unabated. On Christmas Day the Navy requested air cover from the *Luftwaffe* to protect the *Scharnhorst* and *Gneisenau* during a series of planned exercises which Ciliax considered to be necessary after many months of enforced idleness. But Hitler, who had an obsessive belief in the value of surprise, vetoed the proposed training exercises which he feared could warn the enemy that the ships were now ready for sea.

The Führer convened a further conference on 29 December when Raeder and Vice-Admiral Fricke delivered their 'professional assessment' of the various schemes for bringing the battleships back to Germany. Raeder's conclusions came as no surprise. 'According to the evidence so far available,' he told the Führer, 'an escape through the Channel is *not possible* owing to the enormous risks.' Hitler, however, was not impressed by the arguments paraded before him by his senior naval advisers and, returning to his previous obsession that the British were about to attack northern Norway, insisted that the entire fleet must be employed in defence of the Norwegian coast. This meant, whether Raeder liked it or not, bringing the battleships back into the North Sea. He then repeated his veto on training exercises. 'The best strategy,' he reiterated, 'is a complete surprise break-out through the Channel.' Then, having raged about the 'uselessness of the battleships', he warned Raeder that if the OKM continued to view his proposals as 'impossible' he would order the ships to be paid off and their guns and crews sent to Norway.

The Grand Admiral scuttled back to Berlin with his tail between his legs and, as if to wash his hands of the entire matter, handed the problem over to Navy Group West in Paris. Saalwächter, like Raeder, was opposed to the Führer's mad-cap scheme and he, in turn, passed the papers down the line to his fleet commander Otto Ciliax. He then sat down and composed a long letter to the head of the *Kriegsmarine*, setting out his objections to the Channel route. If the projected operation was to end in disaster, as many senior officers expected, the principals involved were taking great care to distance themselves from any apportionment of the blame. Raeder, too, stuck doggedly to his guns and in a memorandum to Hitler dated 8 January he wrote: 'I... cannot bring myself... to recommend such an operation.'

But with the bit now firmly between his teeth the Führer refused to be deterred by the fainthearts and a 'deciding conference' was called at his Wolf's Lair headquarters on 12 January at which all three services were represented. The plan for the Channel breakout, now formally code-named Operation Cerberus and which ran to 120 foolscap pages, was unveiled by Vice-Admiral Ciliax and, while Raeder sat frowning his disapproval in the background, Hitler listened intently as the details were unfolded. He was particularly impressed by Ciliax's key recipe for success: 'I recommend the necessity of leaving Brest under cover of darkness,' the fleet commander told him. 'We can then take maximum advantage of the element of surprise by passing through the Straits of Dover *in daylight*.' The audacity of the plan matched the Führer's own tactical inclinations and he savoured the expressions of frozen horror on the faces of the senior admirals.

Although he offered the plan for discussion it was clear that his mind was already made up. Commodore Ruge explained the intricacies of the mine-clearance operations and how these could be carried out piecemeal to mislead the enemy while Lt-General Jeschonnek, the *Luftwaffe*'s Chief of Staff, after initially complaining that he could not provide adequate protection with the limited resources he had available, subsequently modified his opposition in the face of Hitler's hostile stare, although he still bravely refused to commit his service to a guarantee of 100% air cover.

Hitler finally brought the arguments to an end by announcing that he intended to adopt Ciliax's plan in its entirety. He was, he explained, convinced that the British, caught by surprise when the ships passed through the Dover Straits in daylight, would be unable to respond adequately. 'I do not believe the enemy to be capable of making and carrying out lightning decisions,' he told his advisers, with what seemed to them to be brash over-confidence, and he produced an analogy that has since gone down in history: 'The situation of the Brest group is comparable with that of a cancer patient who is doomed unless he submits to the surgeon's knife. An operation, even though it might be a drastic one, will offer some hope that the patient's life may yet be saved. The passage of our ships through the Channel would be such an operation. It must therefore be attempted.'

After the conference had concluded the admirals and generals met for a meal. The Führer seemed relaxed and at ease now that the die was cast.

'You will find that this operation will turn out to be our most spectacular naval success of the war,' he confided to Raeder. The Grand Admiral nodded dutifully, but his dour expression showed that he did not share Hitler's optimism. 'The decision... was taken against my advice,' he grumbled in his memoirs. 'I could not see the action succeeding.'

The British realized that, sooner or later, the trapped ships must try to escape back to Germany and it was recognized that their most likely route was through the Channel. However, the threat of the *Tirpitz* breaking out from her new base at Trondheim, where she had arrived on 16 January, and the necessity of protecting the Middle Eastern troop convoys, meant that the Home Fleet must remain at Scapa Flow. It was therefore agreed that the Royal Air Force would take the major offensive role if and when the battleships attempted to leave Brest, while the Navy's contribution would be limited to attacks by light surface forces in the narrow waters of the Dover Straits.

From the German viewpoint secrecy was an essential part of the plan. The Channel, for example, needed to be cleared of mines and, as Ruge had explained to Hitler, the operation was broken down into a number of apparently unconnected sweeps so that the increased activities did not unduly arouse enemy interest. It proved to be a superb example of efficient organization and detailed planning, and Ruge, now promoted to Rear-Admiral, conducted the complicated clearance operation with such consummate skill that the movements of his minesweeping flotillas aroused virtually no suspicions on the other side of the Channel. The concentration of *Luftwaffe* fighter squadrons along the French coast, however, and the passage to Brest of the destroyers that were to provide the close escort for the three warships *were* noticed despite a series of carefully orchestrated deceptions. Both the Admiralty and the Air Ministry agreed that a breakout was imminent.

Indeed, on 8 February, the AOC Coastal Command pointed out that there would be no moon on the 15th of the month and this, together with the predicted tidal conditions, made any time after Tuesday, 10 February favourable for the attempt. A later assessment narrowed the probable date to the 12th, an uncannily accurate forecast, for, by this time, Ciliax had fixed the departure of the battleships from Brest for 19.30 on 11 February.

But the man responsible for thwarting Ciliax's plans, Vice-Admiral Sir Bertram Ramsay, still entertained doubts about the effectiveness of the units under his control. He did not, for example, share the Air Ministry's faith in its main striking force of Beaufort torpedo bombers. For, unlike the machines that had struck at the *Gneisenau* in April, 1941, and the *Lützow* two months later, they were in his opinion inadequately trained for attacks on fast-moving ships, and he requested the transfer of the Fleet Air Arm's 825 Squadron with its battle-tested Swordfish from Lee-on-Solent to Manston as a back-up for the RAF machines. It proved to be an inspired if tragic decision. Ramsay also wanted six destroyers from the Nore transferred to his command, but although the ships were placed under his orders berthing difficulties at Dover meant that the flotilla had to remain at Harwich. A similar request for motor torpedo boats was also approved, but, because of casualties in a skirmish with the enemy on 8 February, only three boats were actually available.

Ramsay finally turned his attention to mine-laying. The *Plover* had already laid a series of small fields to the north of Dunkirk in anticipation of an escape from Brest and two further minelayers were now brought in to supplement her endeavours. He then arranged for Bomber Command to air-drop magnetic mines in Germany's home waters off the Frisian Islands. The preparations for Operation Fuller, the code name for the inter-service plan to block the Channel route, were at last complete. Its success now lay in the gift of the gods.

Both sides were straining at the leash. Neither knew exactly what the other had planned but both anticipated a hard-fought struggle. Even as the final minutes ticked away Ciliax tried a final bluff. A fictitious dinner was arranged for the night of 11 February and selected groups of officers from the three warships were invited to a shooting party the following morning. There was, indeed, a shooting party the next day, but the participants were using weapons rather more lethal than 12-bore sporting guns, and the victims they shot out of the sky were not pheasants but Swordfish torpedo-bombers.

Ciliax's plan to leave Brest at 19.30 on the evening of the 11th in order to pass through the Straits in daylight at 11.30 the next morning suffered a last-minute setback when a force of eighteen RAF bombers arrived overhead and delayed the departure by ninety minutes. But, ever resourceful, the Germans turned the raid to their advantage when the *Luftwaffe* commander, General Koller, suggested that the ships went to sea while the harbour was still enveloped in artificial fog. He also delayed sounding the 'All Clear' until dawn so that Allied spies ashore in Brest would not realize that Ciliax's squadron had left until it was too late for them to warn SOE headquarters in London.

The lack of radio reports from the Resistance network in Brest was only the first of many breakdowns in the carefully organized early-warning system on which Ramsay had to rely if he was to succeed in deploying his forces in the right place and at the right time. Far worse was to follow. The submarines *Sealion* and *H-34* which were on standing patrol outside the entrance to Brest had withdrawn out to sea at dusk to recharge their batteries and, in consequence, were not on station when the battleships emerged.

Whether both boats should have left their billet simultaneously is a matter for debate, and it is not without significance that the White Paper, issued by the Board of Enquiry which Churchill set up under Mr Justice Bucknill to examine the failure of Operation Fuller, referred only to the *Sealion* and gave no indication that there had been a second submarine on the patrol line that day.

Everything now depended on the Royal Air Force. A continuous air patrol had been maintained over the approaches to Brest for many weary months; but, as luck would have it, the Hudson carrying out the surveillance on that particular evening had switched off its radar to avoid detection by the *Luftwaffe* night fighters that had taken off in response to the air raid alarm which had sounded when the eighteen Wellington bombers had arrived overhead, and, when the set was switched on again ninety minutes later, it failed to function. Unable to carry out its mission with an unserviceable radar set, the Hudson returned to base at 19.40. The events that followed would have bordered on farce had the stakes not been so high. The replacement aircraft refused to start and the reserve machine, which had to be hurriedly wheeled from its hangar, did not arrive on station until 22.38, by which time the German squadron had passed through the search area and was steaming up-Channel at 27 knots in an attempt to make up the ninety minutes lost because of the earlier air-raid.

The next patrol line, operated by 217 Squadron, lay between Ushant and the Ile de Brehat and, again, the duty Hudson suffered a radar failure at the crucial time and returned to St Eval. On this occasion, and for some unexplained reason, no replacement machine was despatched to fill the gap. Almost unbelievably the final early-warning patrol line between Le Havre and Boulogne also failed when the duty aircraft was recalled to its base on Thorney Island at 06.15 on the 12th because worsening visibility was making landings increasingly hazardous. Had this particular machine remained airborne until the end of its assigned patrol period it would have undoubtedly detected the fast-moving enemy squadron on its radar. But the gods of war, as if rewarding the daring audacity of Hitler's gamble, were clearly favouring Ciliax and his fleeing fugitives at this stage of the game.

For the most part these shortcomings in the British early-warning system were due to electronic malfunctions, adverse weather conditions, and other valid reasons which can be explained if not wholly excused. The decisive failure, however, came much higher up the chain of command. For not one of the Controllers responsible for overseeing the system reported this chapter of accidents to Ramsay's operational nerve-centre in Dover Castle. Their silence was treated as an example of the no-news-is-good-news syndrome and Ramsay's staff officers assumed that, in the absence of any sighting reports, there were no enemy ships at sea. Had the Vice-Admiral realized that the entire patrol network from Brest to Boulogne had broken down he might not have been so sanguine and, in all probability, the air strike units waiting on their airfields in Kent would have been brought to a state of immediate readiness much earlier.

Only a few of the senior officers on board the battleships knew the details of Operation Cerberus. The bulk of the officers and enlisted men making up their crews had absolutely no idea why they had left Brest nor where they were bound. Most assumed that they were in for several days of exercises, while others thought they were about to embark on another raiding sortie against the enemy's Atlantic convoys. They finally learned the purpose of their mission just after midnight as the ships swept past Ushant, and they listened silently as the loudspeaker systems began to relay Admiral Ciliax's Order of the Day:

'Warriors of the Brest Forces. The Führer has summoned us to new work in other waters... Our first task... is to sail through the Channel eastwards into the German Bight. This mission will impose the highest demands on men, weapons and equipment and we are, all of us, aware of the difficulties that lie ahead. The Führer expects from each of us unwavering devotion [and] I lead the Squadron conscious that every man will do his duty to the utmost.'

It was a heartening message and it was greeted by cheers from the listening seamen. It was, however, more than a little ironic that Ciliax had had to borrow so heavily from Nelson's pre-Trafalgar signal to maximize the impact of his announcement.

But despite the confidence of the Admiral's words things were not going quite as smoothly as anticipated. The Squadron's navigational aids had mostly failed and the radar range-finding equipment could not be used in case the enemy detected its pulses. Moreover, they were now paying the price for Hitler's veto on training exercises, for lack of practice soon led to a breakdown in the system of reporting ranges and radio bearings from the shore stations along the coast, many of which, somewhat unwisely, were manned by French operators who had a vested interest in the failure of the mission. But the Fleet Navigator, Commander Helmuth Giessler, kept his nerve and, relying solely on dead reckoning, he guided the ships confidently through the mile-wide swept channel in total darkness at 27 knots. It was an outstanding achievement by any standard.

At 07.30 on the morning of the 12th the three big ships and their escorting destroyers were joined by two fighter squadrons from the 3rd *Luftflotte* and, just under two hours later, as Ciliax's force came abreast of Fécamp, the protective screen was strengthened by two torpedo boat flotillas each of five vessels. Luck, moreover, continued to favour the Germans despite the emergence of a new danger as the ships approached Dieppe. On the previous night the Royal Navy's *Welshman* had laid a minefield athwart their intended course and Ciliax had already left Brest before Ruge's minesweepers discovered the threat. But, working frantically through the small hours, they succeeded in clearing a narrow passage through which the battleships could pass safely. Ciliax was warned of this latest unexpected hazard by radio and, reducing speed to 10 knots, he led the convoy of ships between the two lines of marker vessels. Once clear, he ordered an increase of speed to 27 knots again in readiness for the most dangerous part of the entire operation, the gauntlet of the Dover Straits.

The British were still unaware of the enemy's proximity. It is true that the radar stations situated along the south coast were being jammed, but this was a routine occurrence whenever an inshore convoy was passing up or down the Channel and no significance was attached to the interference. However, some of the more modern Type-271 radar sets were not affected by the jamming and these soon detected an unusual amount of air activity on the French side of the Channel. The information was flashed to Fighter Command but, unfortunately, only a handful of senior officers were privy to the details of Operation Fuller and the majority were unaware that a breakout by the German battleships was imminent. As a result no one considered the reports to be important and no action was taken. Even when a radar plot at Swingate revealed three large ships moving up-Channel at high speed and the information was passed to Dover there were delays and muddles due to the inexperience of the switchboard operator.

Fortunately the Air Liaison Officer at Ramsay's HQ showed a healthy curiosity about the Swingate plot. Requesting the despatch of a reconnaisance flight, he alerted the Fleet Air Arm's 825 Squadron at Manston to bring their Swordfish aircraft to immediate readiness, but, despite this officer's decisive reaction, the misunderstandings and confusions only deepened. Hitler's assessment of Britain's inability to react to the unexpected was proving to be uncomfortably accurate.

By a strange coincidence 825 Squadron was the same unit which, flying from the *Victorious*, had launched the first torpedo strike against the *Bismarck*, but this time the situation was different. Lt-Cdr Eugene Esmonde's obsolete biplanes had been transferred to Manston in anticipation of a night attack and the news that the German ships were already approaching the Straits came as a considerable surprise to the Fleet Air Arm pilots. Ramsay himself fully realized that a daylight strike against such heavily defended vessels – the battleships had even augmented their regular anti-aircraft defences with *army* personnel complete with their own flak weapons – was an invitation to suicide. Loath to send eighteen brave men to almost certain death the Admiral unfairly shifted the responsibility to the squadron's commander, Eugene Esmonde. Having given him the relevant facts, he then left the final decision to the 32-year old Irishman. As a regular officer there was only one decision Esmonde *could* make. 825 Squadron was readied for take-off.

In a last-minute attempt to minimize the risk of a daylight attack Fighter Command arranged for three Spitfire squadrons to fly as a close escort to the lumbering Swordfish biplanes, while a further two squadrons were ordered to support their naval colleagues by carrying out low-level diversionary attacks on the escorting flak ships. Unfortunately, due to various administrative snarl-ups, the majority of these machines failed to arrive on time and Esmonde was forced to take off on his fateful mission with a totally inadequate escort of just ten fighters.

As Esmonde's Swordfish bounced across the grass and turned into wind, he knew that he dare wait no longer for the promised Spitfires. It was vitally important that the attack should be made while the Squadron was still under radar guidance if they were to be spared a tiring visual search during which they would be sitting targets for the *Luftwaffe*'s fighters. It was also tactically desirable to synchronize the air attack with arrival of the motor torpedo boats from Dover and Ramsgate if optimum results were to be obtained. But there were other equally important considerations. The weather was deteriorating rapidly. Indeed Ciliax's own meteorologist was predicting 10/10ths cloud cover and rough seas within the next two hours. There was also another reason for urgency. The battleships were now approaching the shoaling sandbanks that skirted the Belgian coast and an aerial torpedo attack would soon be impossible until such time as the enemy regained the deeper waters of the North Sea.

In the event it was the coastal forces from Dover who made the first contact when, shortly after noon, Lt-Cdr E.N. Pumphrey in *MTB 221* saw the German ships to starboard as Ciliax rounded Cap Gris Nez. It was a fast-moving struggle fought at almost pointblank range and redolent of the destroyer battles that had been waged in the same waters during the First World War. Pumphrey got to within 800 yards of the outer screen of E-boats* before their heavy fire forced him to loose his torpedoes and turn away. *MTB 219* and *MTB 48* were attacked by cannon-armed *Luftwaffe* fighters and were still 4,000 yards off their target when they released their torpedoes, while *MTB 45*, coming in from astern, was driven off by the destroyer *Friedrich Ihn* and was only saved from annihilation by the timely arrival of two of the Dover motor-gunboats.

Meanwhile Spitfire patrols had sighted what was thought to be a number of small craft east of Ostend, but this was not reported to Dover with any degree of urgency and Group 11 responded by despatching a routine

* German motor torpedoboats.

strike-force. Another two Spitfires from Hawkinge actually spotted the main German force and on his return one of the pilots even identified the *Scharnhorst* from a recognition book, yet the sighting was reported to Dover as a coastal convoy and no reference was made to the suspected presence of a major warship. Hitler had prophesied Britain's inability to respond quickly to a surprise situation. He could have hardly foreseen his enemy's total ineptitude.

A short while later, at 10.42, two more Spitfires had found the German squadron and, braving heavy flak, they had descended to low altitude to confirm their prey. But, despite the importance of their discovery, the pilots did not report details of what they had seen until they landed at 11.09 and, even then, a further fourteen valuable minutes were to elapse before the intelligence reached Dover. Ramsay's headquarters reacted immediately and the coast defence battery on the South Foreland was alerted by telephone. At 12.10, as Pumphrey's motor torpedo boats were moving in to attack, the 9.2-inch guns opened fire.

The main targets, however, were still invisible behind billowing smokescreens and the fall of shot had to be spotted by radar, a technology still in its infancy in 1942. Firing at a range of 27,000 yards, it is scarcely surprising that all the shells missed. But the barrage was a foretaste of what the Germans could expect and Ciliax was realistic enough to know that the luck they had enjoyed so far was unlikely to endure much longer. The convoy was still ten miles west of Calais and, staring ahead towards the narrow Straits, the Vice-Admiral recalled Raeder's pessimistic warning to the Führer: 'The return of the Brest forces through the Channel will in all probability result in its total loss − or at least severe damage.' It was not a comforting thought.

In the operations room of his Dover headquarters his opposite number, Vice-Admiral Ramsay, was doing his utmost to bring Raeder's prophecy of doom to realization for, despite the mistakes which had been made so far, the British lion still had sharp teeth. Pumphrey's striking force of five motor torpedo boats and two motor gunboats had already been despatched, Esmonde's Swordfish were about to leave Manston, the shore batteries had joined the action and now heavier metal was being readied for action further to the north where the six destroyers under the command of Captain C.T.M. Pizey had been given orders to intercept the enemy off the West Hinder buoy. Pizey, however, had been monitoring Dover's signals and he realized that his orders were based on inaccurate information: the enemy's speed was not 20 knots as supposed by the staff at Dover but, according to his own plot, was in excess of 27 knots. If he headed for the West Hinder as ordered he would be too late to make an interception. In traditional Royal Navy style he decided to act on his own initiative and, taking his ships across the British minefields guarding the Essex coast, he steered for the Maas estuary which he planned to reach by 15.15.

Although they had secured no hits on the enemy, Pumphrey's cockleshell coastal craft had emerged from the maelstrom of shot and shell miraculously unscathed. As they sped away to rendezvous at the south-east Goodwin buoy Eugene Esmonde's Swordfish, serial number *W 5984*, roared in on full throttle at wavetop height. Indeed it was the splash of his torpedo hitting the water that misled Pumphrey into later claiming a hit on the *Prinz Eugen*.

825 Squadron had left Manston at 12.28 and the torpedo-bombers were only ten miles out from the coast when the first enemy fighters pounced. The depleted Spitfire escort did its best to hold off the Me-109s of the 3rd *Luftflotte* but sheer weight of numbers prevailed and all six Swordfish had been damaged by the time the enemy machines broke off the action. As Swordfish *W 5984* steered resolutely into the wall of flak surrounding the fast-moving ships its lower port mainplane was already little more than a skeleton of twisted spars. But Esmonde, as befitted his Irish ancestry, held his course tenaciously, despite the buffeting blast of the exploding shells. He was still 3,000 yards from the target when a direct hit sent his machine plunging out of control into the sea. The remaining two aircraft making up the first wave suffered a similar fate, although both, like their leader, succeeded in dropping their torpedoes before they crashed. The second flight of three Swordfish perished unseen in the noisy tumult that followed and only five men emerged from the holocaust alive. It was one of the most gallant sorties ever flown by the Fleet Air Arm, and the posthumous award of the Victoria Cross to Lt-Cdr Eugene Esmonde was a symbolic salute to the bravery of each and every member of 825 Squadron.

By the time the Swordfish attack had been beaten off the German force had passed safely through the narrowest part of the Straits and, as the battleships headed for the more spacious waters of the North Sea, Ciliax could not help wondering whether the worst was now over, but his hopes were rudely shattered at 14.32 when the *Scharnhorst* triggered a magnetic mine and shuddered to an involuntary stop. In obedience to standing orders, the *Gneisenau* and *Prinz Eugen* swept past the crippled flagship at 27 knots and vanished into the distance as the destroyer *Z-29* came alongside the battleship to take off Ciliax and his staff. But by good fortune − and the *Scharnhorst* had a deserved reputation for being a lucky ship − the damage to her keel was not serious and, seventeen minutes after the explosion, the battleship was under way again in pursuit of the main force.

The Royal Navy, however, had not yet shot its final bolt for Captain Mark Pizey's six destroyers were still steering an interception course through the mists and poor visibility to the west. They came under spasmodic attack from the *Luftwaffe* and one, the *Walpole*, was forced to return to Harwich with engine trouble. But Pizey's Nelsonic gamble paid off. At 15.17 the *Campbell* picked up two, and then three, significantly large echoes on her radar. With dusk less than an hour away the flotilla captain decided to attack immediately.

But once again muddle and misunderstandings brought near disaster. For even as the flotilla was closing the enemy, a straggling group of RAF Hudson and Beaufort aircraft, badly briefed and unaware of their correct target, fell upon the destroyers with eager enthusiasm and it was fortunate indeed that their attack met with no success. Ironically, a number of German machines who found themselves involved in the mêlée assumed the British vessels to be friendly and withdrew without dropping their bombs.

Shaken, but none the worse for their experience, Pizey's destroyers formed up in line-ahead. The enemy's heavy calibre guns opened fire at 15.45 as the British ships emerged from the misty murk to port and, two minutes later, the *Campbell* and *Vivacious*, both veterans from the First World War, launched their torpedoes before reversing course and beating an understandably hasty retreat. The *Worcester*, however, failed to observe the turn-away of her two companions and continued to close the enemy until, at 15.50, when only 2,400 yards from her target, she was hit repeatedly by large and small calibre shells. Although initially abandoned by her crew due to a misunderstood order, steam pressure was later restored to her engines and the vessel subsequently limped back to Harwich despite increasingly heavy seas and driving winds.

The remaining destroyers launched their torpedoes, but, as they turned away, they came under attack from another wave of Beauforts who forced the *Campbell* to run astern to avoid their torpedoes, a manoeuvre that capsized some of the rafts and floats from the *Worcester* and added to the latter's already substantial casualty list.

In a last-ditch gesture Bomber Command threw an assortment of 242 aircraft at the fleeing German ships.* Each was armed with 500-pound semi-armour piercing bombs but visibility was now so bad that only 39 machines actually succeeded in finding the target and none of these obtained a hit. In desperation the RAF finally deployed minelaying aircraft to the Elbe estuary but, like the bombers, they met with a similar lack of success.

Nevertheless, British mines were to take the edge off the German Navy's triumph. At 19.55, when north of Vlieland, the *Gneisenau* activated an air-dropped magnetic mine but, luckily, damage was minimal

---

* 92 Wellingtons, 64 Hampdens, 37 Blenheims, 15 Manchesters, 13 Halifaxes, 11 Stirlings and 10 American-built Bostons drawn from 2 Group and 5 Group.

and she was making 25 knots within minutes of the explosion. Eleven hours later, at 07.00 on the 13th, she and the *Prinz Eugen* arrived safely in Brunsbuttel at the western end of the Kiel Canal.

The *Scharnhorst*, however, had the misfortune to pass over a second magnetic mine at 21.34 which caused considerable damage and brought her to a standstill for more than an hour. Her port engine was disabled, both steering motors were put out of action, and her turret-training gear, fire-control systems and other vital equipment was smashed. In addition she was shipping more than 1,000 tons of water. But her engineers managed to coax the centre and starboard engines back to life and, limping painfully at 12 knots, she crawled into Wilhelmshaven where she finally berthed shortly before midnight on the 13th.

So far as British public opinion was concerned Operation Cerberus was a decisive German victory, and a sense of national humiliation overwhelmed the country as the details emerged, an anger made all the more bitter by the surrender of the Empire's Far Eastern bastion of Singapore to the Japanese only two days later on 15 February.

The Times newspaper summed up British feelings in its editorial: 'Vice-Admiral Ciliax has succeeded where the Duke of Medina Sidonia failed. Nothing more mortifying to the pride of our sea power has happened since the seventeenth century. And more than pride is involved; for the strength of the naval forces against which we will have to guard will presently be increased by... two battleships and a cruiser [which had previously been] stationary targets for our bombers over Brest.'

Raeder, resentful, perhaps even jealous, of Hitler's successful gamble took an opposing view: 'Although the dash through the Channel was a tactical success, the withdrawal [of the battleships] from the Atlantic was a strategic retreat. With the transfer of the greater part of our naval forces to Norwegian waters... the Battle of the Atlantic, so far as our battleships were concerned, was practically over.'

Churchill agreed with the Grand Admiral's assessment and declaimed in the House of Commons: 'The threat to our convoy routes has been removed and the enemy has been driven to leave this advantageous position... there is no doubt that the naval position in the Atlantic, so far from being worsened, is definitely eased.'

Only a politician of Churchill's calibre could transform defeat into victory within the space of a single sentence.

CHAPTER EIGHT

'At Sea I Am A Coward'

DESPITE THE SUCCESS of Operation Cerberus the two battleships arrived home in a sorry state. The *Gneisenau*, for example, did not possess large-scale charts of either the harbour, the Elbe estuary, or the entrance to the Kiel canal, despite being ordered to berth at Brunsbüttel by Navy Group North. As a result, Captain Fein had to enter the river without detailed pilotage instructions and, caught unawares by an unsuspected current, he ran the battleship onto an unmarked wreck, the shock of the impact causing further flooding of the starboard shaft tunnel.

The *Scharnhorst*, having fallen victim to two mines, was in considerably worse shape. Like the *Gneisenau*, she had lost her navigational aids and gyro compass soon after leaving Brest and, in addition, she was suffering from a distinct, although not serious, list to starboard. Captain Hoffmann fared little better than his comrade-in-arms, Otto Fein, for the Jade estuary was frozen over when he arrived and the local tugmasters and river pilots were showing a marked reluctance to venture through the ice. Hoffmann nevertheless waited off the bar for several hours hoping for assistance until the imminent approach of dawn and the renewed threat of enemy air attack forced him to proceed up-river, literally, under his own steam. With sirens blasting, he inched the *Scharnhorst* through the mist with the ice crunching noisily beneath her bows until, with a certain amount of relief, he gained the welcome security of Wilhelmshaven dockyard.

The *Gneisenau* continued on to Kiel the following morning where she was joined, some time later, by the *Scharnhorst*. As the salvage surveyors came on board to assess the extent of the damage suffered by the two vessels during their Channel ordeal, the battleships' crews were disembarked and taken to rest camps ashore in a fleet of *Kriegsmarine* Mercedes trucks. After several days, spent mostly in probing the underwater damage, the experts submitted their verdict to the two captains in the flagship's conference cabin. It was far from encouraging. Both vessels would need at least six months intensive work before either could be considered fit for combat service. Fein and Hoffmann exchanged glances, and, although neither man spoke, they each shared the same thought. The Channel Dash had achieved precisely nothing. Their ships were still at the mercy of Britain's Bomber Command and were just as vulnerable at Kiel as they had been at Brest. Raeder had been right after all.

The fleet commander, Vice-Admiral Otto Ciliax, who had been awarded the Knight's Cross for his planning of Operation Cerberus, was, of course, far too valuable an officer to be left idle for six months and, given command of Battle Group One at Trondheim, he sailed from Brunsbüttel on 21 February with the *Prinz Eugen* and the pocket-battleship *Admiral Scheer* for Aasfjord where he was to join the *Tirpitz*. The latter had arrived in Norway on 16 January to spearhead the new fleet which Raeder had promised to create in response to Hitler's fears of an impending Allied assault on the northern bastion of Fortress Europe and she had already been unsuccessfully attacked by RAF bombers on the night of 29/30 January, the prelude to a sustained three-year campaign to destroy the battleship from the air.

Now that the *Tirpitz* was in northern waters it was imperative that she should earn her keep, and when a German patrol aircraft sighted the Murmansk-bound convoy PQ-12 seventy miles south of Jan Mayen Island on 5 March Ciliax, who had arrived in Trondheim eleven days earlier*, obtained Hitler's permission to take the battleship and three destroyers to sea for an attack on the merchant ships and their escort of corvettes and destroyers.

The German task force was sighted by the submarine *Seawolf* soon after leaving Trondheim and Admiral Tovey, whose Home Fleet was some 200 miles to the south of the convoy, immediately altered course northwards to establish contact with the enemy, although snow squalls and bad visibility hampered his efforts by preventing the *Victorious* from flying-off an air search for his prey.

Despite spreading his destroyers across the anticipated course of PQ-12 while he took the *Tirpitz* further to the west, Ciliax failed to intercept the Murmansk convoy, although, quite by chance, his destroyers found and sank a Russian straggler from the homeward-bound QP-8 which was also in the immediate area. Tovey was equally unsuccessful and, after casting south-west, east and finally north-east, he took up a covering position to the south of the convoy to await events.

Ciliax, however, had not given up. When the destroyers rejoined the *Tirpitz* he moved eastwards to resume his search for the elusive PQ-12, apparently unaware that the entire British Home Fleet was in Arctic waters

---

* Ciliax's flagship, *Prinz Eugen*, was torpedoed by the British submarine *Trident* as she was approaching the entrance to Trondheim fjord on 23 February. Although the Vice-Admiral was unharmed, the damage sustained by the cruiser kept her out of service for the next eight months.

and actively looking for him. Thanks to the benefits of Ultra intercepts*
Tovey was far better informed than his opponent and, indeed, aided by radio
direction-finding bearings, he even knew the probable position of the *Tirpitz*.
But, despite these advantages, he still failed to find the enemy task force and
by midnight on the 7th he had come to the conclusion that Ciliax had aborted
his intended attack and was now returning to Trondheim. He therefore
moved further south with the hope of launching an air strike from the carrier
Victorious soon after dawn.

Tovey's assumptions, however, proved to be horribly wrong, for by noon
on the 8th the *Tirpitz* had closed to within 80 miles of PQ-12 while the Home
Fleet was many hundreds of miles to the south-west and powerless to help
the merchan. ships if an attack developed. But luck continued to elude Ciliax
and at 18.15 he finally abandoned the chase and ordered his ships back to
Trondheim, a signal duly reported to Tovey by the Admiralty's Operations
Room soon after 02.00 the following morning. Now that he had some positive
information on which to act Tovey seized his opportunity and ordered the
Victorious to fly-off a search unit at dawn which was to be followed at 07.30
by a strike force of torpedo-armed Albacores.

The carrier's search planes found the *Tirpitz* at 08.00 sixty miles west of
Vestfjord and steaming at high speed towards Trondheim with her destroyer
escort. The machines of the strike force did not sight their target until 08.42
but a further half an hour was to elapse before the attack developed because
the slow-moving biplanes, flying into a strong headwind, only had a
thirty-knot speed advantage over the battleship. The *Tirpitz* laid down a
tremendous flak barrage as the aircraft came in at wave-top height but the
Fleet Air Arm pilots, undeterred by the bursting shells and angry tracer
bullets, held on to the last minute before releasing their weapons. Yet,
despite the expenditure of some 4,500 rounds of heavy anti-aircraft
ammunition plus two full broadsides from the main armament 15-inch guns,
only two Albacores were lost. Nevertheless from a British viewpoint the
attack was a failure, although the pilots involved could take some comfort
from Ciliax's subsequent admission that at least two torpedoes had hit the
battleship and failed to detonate.

The Albacore strike, however, marked the end of the sortie and, as the
Tirpitz entered the temporary safety of Narvik's Vestfjord, Tovey and the
Home Fleet withdrew to the west. Three days later, having eluded a flotilla
of British destroyers lying in ambush off Bodö, the battleship returned to
her old lair in Foettenfjord at Trondheim.

---

* By this stage of the war Allied intelligence had gained access to Germany's most secret
communications including signals to and from the Führer's headquarters at Rastenberg. The
decoded information was referred to as an 'Ultra intercept'.

Raeder was furious over the failure of the operation and roundly blamed the *Luftwaffe* for not giving the *Kriegsmarine* the cover and assistance it had required, pointing out that, although the British fleet had been steaming off the Norwegian coast for at least five days, the German Air Force had launched only one attack: with *three* aircraft! He also persuaded Hitler to restart work on the carrier *Graf Zeppelin*, now lying at Gdynia and the last survivor of the 1938 Z-plan, and demanded that pressure should be exerted on Goering to strengthen the *Luftwaffe*'s forces in Norway. Somewhat ambitiously, bearing in mind the circumstances, the Grand Admiral then proposed that a battle fleet consisting of the *Tirpitz, Scharnhorst, Lützow* and *Scheer*, supported by a carrier (as yet uncompleted), various cruisers and a flotilla of some twelve to fourteen destroyers, should be maintained in Norwegian waters. His motives were not entirely altruistic, for, by pandering to Hitler's obsessive fears for the safety of Norway he hoped to ensure the Führer's support in his impending struggle with the *Luftwaffe*. Hitler, however, threw an unintentional spanner into Raeder's schemes by ruling that, in future, the *Tirpitz* must not be risked at sea unless British carriers had been located and neutralized. It was, effectively, an embargo on future sorties by the battleship for, without the assistance of the *Luftwaffe*, the *Kriegsmarine* did not have the resources to meet the Führer's conditions.

Although not personally involved in these high-level arguments, Ciliax, as the Fleet Commander, had more than enough problems of his own. On the night of 30/31 March a force of heavy bombers had been sent to attack the *Tirpitz* and although, for various reasons, none in fact found the battleship, the Vice-Admiral was uncomfortably aware that his Northern Battle Group was likely to be subjected to an air offensive at least equal to that which the *Scharnhorst* and *Gneisenau* had endured at Brest. But overshadowing everything was the spectre of fuel shortages, a problem that was to haunt the *Kriegsmarine* with increasing intensity in the months ahead.

Until the middle of 1941 the *Kriegsmarine* and German industry had obtained adequate supplies of oil from Russia; but this source had been cut off when Hitler invaded the Soviet Union. On 17 February, 1942, four days before Ciliax's appointment to Battle Group One at Trondheim, Navy Group North claimed that the fuel situation was nearing crisis level. Indeed, on 28 March, the Naval Staff in Berlin issued orders that 'heavy naval forces dependent on the consumption of fuel oil must suspend operations'.*

Official statistics released on 2 April confirmed that deliveries of oil from Rumania amounted to only 8,000 tons instead of the anticipated 46,000 tons, and the latter figure represented only 10% of the *Kriegsmarine*'s

---

* The *Tirpitz* and her destroyers had consumed 8,600 tons of oil in the course of Ciliax's abortive attempt to sink convoy PQ-12.

requirements. A few days later Berlin issued a further order: 'All operations are to be discontinued including those by light forces. The sole exceptions to the ban on the consumption of fuel oil are operations made necessary by offensive enemy action.' Clearly something had gone seriously wrong with the Führer's conduct of the war.

On the same day that the *Seekriegsleitung* circulated its secret oil statistics to the *Kriegsmarine*'s senior flag officers, *Scharnhorst*'s popular captain, Kurt Hoffmann, came ashore from his battleship for the last time. He had already been awarded the Knight's Cross for his contribution to Operation Cerberus and, now promoted to the rank of Rear-Admiral, he was leaving to take command of German naval forces in Holland, his place as the vessel's commanding officer being taken by Captain Friedrich Hüffmeier. But Hoffmann's departure was not the only blow to morale suffered by the men of the former Brest squadron, for the RAF, anxious to prove that the ships were no safer in Kiel than they had been in France, showed its mettle again in a series of spectacular and devastating raids.

On the night of 25/26 February a force of more than sixty bombers targeted the floating dock in a vicious raid that destroyed the 13,625-ton depot ship *Monte Sarmiento* and killed nearly 130 seamen. The bombers returned the next night and this time scored a direct hit on the *Gneisenau*'s bows which ignited the inflammable gases rising from the fuel tank ventilation hatches. The stem of the battleship erupted in a fireball of flame that swept the fo'c'sle and threatened to engulf the forward 11-inch turret. By the time the inferno was finally quelled the bow section of the vessel was virtually non-existent and 116 men were dead.

When the *Scharnhorst* and *Gneisenau* were first conceived they were designed to carry a main armament of 15-inch guns, a feature which, it will be recalled, Hitler had vetoed for fear of upsetting his European neighbours. But the war had made a mockery of the old naval limitation treaties and it was decided that, during reconstruction, the battleship should be lengthened by some thirty feet to improve her seaworthiness and that she should be re-equipped with 15-inch weapons as originally intended. It was a massive task which would require complete freedom from the unwelcome attentions of the RAF. So, on 4 April, she was towed to Gdynia; a port which, at that time, was still safely beyond the range of Britain's bombers. By the end of June her damaged bows had been removed and her 11-inch guns lifted out of their turrets, the weapons themselves ultimately finding their way to shore defence batteries in Holland and Norway. Reconstruction work continued for a further six months but was then abandoned and she was left to rust at Gdynia, a pathetic monument to the folly of Raeder's dreams.

The *Scharnhorst*, as usual, enjoyed better luck than her sister. For some unknown reason the RAF called off its offensive against the battleships following the virtual destruction of the *Gneisenau*, even though the *Scharnhorst*, which had escaped damage in previous raids, remained at Kiel. As a result the dockyard was able to proceed with the task of repairing the damage sustained in the Channel Dash without serious interruption and, although not fully operational, she was ready for sea again by August.

The battleships making up Battle Group One in Norway were by now settling down to the routine of their new environment. Net defences were increased in size and complexity, flak positions were strengthened, and everything possible was done to make the lonely anchorage in Foettenfjord impregnable. Neither were the comforts of home forgotten. Captain Karl Topp, the *Tirpitz*'s deservedly popular commanding officer, realized that their stay in Norway was likely to be both long and arduous. Following negotiations with the local authorities, he acquired the holiday island of Salto, situated at the head of the fjord, for use as a rest camp by the battleship's officers and men.

The site was already equipped with log-cabins and these were quickly augmented with substantial rest houses built in matching style. Re-named Tipito it even boasted an open-air theatre where visiting artistes from the Fatherland could entertain the sailors; it proved to be a popular attraction for both officers and men alike, offering a welcome respite from the weary and boring routine of life on a large battleship at anchor for long periods. The winter snows afforded ample facilities for skiing and sledging on the mountains that surrounded the fjord, while the warmer temperatures of spring and summer turned thoughts to boating and fishing.

Despite strict rules which banned hunting, camp fires, and the plundering of the local flora and fauna, life was almost idyllic at Tipito. It was, indeed, a veritable Garden of Eden, until the advent of the serpent Lust and a number of very Nordic blonde Eves. The crew of the *Tirpitz* were, after all, only human and a solitary celibate life held little attraction for virile, twenty-year-old sailors. Before many months had passed parties of girls were being ferried to the island every evening. It may have all been innocent, or it may have had a more sinister side, but when a local fisherman spilled the beans while defending himself against charges of stealing *Kriegsmarine* stores in June, 1942, and the details reached the ears of the *Kommandatur* at Trondheim, Tipito and its fleshpots were promptly closed down.

The war, meanwhile, was never far away. On the night of 27/28 April a force of 31 Halifax and 12 Lancaster bombers carried out an attack on the fjord which, since March, had housed the heavy cruiser *Hipper* as well as the *Tirpitz* and the *Admiral Scheer*. But, learning from their experiences in Brest, German engineers had by now almost perfected their smokescreen defences and only a handful of the aircraft actually found their target. None obtained hits and five machines were shot down by the highly efficient flak batteries of the three ships. There was a second raid the following night but, again, no hits were scored, and two more machines were destroyed.

Despite the threatening presence of the *Tirpitz* at Trondheim, Britain continued to run a steady stream of convoys, carrying aircraft, tanks, ammunition, and other vital war materials, to Murmansk and Archangel. But although the battleships and other heavy units could not venture to sea because of the ever-deepening oil crisis — light forces, notably the 8th Destroyer Flotilla under the command of Admiral Schmundt — Doenitz's U-boats and units of the *Luftwaffe* continued to maintain pressure on the Russian convoy route. PQ-13, for example, was attacked by the destroyers *Z-24*, *Z-25* and *Z-26*, Ju-88 bombers from III/KG30 and the submarines *U-209*, *U-376*, *U-435*, *U-436*, *U-454*, *U-456*, *U-585* and *U-589*. The three-day battle cost Germany the destroyer *Z-26* and one of the U-boats, while the Royal Navy almost lost the cruiser *Trinidad* which had the singular misfortune to torpedo herself. Several British destroyers were also seriously damaged. With six of the convoy's merchant ships sunk, the Naval Staff in Berlin were quietly satisfied with the results despite the losses sustained, but Admiral Schmundt, apparently unaware of the restrictions placed upon Ciliax by the oil crisis, complained bitterly about the lack of battleship support for his destroyers.

Bad weather kept Schmundt's ships in harbour when the next convoys, PQ-14 and QP-10, sailed and this time the honours were shared between the U-boats and the aircraft of III/KG30, with the submarines claiming four victims and the *Luftwaffe*'s Ju-88s a further two. More importantly, however, the air attacks had forced sixteen ships from PQ-14 to turn back and return to Iceland, by any yardstick a major strategic victory. Impressed by the results obtained, Hitler decided that the *Luftwaffe* should in future have its own force of torpedo-carrying aircraft for anti-shipping operations. Goering had favoured aerial torpedo attacks for some time but his plans had always been thwarted by Raeder, who, despite his regular protests that the Air Force was not giving the *Kriegsmarine* adequate support, had resolutely opposed the release of torpedoes to the *Luftwaffe* because he regarded them as solely naval weapons. By an odd coincidence, however, the wrangle, which had originated before the war, had been resolved earlier in the year when Raeder had finally yielded to Goering's pressure. The first unit of twelve machines had arrived at Bardufoss in northern Norway only a matter of days before the Führer made his decision known.

This particular conference also saw a sharp change in Hitler's attitude to the sea war when, in an unexpected *volte-face*, he told Raeder that every effort must now be made to stop the convoys from getting through to Russia and that plans should be drawn up for a joint air-and-sea offensive in June.

To the Grand Admiral's astonishment he also gave orders for the *Admiral Scheer* to be despatched on another raiding sortie.

As a consequence of the *Kriegsmarine*'s new dynamic strategy much of May was taken up with high-level planning meetings and the movements of ships and units in preparation for the promised offensive. The *Scheer*, with the torpedo boats *T-5* and *T-7* and her support vessel *Dithmarschen*, left Trondheim and moved north to Narvik, while the damaged *Prinz Eugen* returned to Germany on 18 May for repairs. On the same day the battleship *Lützow*, now officially reclassified as a heavy cruiser, left Kiel and, a week later, joined her sister-ship *Scheer* at Narvik, the two vessels forming the nucleus of Vice-Admiral Kummetz's newly formed Battle Group Two.

While Germany's heavy ships were playing musical chairs Raeder flew from Berlin to Trondheim to discuss details of the planned strike against the Russian convoy route with Ciliax's successor as Fleet Commander, Admiral Otto Schniewind, and his deputy, Vice-Admiral Kummetz. The three men were subsequently joined by General-Admiral Rolf Carls who, in his capacity as Flag Officer Navy Group North at Kiel, was in overall command of operations in Arctic waters. The target they selected for attack was convoy PQ-17 which was expected to sail towards the end of June, the plan being identified by the code name *Rösselsprung* or Operation Knight's Move. The senior admirals were convinced that they were at last on the verge of a resounding victory even though the movements of the *Tirpitz* continued to be restricted by the Führer's earlier order which he had not seen fit to rescind when he met Raeder on 15 June: 'Before any attack is made by our battleships the position of enemy aircraft carriers must be established; and they must also first be rendered harmless by our dive-bombers.' It is interesting to note that, by reclassifying the *Lützow* and *Scheer* as heavy cruisers, the two pocket-battleships were not subject to Hitler's reservations. Bearing in mind Raeder's machiavellian cunning, it is impossible not to wonder whether this was the true purpose for the otherwise inexplicable reduction in their status.

There were clashes of policy on the British side as well, for Admiral Tovey was opposed to large convoys — PQ-17 with thirty-six ships was to be the biggest yet — and wanted the vessels to sail in two separate groups. Dudley Pound, the First Sea Lord, disagreed and insisted that concentration was essential if enemy air and submarine attacks were to be successfully resisted. With the bitter experience of recent operations in mind during which the *Trinidad* and *Edinburgh* had both been lost*, Tovey was not in favour of sending his cruisers too far to the east because the proximity of the

---

* After surviving PQ-13 the *Trinidad* had been sunk by enemy aircraft on 14 May. The *Edinburgh* was lost while defending PQ-15.

Luftwaffe's bases in northern Norway increased the risk of air attack. Pound accepted the Commander-in-Chief's reservations but took the argument a stage further by suggesting that, once east of Bear Island, the convoy should be dispersed and the individual merchantmen allowed to proceed to Murmansk independently and without escort. Tovey was appalled by the idea which he castigated as 'sheer bloody murder'. Wilting before the blast of Tovey's wrath the First Sea Lord withdrew his suggestion. But he insisted that, in accordance with the Admiralty's traditional policy, the convoy would be ordered to scatter if threatened with an attack *by surface ships*.

PQ-17, reduced for various reasons to 33 merchant vessels plus the tanker *Aldersadale*, together with a close escort of six destroyers, four corvettes, and numerous armed trawlers and anti-aircraft ships, left Reykjavik on 27 June. The homeward-bound QP-13, a convoy of 23 merchantmen guarded by five destroyers and three corvettes, sailed from Murmansk the same day. Twenty-four hours later Tovey's covering force − a formidable fleet which included the battleships *Duke of York* and the *USS Washington*, the carrier *Victorious*, two cruisers and ultimately a total of fourteen destroyers − left Scapa to take station between Iceland and Bear Island.

Confirmation that PQ-17 had sailed came on 1 July when the *B-Dienst* monitors established its position by means of radio intercepts and a few hours later visual contact was made by Lt-Cdr Reche's *U-255* some 60 miles east of Jan Mayen Island. Shadowing the convoy from astern, Reche transmitted a series of homing signals, a clarion call to which no fewer than nine other U-boats responded. During the afternoon the homeward-bound QP-13 hove into sight and passed westwards unchallenged. Empty ships were not the prize which the *Kriegsmarine* was seeking.

Now that the position, course and speed of PQ-17 had been confirmed it was time for the battleships to enter the fray and, on the afternoon of 2 July, Schniewind's Battle Group One, headed by the *Tirpitz*, started the long trek down Trondheimsfjord towards the open sea, its departure having been delayed for nearly 24 hours by Hitler's absence from his East Prussian headquarters. For, ever mindful of his own precarious position, Raeder insisted on obtaining the Führer's personal approval before the ships actually sailed. It was during this temporary hiatus that a group of Heinkel He-115 torpedo-bombers swooped on the convoy as it trundled eastwards at a steady nine knots. It was the first direct attack on PQ-17, the prowling U-boats having been driven off by the escorts earlier in the day, and its lack of success raised morale as effectively as the Royal Navy's traditional tot of rum.

Vice-Admiral Kummetz's Battle Group Two sailed from Narvik the following night. It left in thick fog and was soon in trouble when, at 03.00, while the ships were negotiating the narrow channel guarded by the Storboen lighthouse, the *Lützow* ran aground and was forced to return. It was not the most auspicious beginning for Operation *Rösselsprung*, but worse was to come. With the intention of escaping British air reconnaissance both Battle Groups were routed close inshore along a coast notorious for its fogs, treacherous currents and navigational hazards, and, soon after dawn, Schniewind's force met disaster when three of its four destroyers – *Karl Glaster*, *Hans Lody* and *Theodor Reidel* – struck uncharted rocks off Gimsöy. The Admiral hastily dropped anchor and waited impatiently while the extent of the damage was determined. The verdict of the experts did little to relieve the gloom and, leaving the three ships behind, the *Tirpitz* and *Hipper* together with the remaining destroyer *Friedrich Ihn*, continued on their way to Altenfjord where they joined Kummetz and the *Scheer* at 10.30 the following day.

There had, however, been some confusion in the interim while the ships were still anchored off Gimsöy. For Schniewind had made use of the hiatus to send one of the flagship's seaplanes back to Narvik with instructions to despatch a teleprinter message to Admiral Schmundt, the Flag Officer Northern Norway, asking him to inform Carls of his intention to sail against the convoy the next morning. The signal left Schmundt in a quandary, for the executive order authorizing the launch of Operation *Rösselsprung* had not yet been issued by Navy Group North and Schniewind was clearly guilty of jumping the gun. Anxious to conceal the fleet commander's impetuosity, Schmundt ignored the teleprinter message and, instead, called Carls by telephone on his own initiative. Fortunately the latter shared Schniewind's eagerness to seek battle and, unaware that the *Tirpitz* had already left Narvik, Carls transmitted a direct order to the flagship by radio: *Transfer to Altenfjord. Request intentions*. By the time Schniewind received Navy Group North's authorization to proceed he and his remaining ships had left Gimsöy and were already well on their way to join Kummetz.

British air reconnaissance had established that the two groups of German warships had sailed from Narvik and Trondheim and the Admiralty was also aware, from secret intelligence sources, that Raeder planned to launch a full-scale battleship sortie against the convoy. A report was then received that the *Scheer* was in Altenfjord and, on the evening of the 4th, an Ultra intercept indicated that the *Tirpitz* had been ordered to join the pocket-battleship in her northern lair that morning. Although he lacked confirmatory evidence, the First Sea Lord, Admiral Pound, was forced to assume that the *Tirpitz*, too, had reached Altenfjord. But a nagging doubt remained. Had the ships left again and were they now at sea and steering for the convoy? There was, however, no firm news. Indeed there had been no reports of the battleships leaving Altenfjord from either the submarines patrolling outside, the Norwegian secret agent keeping watch on the entrance, or intercepted wireless traffic. Nevertheless Commander Denning, the Admiralty officer responsible for sifting all intelligence information about the battleships, could not give Pound the assurance he needed, for without positive confirmation that the *Tirpitz* was still in Altenfjord the only evidence available was merely circumstantial. Pound, forced to act on the basis of a worst-case scenario — that the *Tirpitz* was at sea and already closing on PQ-17 — came to a fateful decision. The convoy was to disperse.

At 21.11 on 4 July, while the *Tirpitz* and the other ships were still waiting in Altenfjord for the executive signal from Berlin and Schniewind's frustration was deepening by the hour, the British Admiralty flashed a signal to Rear-Admiral Hamilton whose close-covering force of cruisers was now standing sentinel to the north of the convoy: *Secret. Most immediate. Cruiser force to retire westwards at high speed*. Twelve minutes later Commander Jack Broome, in command of the close escort, was given his orders in similarly urgent style: *Secret. Immediate. Owing to threat from surface ships, convoy is to disperse and proceed to Russian ports.*

The situation to which Pound was responding existed only in his own mind. In reality the German battleships were still at anchor in Altenfjord awaiting orders — orders which could not be issued until the precise location of the Royal Navy's carriers had been established. Hitler's instructions regarding the elimination of the enemy's carriers had been crystal clear, and no senior officer in the *Kriegsmarine*, from Grand Admiral Raeder downwards, was prepared to flout the Führer.

At 21.36 Pound sent the final and fatal signal to PQ-17: *Secret. Most immediate. Convoy is to scatter.* Broome could scarcely believe his eyes when his Chief Yeoman of Signals Jim Blood handed him the decoded message slip. Almost instinctively both men searched to the south with their glasses, each expecting to see the masts and smoke of German battleships already in sight above the rim of the horizon. Surely such a peremptory signal could only mean that the enemy was on the point of attacking? Broome's destroyer, *Keppel*, raced through the convoy with the scatter signal flying from its masthead and then, gathering the other escorting destroyers under his wing, he turned eastwards as the ships of PQ-17 broke formation and scattered in all directions like frightened chickens running from a fox.

There was similar uncertainty about the enemy's strength and position among the senior officers of the *Kriegsmarine*'s High Command. A *Luftwaffe* pilot had sighted Hamilton's cruisers on the night of the 3rd, while the *Tirpitz* was still en route to Altenfjord, and wrongly identified them as a force of *battleships* and cruisers. The mistake was not rectified until the next morning (4th) but had then been inadvertently repeated, almost within hours, by the *U-457*. To make matters worse a *Luftwaffe* shadower had sighted two floatplanes on anti-submarine patrol from the *USS Wichita* and reported them as being torpedo-bombers.

To Raeder, agonizing over the contradictory signals, the *Luftwaffe* report could mean only one thing: there was at least one British carrier in the vicinity of PQ-17, and until she could be eliminated the *Tirpitz* must remain where she was. Carls, increasingly irritated by the indecision in Berlin, informed Raeder that if the operation did not begin within 24 hours he intended to recall Schniewind's ships to Narvik. The Grand Admiral wearily agreed.

But the confusion and lack of clear-cut decisions remained until, just before midnight on the 4th, *U-456* reported that the cruisers were withdrawing westwards at high speed. Carls promptly requested permission to send the Battle Group to sea but was again rebuffed by Raeder who was still worried about the threat posed by the British carrier. Finally at 06.55 (5th) a lone *Luftwaffe* reconnaissance aircraft sighted the Home Fleet and the carrier *Victorious* to the north-west of Bear Island, 800 miles away from the probable scene of action. Carls repeated his request to Raeder and this time Raeder passed it on to the Führer. Hitler's approval reached Berlin at 11.30 and was forwarded to Carls at 11.40. One minute later Navy Group North transmitted the executive signal to the Fleet Commander at Altenfjord. But, as if regretting his previous temerity in seeking permission to attack, he hastily qualified his order to Schniewind in terms that undoubtedly reflected Hitler's personal views: 'A brief operation with partial success is more important than a total victory involving major expenditure of time. Report at once if overflown by enemy aircraft. Do not hesitate to break off the operation if situation doubtful. On no account grant enemy success against the nucleus of our fleet.'

It was a less than inspirational call to battle. What had happened to the fighting spirit of the old Imperial German Navy? Where were men like Hipper who, at Jutland, had ordered the battle-cruisers: *At the enemy! Charge! Ram!*? The answer rested in the character of the evil genius who had created, and was now in the process of destroying, the Third Reich, Adolf Hitler. 'On land I am a hero,' he had once confided to a staff officer, 'At sea I am a coward.' It was the misfortune of the *Kriegsmarine* to be led by such a man.

Schniewind had once again pre-empted his orders by leaving Altenfjord before Carls' formal authority to execute Operation *Rösselsprung* was received and, by 15.00, the combined Battle Group was already steaming through the Barents Sea at 25 knots. Any hopes of falling upon PQ-17 without warning vanished, however, at 17.00 when the Soviet submarine *K-21* intercepted the *Tirpitz* and fired a full salvo of torpedoes, none of which came anywhere near the flagship. The ships were seen by an RAF Catalina an hour later and this contact was followed, some time after 20.00, by a further sighting report from the British submarine *Unshaken*. As the *B-Dienst* monitors decoded the various signals and passed them back to the Admiralty in Berlin, Raeder lost his nerve again and at 21.00 he ordered the task force to be recalled to Altenfjord. Carls' signal to Schniewind, *KR-KR-KR Break Break Break*, was transmitted from Kiel at 21.15.

And so, despite the promise and optimism that had surrounded the initial planning stages of the operation, the *Tirpitz* and her companions turned back without firing a single shot from their guns. Schniewind and his senior officers were furious, the junior officers frustrated and the enlisted men bemused. Morale plummeted as the ships felt their way into the fjord in the early hours of 6 July, and the resentment remained when they left again that evening and proceeded south to Narvik. Yet, had they but known it at the time, they had achieved a stunning victory. The threat of a surface attack had caused Dudley Pound to disperse PQ-17 and withdraw its escorts. By so doing he exposed the helpless and defenceless merchant ships to the fury of the waiting U-boats and the venom of Goering's *Luftwaffe*.

PQ-17 was decimated. The U-boats sank nine ships totalling 56,611 tons, while German aircraft disposed of another eight amounting to 40,376 tons. They also damaged a further seven ships of 46,982 tons which the submarines finished off at their leisure. 3,350 vehicles went down with the ships together with 430 tanks, 210 aircraft, and nearly 100,000 tons of war materials and equipment. In return Germany had lost just five aircraft. The *Tirpitz* and her Battle Group may not have fired their guns in anger or even seen the enemy, but they had been responsible for the greatest convoy success in the history of modern sea warfare.

The failure of the battleships to engage the enemy led, not unnaturally, to recriminations. Schniewind cautiously avoided apportioning blame but observed somewhat caustically that 'without some offensive spirit war-like operations cannot be carried out with any hope of success'. Raeder was even more circumspect. 'Our heavy units had to return to their bases in accordance with their standing orders,' he noted in his memoirs. 'Hitler had limited their scope of operations . . . [as] a direct consequence of the loss of the *Bismarck*.' It was left to a relatively junior officer, Captain Gerhard Wagner, the Chief of Operations at the Admiralty in Berlin, to put the blame where it belonged: 'Every operation by our heavy surface forces has been hampered by the Führer's desire to avoid losses and reverses at all costs.'

The massacre of PQ-17 led the British Admiralty to suspend all further Russian convoys during the summer months, but before the new policy could be implemented Churchill insisted on the despatch of one more convoy, PQ-18, which began its perilous journey to Murmansk on 2 September. The close escort and the covering force were both strengthened, but, due to refitting, the *Victorious* was not available and the convoy sailed without the protection of a fleet carrier, although a smaller escort carrier, the *Avenger*, formed part of the escort force. The absence of the *Victorious* should have been an open invitation for a sortie by the *Tirpitz* and the pocket-battleships, but the Führer, failing to appreciate the underlying reason behind the destruction of PQ-17 — the threat of a surface attack — considered that the German success had been solely due to the joint efforts of the U-boats and the *Luftwaffe*. He therefore ruled out any further battleship attacks on the outward-bound convoys to Murmansk and limited further sorties to operations in the Barents Sea against the QP convoys. As a result of the Führer's hasty and superficial analysis PQ-18 proved to be another lost opportunity for Schniewind's Battle Group. Raeder's tentative plan, Operation *Doppelschlag*, for the *Scheer* and the cruisers *Hipper* and *Köln* to attack the convoy while the *Tirpitz* provided long-range support, was dropped on 13 September following a personal telephone call from Hitler.

Despite the absence of the *Kriegsmarine*'s heavy ships, PQ-18 suffered a severe mauling at the hands of Doenitz's U-boats and the *Luftwaffe*'s aircraft, losing thirteen ships totalling 75,657 tons, the majority falling victim to air attack. By way of compensation the British escorts sank three U-boats, *U-88*, *U-457* and *U-589*, and shot down no fewer than twenty-two aircraft, a tally of success that left the honours roughly even in the final analysis.

Hitler's earlier order to despatch the *Scheer* on a commerce-raiding mission was implemented sixteen days before PQ-18 sailed, and in a sortie code-named Operation *Wunderland*, the pocket-battleship, arguably the most successful of the German Navy's seven heavy ships, left Narvik under the command of Captain Meendsen-Bohlken on 16 August and entered the Kara Sea seventy-two hours later. The cruise, however, opened on a disappointing note, for, although her float-plane sighted three small convoys on the 20th, rolling banks of mist, sea-ice and bad weather in the vicinity of Krakovka Island combined to prevent the *Scheer* from getting close enough to use her guns.

The battleship next appeared off the Soviet polar settlement at Cape Zhelaniya at dawn on 25 August and, standing-off from the shore at short range, she proceeded to bombard the installations with her 11-inch weapons, destroying warehouses, living quarters, and the meteorological station and damaging the building that housed the settlement's wireless equipment. Then, having completed her orgy of destruction, the *Scheer* continued on her way to her next objective, Novy Dikson. En route she intercepted the Soviet icebreaker *Sibiryakov* from whom she demanded up-to-date information about ice conditions in the Kara Sea. Captain Kacharava tried to play for time. There was a convoy in the vicinity and it was his task to delay the Nazi battleship until it had passed safely out of danger. Following the accepted rules of the sea, he asked the *Scheer* for her name. A signal lamp flashed from the battleship's bridge: *Shishiyama*. Unfortunately Meendsen-Bohlken's attempt to hide behind Japanese neutrality* was promptly scuppered when someone ran an American ensign up the *Scheer*'s masthead. Despite the confusion, Kacharava had little doubt about the true identity of his opponent and, although hopelessly outgunned, he opened fire on the raider. It was a challenge that exactly mirrored the sacrifice of the *Jervis Bay* almost two years earlier and it had a similarly tragic conclusion. Crushed by superior firepower, the icebreaker went to the bottom with all hands and, not waiting to search for survivors, the *Scheer* moved eastwards in pursuit of the convoy.

The ice barrier put an end to the hunt some hours later, however, and baulked of her prey, the battleship turned westwards again. At 01.05 on 27 August she was sighted approaching Novy Dikson, moving through the mists like a silver wraith as she closed the harbour. At 01.37 her 11-inch guns opened fire at a range of three miles. But, unlike the settlement at Cape Zhelaniya, Novy Dikson was defended and the shore batteries replied spiritedly, the army's guns soon being joined by the weapons mounted on the merchant ships berthed in the harbour. Two direct hits from the coastal-defence batteries forced the *Scheer* to break off the engagement after some twenty-three minutes and she beat a hasty retreat under cover of a smoke-screen to escape further damage. She returned to the fray half an hour later but, on being hit for a third time, she withdrew out to sea, having expended more than a hundred 11-inch shells on the town and its harbour causing considerable structural damage to buildings, as well as hitting the icebreaker *Dezhnev* and the steamer *Revolutsioner*.

But the attack on Novy Dikson proved to be the final flourish of Operation *Wunderland*. Calling an end to what had been a disappointing sortie, Meendsen-Bohlken continued westwards out of the Kara Sea to bring the *Scheer* back to Narvik on 30 August where, like a great wounded animal, she was left to lick her wounds.

The *Tirpitz* was by this time also in dire need of refitting, but Hitler refused to allow Germany's largest battleship to leave Norway for expert attention at Kiel or Wilhelmshaven and a frustrated Raeder decided to send her south to her former berth in central Norway. She sailed on 23 October and on reaching Trondheimsfjord she steamed slowly past the guardships and net defences to enter Foettenfjord, a stretch of water some forty miles from the sea, where dockyard repairmen, shipped by Raeder from Kiel to Norway for this specific purpose, were already waiting to begin work. Lacking proper dockyard facilities, they faced a number of daunting tasks, one of which involved unshipping the battleship's enormous rudder. But

---

* Japan and Russia were not at war with each other in 1942.

they worked steadily and the refit was ultimately completed by January, 1943.

The Royal Navy, however, was determined to encompass the destruction of the *Tirpitz* by one means or another. The first scheme to be adopted featured an attack by 'chariots' — two-man human torpedoes which had been copied from the Italian Navy's highly successful *Maiali* that had crippled Britain's Mediterranean Fleet at Alexandria in December, 1941. Preparations had begun in the Spring of 1942 and, as soon as the volunteer charioteers had been trained, a plan was drawn up for the torpedoes to be towed across the North Sea by a fishing-boat, in this instance a vessel that had already taken part in numerous clandestine operations along the Norwegian coast. Agents keeping watch ashore reported the battleship's arrival in Foettenfjord to London within hours and the following day the chariot attack, code-named Operation Title, was authorized for 31 October.

From a British viewpoint the venture ended in disaster. The fishing-boat developed engine trouble, enjoyed a narrow escape when she was stopped by a German patrol-boat and, finally, during the run up Trondheimsfjord in increasingly foul weather, the towing hawsers snapped and both chariots were lost. It was the end of a gallant endeavour and, on getting ashore, the survivors split into two parties and made for the Swedish frontier. All except one, Able Seaman Bob Evans, safely crossed the border. But the latter, challenged by Norwegian guards, was shot and wounded and, later, handed over to the Gestapo. He was subsequently executed on direct orders from Hitler, a crime for which the *Kriegsmarine* was, happily, blameless.

The temporary suspension of the Russian convoys came to an end with the approach of winter when the British Admiralty decided to re-open the Arctic route in order to bring home the empty merchant ships stranded at Murmansk and Archangel before the sea froze over and they were iced in. The convoy, QP-15, left the Kola Inlet on 17 November and Kummetz was warned to bring the cruiser *Hipper* and two destroyers to immediate readiness. But at the crucial moment the Luftwaffe failed to provide the necessary air reconnaissance and Raeder, unwilling to take chances, cancelled the sortie. QP-15 was therefore left to the U-boats but, on this particular occasion, they did not enjoy their usual success and only two of the merchant ships were sunk.

The failure to destroy QP-15 was fresh in Raeder's mind when he attended the monthly routine conference with Hitler at the *Berghof* on 19 November and he took the opportunity to set out his usual list of grievances: lack of support from the *Luftwaffe*; the British minelaying offensive in northern waters; the prolonged refit of the *Tirpitz*; and, finally, the chronic fuel shortage which was strangling every effort to get the surface ships to sea. His general mood of irritability and defeatism did nothing to lighten the general atmosphere of gloom at the Führer's headquarters. Perhaps the most significant feature of this particular conference was the Grand Admiral's proposals to attack only the homeward-bound QP convoys 'since it is expected that they will not be heavily guarded' − a tacit admission that the Royal Navy was winning the battle for control of the Arctic sea-lanes.

Two matters loomed large in the discussions: the crippling effect of the *Kriegsmarine*'s shortage of fuel oil and Hitler's obsession with the probability of an Allied invasion of Norway. With a view to strengthening Germany's defences against the latter contingency, the Führer insisted that further light forces must be transferred to the northern zone. He also demanded that at least twenty-three U-boats should be kept available for service in Arctic waters. Raeder, for his part, was equally anxious to get more of the *Kriegsmarine*'s heavy units to Norway so that he could wage an offensive, albeit restricted, war against the Allied convoys. He pointed out that with the heavy cruisers *Hipper* and *Prinz Eugen* and the battleship *Lützow* fully operational again, now was the time to reinforce Schniewind's battle group. The Führer, however, would only consent to the transfer of the diesel-powered *Lützow*, arguing that the severe shortage of fuel oil made it impossible to send the two cruisers into northern waters.

In accordance with the decisions taken at the *Berghof* in November the *Lützow* left Gdynia on 10 December and arrived in Altenfjord a week later. But the balance of naval strength in Norway remained unchanged, for, as a consequence of the damage she had sustained during Operation *Wunderland*, the *Scheer* was forced to return to Germany for repairs and refitting. To make up the deficiency Raeder obtained the Führer's reluctant consent to move the heavy cruiser *Hipper* to Altenfjord as well, as part of the agreed plan to strengthen the *Kriegsmarine* in northern waters. The *Tirpitz*, of course, was still undergoing major surgery at Trondheim in central Norway and would not be available for operations until January.

On 15 December the first section of a Murmansk-bound convoy, JW-51A*, left Loch Ewe with a heavy escort of two cruisers and nine destroyers. Support cover was supplied by the battleship *King George V* plus the cruisers and destroyers of the Home Fleet. The *Kriegsmarine*, lacking the resources for efficient air reconnaissance and, in any event, hampered by bad weather, had no idea that the convoy had sailed and the ships, carrying more than 100,000 tons of much-needed war materials reached the Soviet Union without interference on Christmas Day. The news, when it reached the *Wolfsschanze*, did little to restore Hitler's confidence in either his admirals or his navy. The war in Russia was not going well and the

---

* The destruction of PQ-17 had so unnerved the British Admiralty that the PQ prefix was abandoned in the autumn of 1942 in favour of JW.

annihilation of the 6th Army at Stalingrad was imminent. Not surprisingly he used the *Kriegsmarine* as a scapegoat and returned to his familiar complaints about the battleships 'lying uselessly in the fjords' — a situation made all the more bitter since it exposed his own miscalculations concerning future Allied strategy. For instead of invading Norway, as the Führer had anticipated, the British and Americans had opened their 'second front' with massive landings in North Africa on 8 November. Thanks to Hitler's Norwegian obsession the battleships and cruisers of the *Kriegsmarine* were some 2500 miles away from the action when the Allies struck.

The second half of the convoy, JW-51B, sailed on 14 December. But, less fortunate than its predecessor, it was sighted, first by a *Luftwaffe* aircraft, and then by U-boats. The relevant details were passed to Berlin and Raeder wasted no time in seeking Hitler's permission to attack, the Führer's approval now being mandatory for all operations involving battleships. The prognosis was good, for the convoy was reported to be only lightly escorted and the U-boats had confirmed that there were 'no superior forces accompanying' the merchantmen and their close escort. It promised to be a repeat performance of PQ-17, only this time the surface ships would play the leading role. Hitler gave his approval and, scenting victory, asked Vice-Admiral Krancke, Raeder's representative at Führer headquarters, to keep him informed of developments.

Command of the sortie, codenamed Operation *Regenbogen*, was given to Vice-Admiral Oskar Kummetz whose battle-plan envisaged an assault by the *Lützow* and *Hipper* during the brief two-hour period of twilight that punctuated the 24-hours of darkness that marked the Arctic night in mid-winter. The attack itself was to be in the form of a pincer movement with the *Hipper* and three destroyers sweeping around the convoy and then driving the hapless merchant ships into the arms of Captain Rudolf Stange and the *Lützow*'s powerful 11-inch guns.

The force left Altenfjord during the afternoon of 30 December and passed through the boom defences at around 17.00. But before the ships had cleared the exit to the fjord Kummetz was handed an urgent signal from Admiral Kurt Fricke, Raeder's Chief of Staff in Berlin: *In spite of operational orders discretion is to be exercised in the face of an enemy of equal strength. It is undesirable to run excessive risk with the heavy ships.* Fricke intended the signal to be no more than a timely reminder to the force commander of Hitler's overriding requirement to avoid 'unnecessary risks'. But Kummetz, not unnaturally, read it as a further restriction on his freedom of manoeuvre. Those few ill-chosen words were destined to bring Hitler's battleships to the brink of extinction.

In accordance with the tactical plan which Kummetz had drawn, the battle group divided into two separate units at 02.30 on New Year's Eve and began their search for JW-51B. At 07.54 Kummetz's flagship, the *Hipper*, found the convoy − little more than fleeting wraith-like shadows in the freezing polar darkness − and the Vice-Admiral ordered his three destroyers to take up shadowing stations in readiness for a dawn attack. Half an hour later the German ships were sighted by a corvette and the *Obdurate*, one of the four destroyers making up the convoy's close escort, turned to investigate. Bad visibility made identification of friend and foe difficult but at 09.15 any doubts were resolved when the *Friedrich Eckoldt* opened fire. Kummetz, however, was also hampered by the arctic mists and poor levels of light and, prudently anxious to avoid firing at his own ships, ordered the *Eckoldt* and her two flotilla mates to break off and rejoin the *Hipper*. Fourteen minutes later Captain Sherbrooke, keeping watch on the bridge of the destroyer *Onslow*, sighted the German cruiser and moments later, as the ships emerged into an area of clear visibility, the *Hipper* opened fire with her 8-inch guns. The battle for JW-51B had begun.

Kummetz's signal: *Am engaging the enemy*, transmitted at 09.36, was greeted with enthusiastic excitement at the Führer's headquarters for, according to the latest available intelligence, the convoy lay at the mercy of the *Lützow* and *Hipper*. JW-51B's close escort was barely adequate for its task, and it was certainly, in theory, too weak to ward off an attack by enemy heavy ships. But Captain Robert St Vincent Sherbrooke had no time for theories. His job was to protect the convoy. Placing the *Onslow* and *Orwell* between JW-51B and the northern sweep of Kummetz's pincer movement, he kept the cruiser away from the merchantmen for more than thirty minutes until, at 10.19, his ship was hit by a salvo of 8-inch shells which caused heavy casualties and damage. But as the stricken *Onslow* withdrew behind smoke, the *Obedient* moved forward to seal off the gap her departure had created in the defensive screen and Kummetz was again denied his prey.

The *Lützow*, further to the south, had sighted JW-51B at 09.30, but, worried by the poor visibility, Stange recalled his destroyers minutes after they had altered course to close the convoy. Contact with the enemy was lost for the next hour but at 10.45 visual contact was renewed, only to be lost again as the vague shadows vanished into a snow squall. Radar contact was established soon afterwards but Stange, who had never been in combat before, was not prepared to risk his ships in such treacherous conditions and, refusing to investigate the radar echoes to port, he maintained course. It proved to be a costly mistake for, unbeknown to Stange, the *Lützow* and her destroyers had passed across the head of JW-51B and were now on the same side of the convoy as the *Hipper*. Kummetz's carefully planned pincer movement had failed.

Hipper in the meanwhile had closed its target again and at 11.32 a further signal from Kummetz was received at the *Wolfsschanze*: *Engaging close escort.*

No cruisers with convoy. It was confirmation of the Führer's wildest dreams. Unopposed by enemy heavy ships there was now nothing to stop a total and annihilating victory. The roseate picture was confirmed independently at 11.45 by a signal from the *U-354*: *Observation of scene suggests battle has reached a climax. Only a red glow can be seen in the Arctic twilight*. The wording of *Kapitanleutnant* Herbschleb's report could only mean one thing. The surface ships had got in amongst the convoy and the helpless merchantmen were ablaze. Even Hitler smiled when Krancke repeated the gist of the signal to him. This was the victory Germany needed.

In reality the tactical situation in the Barents Sea was deteriorating with frightening rapidity. Within minutes of Kummetz's optimistic report that the convoy's escort contained no heavy ships the British cruisers *Sheffield* and *Jamaica* emerged from a white wall of snow with their radar-directed guns already pointing menacingly at the German flagship. A shell burst in the *Hipper*'s No 3 boiler room, temporarily reducing her speed by some five knots and, as Kummetz altered course to parry this new and unexpected threat, two more shells exploded inboard, one of which started a fierce fire in the aircraft hangar.

At that precise moment, and by an ironic coincidence, Kummetz was handed a stark three-word signal issued, apparently, in response to the report he had sent at 09.36. It read simply: *No unnecessary risk*. As the *Hipper* squared up to meet the two enemy cruisers, the task force commander recalled Fricke's earlier warning: 'Discretion is to be exercised in the face of an enemy of equal strength'. Realizing that he must bow to the strategic requirements of higher authority, Kummetz turned away and ordered his destroyers to break off the action and retire westwards. But, tragically for one of the flotilla, his order came exactly three minutes too late. At 11.34 the *Friedrich Eckoldt* had come under fire from a cruiser which, in the confusion of battle, her captain, Commander Bachmann, had mistakenly identified as the *Hipper*. Before the error could be rectified she had been hit in short succession by seven salvoes of 6-inch shells and sunk with all hands.

At 12.03 the *Lützow*, which had hit and severely damaged the *Obdurate*, was also ordered to cease fire and withdraw. As the surviving German ships retired to the west away from the JW-51B Kummetz sent a brief signal to Berlin reporting that the engagement had been broken off, but giving no other details. Anxious not to reveal his position to the enemy, he steadfastly maintained radio silence until his ships arrived in Aktenfjord at 07.00 on New Year's Day.

A mood of optimism had swept both the Admiralty in Berlin and the Führer's headquarters in Rastenberg in the wake of Kummetz's initial reports. Hitler was convinced that a great victory had been achieved and joyfully told every new arrival at his New Year's Eve party the good news, even though there was not a shred of evidence to support it. But as the hours passed and no further details were received from Kummetz his impatience increased. He ordered Krancke to demand an immediate report from the fleet commander but even this message, transmitted to Altenfjord, was delayed by a breakdown of the German teleprinter service in Norway. To make matters worse a Reuter's news flash, based on British sources, claimed that a German attack on an Arctic convoy had been beaten off and that an enemy destroyer had been sunk and a cruiser damaged.

The Reuter's report, received at the *Wolfsschanze* after a sleepless night, did little to improve Hitler's temper, and by noon he was literally raging with fury. According to Krancke, whom Raeder castigated for making tactless remarks, '[the Führer] said it was an impudence that he, as Supreme Commander, had not received any news for 24 hours after the action . . . [and] he spoke of the uselessness of the battleships, of lack of ability, and lack of daring on the part of the older naval officers, and so on.'

Kummetz's report, when it was finally received that afternoon, only served to increase Hitler's irritation and at the routine situation conference that evening he lost control and was almost hysterical with rage. 'I have made the following decision,' he shouted at the unfortunate Krancke, 'and order you forthwith to inform the Admiralty that it is my unalterable resolve. The heavy ships are a needless drain on men and materials. They will accordingly be paid off and reduced to scrap. Their guns will be mounted on land for coastal defence.'

It was the identical threat which the Führer had voiced at the time of the Channel Dash, but this time he meant every word of it.

Krancke, stung into a defence of his *Kriegsmarine* comrades, retorted that if the ships were disarmed 'it would be the cheapest victory Britain could possibly win'. But the Führer was beyond persuasion and, according to Raeder, insisted that 'his views [were] recorded in the official War Diary as his irrevocable decision on the matter'. He then told Krancke to telephone Raeder and order him to report to the *Wolfsschanze* immediately. The Grand Admiral, however, was well versed in handling the Führer. He pleaded illness and obtained a six-day delay in the confrontation, an interval during which he hoped to gain the evidence he needed to change Hitler's mind.

Raeder arrived at the Rastenberg headquarters on the evening of 7 January, but before he had had an opportunity to state his case he was verbally swamped by a 'completely spiteful' tirade from the Führer that lasted a full ninety minutes! Raeder listened in silence. 'I considered it beneath my dignity to challenge the details of this completely fabricated story,' he confided in his memoirs. When Hitler had finished his oration the Grand Admiral requested a private audience during which he asked to be relieved of his post as Commander-in-Chief.

The Führer, somewhat aghast at the effects of his rhetoric, tried to placate the Admiral by hastily explaining that he was only criticizing the big ships; the *Kriegsmarine*'s light forces and U-boats were doing an excellent job in difficult circumstances. Reminding him of the recent dismissals and resignations among the Army's most senior generals as a direct result of the stagnating situation on the Eastern Front, the Führer asked Raeder to reconsider, but the Grand Admiral, a man of honour despite certain flaws in his character, refused to rescind his request. However, in order not to embarrass Hitler, he offered to postpone his departure to 30 January, 1943, the 10th anniversary of the Führer's accession to power and the founding of the Third Reich, a choice of date that would suggest, publicly, that he was stepping down in the natural order of things to make way for a younger man.

On 15 January, at Hitler's own suggestion, Raeder submitted a detailed memorandum which supported the retention of the *Kriegsmarine*'s battleships and cruisers as an integral part of the operational fleet. Pulling no punches, he reminded the Führer that the war had broken out five years earlier than he had been told to expect and that this had wrecked the Z-plan. He also blamed the *Luftwaffe* for it's 'failure to provide enough aircraft for reconnaissance or naval [air] cover' and lamented 'the fading possibility of our ships being given the protection of an aircraft carrier'. Finally, he pointed out that the Führer's personally imposed policy of taking no unnecessary risks had prevented the heavy ships from fighting as their admirals wished and, on several occasions, had prevented victory.

But Hitler was unmoved by the argument. His decision remained irrevocable. On Saturday 30 January Erich Raeder stepped down as the Supreme Commander of the *Kriegsmarine* in favour of his successor, Admiral Karl Doenitz, the former Commander-in-Chief U-boats. With Doenitz, a dedicated submarine enthusiast, at the helm the decommissioning of Germany's battleships now looked inevitable.

CHAPTER NINE

'We Shall Fight To Our Last Shell'

WHILE THEIR COMRADES WERE FIGHTING for their lives in the snow-swept wastes of the Barents Sea, the men of the *Tirpitz* celebrated New Year's Eve with traditional cheer. The mess decks were decorated with fir branches and paper streamers and, despite wartime shortages, the ship's company sat down to a festive meal after which each member of the crew received a bottle of wine, a box of cigarettes, a packet of chocolate and a book.

At midnight Captain Karl Topp marked the passing of the old year by addressing the men over the battleship's loudspeaker system. He commiserated with them for the lack of action and the boredom of life in Norway and used the opportunity to thank them for their loyal discipline and the cheerful willingness with which they tackled the routine tasks of shipboard life. There were also, of course, the obligatory references to the Führer, the glory of the Third Reich, and the high moral purpose of Germany's war aims. 'We enter this new year [1943],' he concluded solemnly, 'in the certain knowledge that when the moment comes... we shall be ready for it. I wish you all a happy new year.'

So far as Topp was concerned 1943 certainly proved to be both happy and prosperous. For in February the *Tirpitz*'s popular skipper, who had guided the fortunes of the battleship from the day of her commissioning into the *Kriegsmarine*, left to become the Director of the Shipbuilding Directorate in Berlin, following his well-deserved promotion to the rank of Rear-Admiral. His place was taken by Captain Hans Meyer, a doughty veteran of the 1919 mutiny during which he had lost an arm fighting against the socialists. But if Hitler did not withdraw his decision to demilitarize the battleships, would Meyer still have a ship to command in a few weeks' time?

The question mark hanging over the *Kriegsmarine*'s big ships was underlined by a directive which the Führer presented to the Commander-in-Chief designate, Karl Doenitz, on his arrival at the *Wolfsschanze* on 25 January. It was stark and to the point:

1. All construction and conversion of heavy ships is to cease with immediate effect...

2. Battleships, pocket-battleships, heavy cruisers, and light cruisers, [are] to be paid off, except where they are required for training purposes...

3. The surplus dockyard capacity [resulting from this] is to be applied to an intensification of U-boat repair and U-boat construction.

The document, dictated by Hitler himself, was intended to sound the death-knell of the battleships. Indeed, the directive seemed to offer Doenitz, the former C-in-C U-boats, the authority he needed to concentrate on underwater warfare without the encumbrance of a surface fleet. But the new Grand Admiral was a shrewd and highly professional officer. He realized that the submarine arm of the navy needed the strategic support of the surface fleet, and, although he paid lip-service to the Führer's wishes, he played his cards close to his chest. Only a week after his appointment, on 8 February, he submitted that, for the time being, the *Tirpitz* and *Scharnhorst* should be retained as 'mobile batteries', although he was prepared to accept that the cruisers *Hipper*, *Leipzig* and *Köln* should be paid off. He protected the remaining big ships by creating a training squadron, a convenient escape route that had been inadvertently provided by Paragraph Two of the Directive. Hitler shrugged when he read the proposals but raised no objections.

Having gained a temporary stay of execution for the battleships, Doenitz returned to the offensive on 26 February when, during a meeting with Hitler in Rastenberg, he drew attention to the situation on the Russian front and told the Führer that Germany still needed a Battle Group in northern Norway. He therefore proposed to transfer the *Scharnhorst*, which he had previously promised to pay off in July, to Norway to join the *Tirpitz*. Hitler promptly objected to the proposal and once again listed out the sorry history of failure that had pursued the navy's heavy ships throughout the war. Doenitz listened unmoved, and when the Führer had finished his rambling dissertation he boldly returned to the attack by pointing out that 'the fighting ability of the ships had been severely hampered by their obligation to remain afloat'.

Realizing that he was in danger of losing the argument, Hitler hurriedly tried to distance himself from any personal blame for the 'no risks' policy. 'If our ships meet with the enemy,' he grumbled, 'they must fight.' Doenitz suddenly realized that he had won the battle which Raeder had come so close to losing. 'In that case, *mein Führer*,' he said quietly, 'I take it that I may send the *Scharnhorst* to Norway.' According to Doenitz's memoirs: '[The Führer] was highly astonished and indignant, but in the end he accepted it, albeit reluctantly and with bad grace.'

Having gained Hitler's approval, Doenitz wasted no time in exploiting this dramatic reversal of policy. After two abortive attempts to get away from Gdynia, both of which were foiled by the RAF, the *Scharnhorst* finally left on 3 March and, after a diversionary five-day exercise in the Baltic, she steamed out through the Skagerrak and set course for Norway, driving northwards at 25 knots in fierce snow storms and gale-force winds. She joined the *Tirpitz* and *Lützow* at Narvik on 14 March and the three ships then continued on to Altenfjord which they reached later in the month. But, ironically, although Doenitz had succeeded in concentrating his battleships in northern Norway despite Hitler's earlier 'irrevocable decision' to scrap them, he found himself in the unfortunate position of a fox confronted by an empty chicken-run after a long struggle to breach the fence. For, as a direct result of the PQ-17 disaster, and the proven success of the winter sailing schedules, the British Admiralty had decided to suspend the despatch of all Russian convoys during the summer months when better weather conditions and short nights would tilt the balance in favour of the enemy.

Without targets there was nothing for the battleships to attack, although, admittedly, their mere presence in Norway posed a threat which the British could not ignore. In addition, the continued shortage of fuel oil meant that no regular programmes of exercises and gunnery practice were possible, although Kummetz did, at one point, manage to undertake a short 200-mile cruise to Bear Island to blow away the cobwebs. But even inactivity brought its share of disaster. On 8 April the ammunition stored in the magazine of the *Scharnhorst*'s after 11-inch turret detonated spontaneously and the resulting explosion caused considerable structural damage as well as killing seventeen members of the battleship's crew. Nevertheless, despite the tragedy, the *Scharnhorst* maintained her reputation as a lucky ship, for many vessels had been totally destroyed by internal explosions in the past, the Royal Navy having lost the *Bulwark*, *Vanguard* and *Natal* in similar circumstances during the First World War.

As the long summer months passed in enforced idleness the lack of leisure facilities which the *Tirpitz*'s crew had enjoyed at Trondheim dampened spirits, for even in July and August Altenfjord, some 400 miles inside the Arctic Circle, was a godforsaken place. But by September Kummetz had managed to accumulate sufficient fuel oil to take his Battle Group to sea and, having considered the options, decided in favour of a morale-boosting attack on Spitzbergen, an isolated group of islands in the Arctic Sea which at first the Germans and subsequently the Allies used as a weather observation station.

The *Tirpitz* and *Scharnhorst* left Altenfjord on the evening of 6 September and arrived off Spitzbergen in the early hours of the 8th. A 600-strong contingent of commando-style troops were put ashore from the destroyers to carry out demolition work and round up prisoners while the *Tirpitz* stood off in deep water and bombarded Longyearbyen and Barentsburg. The *Scharnhorst*, with her shallower draught, penetrated Sveagruvafjord in search of suitable targets; but, despite the devastating power of the two battleships, the Norwegian defenders, armed with nothing larger than 3-inch field guns, fought back fiercely and, against all the odds, succeeded in damaging two of Kummetz's destroyers before they were finally overwhelmed.

Having levelled virtually every structure and building on the islands, the German ships withdrew at 11.00 and by the time Admiral Bruce Fraser's Home Fleet arrived on the scene the German squadron had fled and was safely back at its moorings in Altenfjord. Although the food looted from the islands' storehouses helped to raise spirits, morale plummeted again a few days later following an unseemly dispute over the distribution of Iron Crosses. The Spitzbergen expedition, however, deserves a special place in the history of naval warfare, for it proved to be the only occasion that the *Tirpitz* fired her main 15-inch armament at surface targets, even though her objectives were only defenceless buildings incapable of hitting back.

Spitzbergen, however, turned out to be the only oasis of excitement that summer, for the anticipated air attacks on Altenfjord did not take place, the RAF being denied suitable facilities for its heavy bombers in Russia, while the Home Fleet lacked a modern aircraft carrier. Fraser's only carrier, the *Furious*, was far too antiquated to undertake a major air strike. It was, from a German viewpoint, unexpectedly quiet. Ominously quiet. Nevertheless, the British had not given up hopes of sinking the battleships in their Norwegian lair. The two-man torpedoes, the chariots, may have failed, but the Royal Navy and the Royal Air Force had other surprises up their respective sleeves of which the enemy had neither warning nor knowledge. Perhaps, hopefully, one of these could deliver the knockout blow.

On the night of 21 September, having obtained Kummetz's prior permission, Captain Frederich Hüffmeier took the *Scharnhorst* down the fjord and anchored off the island of Aaroy in readiness for an anti-aircraft exercise at first light the following morning. The *Lützow*'s berth was also empty for, scheduled to return to Gdynia for a routine refit, the pocket-battleship had already shifted to a new anchorage closer to the open sea to avoid delaying her departure the next day. The night passed quietly. The men guarding the net defences that protected the entrance to Kaafjord, in which the *Tirpitz* was lying, failed to observe the dark shape that had trailed the wake of a small coaster as it passed through the gates of the boom shortly before 05.00. A petty officer on board the battleship who saw a strange flurry of water and glimpsed a black object momentarily exposed on the surface at 07.07 merely shrugged it off as being no more than a seal diving for prey.

As the petty officer looked away and returned to the task at hand a small submarine suddenly bobbed to the surface, its unexpected appearance being greeted with a volley of small-arms' fire from the battleship's deck sentries. But as Captain Meyer hurriedly abandoned his half-eaten breakfast and made his way to the bridge the little submersible dipped beneath the waters of the fjord and disappeared from view. Realizing that his ship was under attack from a new and unknown weapon, Meyer gave orders to prepare for sea and sent a team of divers over the side to check the hull for limpet mines. Suddenly the midget submarine reappeared on the surface to port and its crew scrambled out of its hatch with their hands raised in surrender as a patrol launch came alongside. Only four minutes later a second submarine revealed its sinister presence and Meyer, realizing that his ship might be safer *inside* the net defences, belayed his previous order to prepare for sea and instructed the officer of the watch to veer the bows to starboard by means of cables in a hurried attempt to reduce the target area.

But Meyer's precautions came too late to save his ship. At 08.12 the *Tirpitz* shuddered with a 'most God Almighty bang' and for a few minutes chaos reigned supreme with crewmen running in all directions, the secondary armament weapons firing wildly at unseen and non-existent enemy vessels, all internal lights extinguished, and the automatic sprinkler system dousing all and sundry with foam. More seriously, the shock of the blast had lifted *Anton* turret off its turntable mountings, as well as inflicting other structural damage. A second charge, exploding beneath the after end of the battleship a few moments later, smashed the port rudder and jammed all three propellers, in addition to crippling the rotating mechanism of *Caesar* turret. Despite the protection offered by the vessel's massive armour, the combined explosions had wreaked havoc in many other directions: delicate fire-control and radar equipment had been knocked out, a generator room and the after steering compartment were flooded and even the steel decks had been buckled by the blast. Thanks to her stout construction the *Tirpitz* did not sink, but she was, for the moment at least, crippled. It would take many months of work to repair the damage.

Operation Source, as the British code-named the midget submarine attack on the *Tirpitz*, was one of the Royal Navy's greatest successes of the Second World War. But, contrary to popular belief, the tiny X-craft submersibles used in the sortie were not inspired by Japan's midget submarines, for work on the first boat began at least six months before the Japanese Type-A vessels grabbed the headlines at Pearl Harbor in December, 1941. However, technical and operational problems caused serious construction delays and the prototype, the *X-3*, did not take to the water until 15 March, 1943. A month later she and her five identical sisters were organized into the 12th Submarine Flotilla and placed under the command of Captain W.E. Banks in the depot-ship *Bonaventure*.

The attack was set for dawn on 22 September and the six-boat flotilla left its base at Cairnbawn on the 11th with each midget, manned by a passage crew, in the tow of a larger conventional submarine. The teams selected to carry out the attack itself, the combat crews, remained on board the mother-submarines until the final stage of the operation. The flotilla, however, encountered a number of problems while on passage to Norway. *X-9* and her passage crew vanished and were never seen again after the towing hawser linking her to the *Syrtis* broke; the *X-8* also developed technical trouble and, after losing her tow from the *Seanymph*, was ultimately scuttled.

The remaining four submarines – *X-5* (Lt Henty Henty-Creer RNVR); *X-6* (Lt Donald Cameron RNR); *X-7* (Lt Godfrey Place RN); and *X-10* (Lt Kenneth Hudspeth RANVR) – slipped their tows during the early evening of 20 September and headed east through the German minefields that protected the entrances to Stjern Sound and Soroy Sound. *X-10* was within sight of the island of Brattholm, directly opposite Kaafjord, when she, too, fell victim to electrical problems. Although her Australian skipper spent the next fourteen hours submerged on the bottom of Altenfjord struggling to pin-point that source of the fault, he was finally forced to abort the mission. His boat was subsequently recovered from Ofjord on the 28th, over a week after *X-10* had set out from Cairnbawn.

The surviving submarines managed to evade the enemy's surface patrols in Altenfjord and, having overcome the minefields and net defences, all three were inside Kaafjord and close to their target by 07.00. Henty-Creer's *X-5* was never seen again and is believed to have been sunk by depth-charges shortly before 09.00. However, both Cameron and Place in *X-6* and *X-7* succeeded in their mission and, as related earlier, the former was taken prisoner by the Germans before the charges exploded. Having been picked up by a launch and taken back to the *Tirpitz*, they spent several terrifying minutes on the battleship's quarterdeck surrounded by guards armed with tommy-guns until Captain Meyer intervened and ordered the bedraggled British submariners to be taken below and given hot coffee and schnapps. Although interrogated, they refused to give more than their names, ranks and numbers and the Germans made no attempt to coerce them, unlike the unlucky Italian frogmen captured by the British after a similar attack on the Mediterranean Fleet at Alexandria in 1940 who were placed in the lowest recesses of the battleship *Valiant* on the orders of Admiral Cunningham in an unsuccessful attempt to break their morale and 'persuade' them to reveal where they had placed their explosive charges.

168

X-6's team was joined a short while later by Godfrey Place and Sub-Lieutenant Bob Aitken, the only two members of the *X-7*'s crew to survive. The six men had the grim satisfaction of experiencing the detonation of the limpet mines at firsthand. Yet, despite the crippling damage to his ship, Captain Meyer continued to treat his prisoners in a humane manner and, aware of what had happened to the captured survivor of the earlier chariot attack who had fallen into the hands of the Gestapo, he sent the submariners ashore to Tromsö hospital the next morning and ensured that they were transferred to POW camps in Germany where, protected by the Geneva Convention, they were safe from the clutches of the Nazi's notorious secret police.

As a result of Operation Source the *Tirpitz* was, for the moment, more of a liability to the *Kriegsmarine* than an asset. The first plan was to bring her back to Kiel or Wilhelmshaven where she could be dry-docked for repair. But, unable to move under her own power, this would entail a hazardous towing operation over a distance of more than a thousand miles during which she would be exposed to attacks by Royal Air Force and Fleet Air Arm aircraft, not to mention the Royal Navy's submarines. With unpleasant memories of what had happened to the *Gneisenau* and the *Lützow* in the same waters, wiser counsels prevailed and it was decided, after consultation with various experts, to carry out repairs in situ using special cement to seal the underwater holes and constructing a coffer-dam so that the repair teams could get at the rudders and propellers. Within three weeks some eight hundred specialist dockyard workers had arrived at Kaafjord aboard the repair ship *Monte Rosa* and the task of restoring the *Tirpitz* to a seaworthy condition began.

With the *Lützow* safely back in Gdynia for her much-needed refit the *Scharnhorst* was now the only battleship available to the *Kriegsmarine* for operational service. The *Scheer* was still under repair, while the unfortunate *Gneisenau* was little more than a deserted hulk, all work on her having been abandoned in the aftermath of Hitler's 'irrevocable decision' to consign all of his battleships to the scrapheap. There were changes, too, at command level, for in November Vice-Admiral Kummetz returned to Germany on 'indefinite sick leave' − a euphemism frequently adopted to conceal fundamental disagreements between the top brass in Berlin and the fleet commander − and Rear-Admiral Erich Bey, the Flag Officer Destroyers with Battle Group One, assumed temporary responsibility for the units based in Altenfjord.

Having removed, at least for the time being, the threat of the *Tirpitz* and now faced only by the *Scharnhorst* and a handful of destroyers, the British decided to resume the shipment of war materials to Russia with the onset of winter, although the continued presence of the latter in Arctic waters meant that the convoys would still require battleship protection. Indeed, Admiral Bruce Fraser, the new C-in-C Home Fleet, was convinced that the enemy would launch a surface strike against the convoys. But with the Royal Navy's superior radar technology and, thanks to Ultra, its new-found ability to penetrate the enemy's naval codes, he was itching for a fight.

A Royal Navy escort force arrived at Archangel at the end of October to bring back the unladen ships waiting to return home, a first and necessary step before the Russian convoys could be reinstated. During the same month the *Scharnhorst*'s commanding officer, Captain Friedrich Hüffmeier, was replaced by Captain Fritz Hintze who, within a matter of weeks, showed himself to be a worthy successor to the popular Kurt Hoffmann. Hintze and the Battle Group's new Admiral, 'Achmed' Bey, looked likely to be a promising combination, for both men were known to favour taking the fight to the enemy, despite the latter's grumbling preference for his beloved destroyers. Morale, shaken by the *Tirpitz* incident, quickly improved with the appointment of the two new leaders and the prospect of combat.

Convoy RA-54A, the homeward-bound empty ships from Archangel, sailed on 1 November and arrived in Britain unscathed. On 15 November the first half of JW-54, a total of eighteen ships, left Loch Ewe for Russia and was followed a week later by the remaining half, JW-54B. Like RA-54A both groups arrived at their destination without incident. But Fraser was not lulled into a false sense of security by the *Kriegsmarine*'s failure to respond, and when the 19-ship JW-55A sailed from Loch Ewe on 12 December his flagship, the battleship *Duke of York*, remained with the convoy all the way to Russia, a complete reversal of the Royal Navy's previous 'play safe' policy of not employing its big ships east of the North Cape. Fraser arrived at Archangel on 16 December and, after discussions with his opposite number, Admiral Golovko, left again on the 18th to cover JW-55B after first making a quick dash to Iceland for refuelling. In the meanwhile JW-55A arrived in the Kola Inlet and berthed safely in Archangel on the 22nd.

The day after Fraser sailed from Russia to cover the passage of JW-55B Doenitz visited the *Wolfsschanze* for his routine monthly situation conference with the Führer. The situation on the Eastern Front was deteriorating rapidly and the reinstatement of the Allied supply line to northern Russia was causing Hitler and the Army generals considerable concern. Doenitz, shrugging aside the Führer's previous doubts about the *Kriegsmarine*'s heavy ships, offered the navy's assistance and submitted that the *Scharnhorst* and the five remaining destroyers still based at Altenfjord should attack the next British convoy. Hitler, it seems, neither supported nor opposed the plan. He had, by now, become so disillusioned by the failure of his battleships that he expected nothing from them except defeat and disaster, but, reluctantly, he signified his approval and left Doenitz to get on with it.

On the day that the conference ended, 20 December, the next Russian convoy, JW-55B, left Loch Ewe. Two days later a homeward-bound group of empty ships, RA-55A, sailed from Murmansk. The stage was set for the ultimate showdown. But could the *Scharnhorst*, operating alone and without the support of the mighty *Tirpitz*, provide the much-needed success which Doenitz had promised the Führer?

Both convoys were allocated the usual close escort of destroyers, corvettes, AA ships and armed trawlers, but this time the British divided their covering force into two separate groups. Rear-Admiral Burnett's cruisers, identified as Force One, was to cover RA-55A from the Kola Inlet to Bear Island where the two convoys were scheduled to pass each other. He was then to return eastwards with JW-55B under his wing. Admiral Fraser's Force Two, comprising the 14-inch gunned *Duke of York*, the cruiser *Jamaica* and four destroyers, was to provide long-range heavy support for JW-55B in the usual manner, but, in a change of tactics, the Admiral this time intended to loiter in the vicinity of the North Cape in the hope of ambushing the *Scharnhorst* should she venture out to attack either of the two convoys.

The drama unfolded quickly. JW-55B was sighted off the Faeroes by a *Luftwaffe* patrol aircraft on 22 December and Schniewind, the C-in-C Navy Group North, ordered all eight U-boats operating in Arctic waters to concentrate in the Bear Island passage. At the same time he sent a teleprinter order to Bey to raise steam for three hours' notice, a routine precaution when enemy warships were known to be within striking distance. On the following day the *Luftwaffe* reported the convoy as being 300 miles SE of Jan Mayen Island and 24 hours later the merchantmen were sighted again, this time 220 miles further to the east. The second convoy, RA-55A, had not been detected, however, and Schniewind was similarly unaware that Burnett's covering cruiser force was steaming westwards from the Kola Inlet. Even more importantly, he did not know that Fraser was closing the Bear Island passage at high speed after his hasty refuelling stop in Iceland. Nevertheless, given the whole-hearted co-operation and support of the *Luftwaffe*, there is little doubt that both groups of enemy warships would have been reported to Navy Group North's headquarters in Kiel within a matter of hours.

Unfortunately the *Luftwaffe* chose this critical moment to throw a sizeable spanner in the works. The 5th Air Fleet's headquarters in Oslo suddenly informed Kiel that it had no strike aircraft in northern Norway and that insufficient machines were available to provide the continuous and extended reconnaissance missions required by the navy unless — and the sarcasm was barely disguised — the *Kriegsmarine* had the firm intention of launching a surface attack on the convoy. Even then, reconnaissance in depth could not be guaranteed. The fact that the morrow was Christmas Day and the aircrews wanted to enjoy the festivities in comfort was probably not without significance.

Schniewind was no stranger to the *Luftwaffe*'s double-dealing methods: he had been Raeder's Chief-of-Staff in 1939 and the Fleet Commander during the PQ-17 operation. The near-disaster of JW-51B was also still fresh in his mind and he knew better than most that Rear-Admiral Bey's Battle Group would be seriously at risk without air reconnaissance. Unwilling to accept responsibility for the operation unless the conditions were 'really promising' – he had already noted that 'the chances of success are small and the stakes are high' – he telephoned Berlin to obtain Doenitz's views on the situation. But, by chance, the Grand Admiral was on a visit to Paris and all decisions had to be deferred for twenty-four hours.

When Christmas Day dawned the *Kriegsmarine*'s High Command was still unaware that Fraser and the *Duke of York* were off the North Cape, for, not only had the *Luftwaffe* failed to carry out the necessary reconnaissance flights, but the usually reliable *B-Dienst* monitors had missed the two occasions when Fraser had broken radio silence to make last-minute changes in his operational orders. At 14.15 Doenitz issued the executive order to launch Operation *Ostfront*, the codename for the battleship sortie against JW-55B. Within minutes Schniewind's headquarters in Kiel had despatched a terse *Ostfront 17.00* to Rear-Admiral Bey in Altenfjord.

Doenitz, however, still had reservations. Following the earlier muddles caused by over-centralized command, he had insisted, some months previously, that the fleet commander should be allowed complete freedom of action and that Navy Group North should not interfere with his operational decisions. Now, however, he was having second thoughts and, contrary to his usual attitude of confident detachment, he began to demonstrate a nervous Raeder-like inclination to retain some sort of personal control over the forthcoming operation. A five-point order was therefore despatched to Bey outlining the reasons for *Ostfront* – as if such an explanation was necessary – and which included a significant restatement of OKM policy: 'Tactical situation to be exploited skilfully and boldly. Engagement not to be broken off until full success achieved... *Scharnhorst*'s superior firepower is crucial... disengage at own discretion, and automatically if heavy forces encountered.' For all the brave words it was the old 'no unnecessary risks' policy all over again. Like his unfortunate predecessors, Bey was going into battle with one hand tied behind his back.

The Rear-Admiral, who had spent the morning aboard his official flagship, the *Tirpitz*, made his way back to the *Scharnhorst* on receipt of Group North's *Ostfront 17.00* signal. His original plan envisaged an attack on the convoy by the destroyers with the *Scharnhorst* playing a long-range support role. Doenitz's subsequent signal, however, meant that the battleship was now to be the centre-piece of the assault. As the ships steamed slowly down Altenfjord, some two hours behind schedule, Bey was sitting in his day cabin frantically redrafting his battle orders. There were similar, and familiar, scenes of turmoil at Group North's headquarters in Kiel, and when Schniewind learned that bad weather had forced the *Luftwaffe* to cancel all reconnaissance flights for Boxing Day he telephoned Berlin and suggested that *Ostfront* should be aborted. Doenitz, however, did not agree. At 20.46 that evening Schniewind despatched another message to Berlin, this time by teleprinter, repeating his request for the operation to be cancelled. But Doenitz again refused. Hitler had been promised victory and, if the Navy was to survive, victory there must be.

Despite the atrocious weather conditions six flying-boats, manned by *Kriegsmarine* volunteers, took off on the morning of 26 December and headed out into the Arctic. At 10.12, quite by chance, one of the machines detected the *Duke of York* on its radar and reported the presence of 'one large and several smaller ships'. But once again lethargy and muddle intervened. The sighting was not received in Narvik until 13.41 and nearly two more hours passed before the signal was repeated to Bey in the *Scharnhorst*. More importantly Navy Group North doctored the flying-boat's original report and, for reasons best known to Schniewind's staff, deleted the reference to 'one large ship'.

The *B-Dienst* service, too, intercepted a vast volume of enemy radio traffic which, in contrast to the early days of the war, its experts were unable to decipher. The signals, however, were thought to indicate a possible 'heavy covering force [heading] towards the target [*Scharnhorst*]'. But this assessment was considered to be too vague by the staff at Navy Group North and it was decided not to pass the information on to Bey, who was now in the position of a blind man who had been deprived of both his guide dog and his white stick by an over-solicitous friend. Meanwhile the overall tactical situation was becoming increasingly uncertain, a scenario exacerbated by the *Luftwaffe*'s continued failure to launch a properly organized air search for the enemy's heavy ships. Yet, even at this stage, no one seemed prepared to intervene and cancel the operation which, by now, was exhibiting all the signs of degenerating into a suicide mission. As Richard Garrett observed in *Scharnhorst and Gneisenau – The Elusive Sisters** 'the destruction of the *Scharnhorst*... could never have been achieved without the unwitting collaboration of senior officers within the Germany Navy.'

Shortly after 07.00 [26 December] Bey, who was operating in the dark in more than one sense of the word, turned the *Scharnhorst* on to a south-westerly course and ordered his destroyers to fan out ahead of the

* David & Charles, 1978.

battleship in search of the convoy. But, far from being the predator, the *Scharnhorst* was, in reality, the prey. For at 08.40 the cruiser *Belfast*, a unit of Burnett's Force One, had detected the battleship on radar and, steadily closing the range, had established visual contact with the enemy at 09.21. Just four minutes later the 8-inch guns of the *Norfolk* opened fire, but Bey skilfully evaded the enemy's shells by a sudden sharp turn to the south followed by an unexpected reversal of course northwards. Then, exploiting the *Scharnhorst*'s superior speed, he gradually pulled away from his frustrated pursuers and at one point even vanished off their radar screens. But Burnett's cruisers found the battleship again at 12.05 and there was another exchange of fire some twenty minutes later during which the *Scharnhorst* hit and damaged the *Norfolk*.

Although Bey was now steering south-south-west at maximum speed, it proved impossible to escape from the enemy's radar. Denied the vital intelligence which Navy Group North had chosen not to pass on to him, the unfortunate Admiral had no idea that he was steering directly towards Fraser and the overwhelming firepower of the *Duke of York*. Nevertheless, some intuitive sixth-sense warned Bey of impending danger and, mindful of the dangers that might lie ahead, he took pity on his destroyers and ordered their captains to return to Altenfjord, leaving the battleship alone and friendless like a fugitive fox fleeing from a pack of howling dogs.

Fraser sprung the trap at 16.17 when the pulsing echo of the *Scharnhorst* suddenly glowed on the *Duke of York*'s radar screens at a range of 22 miles. It took the flagship more than thirty minutes to close the invisible target but at 16.50 a starshell, arcing high into the sky, exposed the enemy battleship and the *Duke of York*'s 14-inch guns opened fire with deadly effect. She was joined a short while later by the 6-inch weapons of the cruiser *Jamaica* and Bey swung eastwards in a desperate bid to escape, the *Scharnhorst* yawing to starboard at frequent intervals as the fleeing battleship tried to keep her tormentors at a respectful distance with a series of savage nine-gun broadsides.

With the advantage of radar gunnery control, however, the *Duke of York* was soon scoring hits. Indeed, her very first salvo had jammed the rotating gear of the *Scharnhorst*'s turret *Anton*, starting a flash fire that had spread back to turret *Bruno*, forcing Captain Hintze to flood the vulnerable powder store directly beneath the barbette. By 17.27 the action had developed into a wild chase through the Arctic darkness during which the *Scharnhorst* successfully outran the cruiser's lighter guns. But Fraser hung on tenaciously as shell after shell slammed into the German battleship. Turret *Bruno* was knocked out at around 18.20, while a direct hit on No 1 boiler room temporarily reduced the *Scharnhorst*'s speed to ten knots, although this was quickly restored to some 20 knots thanks to the heroic efforts of the engine-room staff. But the end was near and, as the British destroyers closed in for the kill, Captain Hintze sent a last signal to the Führer: *We shall fight to the last shell*.

The crippled battleship attempted to hold off the destroyers with her secondary armament but by now her fire was ragged and poorly controlled and in the ensuing mêlée four torpedoes struck home, causing severe underwater damage that led to serious flooding and another sharp reduction in speed. But the *Scharnhorst* could still fight and the destroyer *Saumarez*, the main recipient of her venom, staggered out of line after being hit by several 11-inch shells.

Both the *Duke of York* and the *Jamaica* had by now caught up with the crippled battleship again and, at 19.01, firing under radar control, their main armaments began to pound the German flagship to death. After fifteen minutes of relentless punishment the *Scharnhorst*'s last remaining 11-inch turret fell silent and the cruisers and destroyers of Burnett's Force One closed in and smothered their helpless victim with a merciless hail of fire. Struck by no fewer than eleven torpedoes and at least thirteen 14-inch shells the battleship was now no more than a blazing shambles of torn and twisted steel with the dead and dying lying in bloody heaps among the fire-blackened wreckage. Her agony ended at 19.45 when a tremendous explosion, probably caused by the detonation of a magazine, reduced the ship to a million pieces of white hot metal. When the smoke cleared the battleship had disappeared.

Both Rear-Admiral Bey and the *Scharnhorst*'s captain, Fritz Hintze, went down with their ship. Of the 1,968 officers and men who had sailed down Altenfjord on the afternoon of Christmas Day only 36 survived to tell the tale. The *Scharnhorst*'s legendary luck had finally run out.

Ignoring his own contribution to the tragic failure of Operation *Ostfront*, Doenitz attributed the loss of the *Scharnhorst* to Britain's superiority in radar technology. Hitler was equally unsympathetic. He had long given up any expectation of a German battleship emerging victorious from a clash with the Royal Navy, and he once again picked on the apparent reluctance of his admirals to stand and fight, blaming the unfortunate man on the spot, Rear-Admiral Bey, rather than the top-heavy higher command structure which was too prone to interfere and which, in this instance, had even doctored the signals which it had repeated to the fleet commander. Of course he levelled no criticism at the *Luftwaffe* whose failure to provide adequate reconnaissance facilities was probably the prime cause of the disaster.

'How could the Admiral have made the grave error of assuming that he was confronted by heavy ships when only heavy cruisers were involved?' he demanded, and, like Pilate, he did not stay for an answer. 'Our battleship... ran away from the enemy cruisers even though she was superior to them in both armour and fighting power. I always suspect that such happenings occur because too much consideration is given to the safety of our battleships – as we saw in the case of the *Graf Spee*.' The Führer clearly had a long memory.

With the *Gneisenau* now reduced to little more than a floating hulk at Gdynia and the *Scheer* and *Lützow* relegated to training duties in the Baltic as a consequence of the Führer's January directive, the *Kriegsmarine* now possessed only one operational battleship, the *Tirpitz*, and even she was still *hors de combat* following the damage inflicted upon her by the British X-craft the previous September. Somewhat surprisingly the first attempt to attack her was launched by the Russian Air Force, an organization not usually noted for mass precision bombing, when on the night of 10/11 February a force of fifteen Soviet bombers set out from their base in northern Russian to strike at the battleship in its Norwegian lair. Each machine carried a 2,000-pound bomb but faulty planning and poor navigation resulted in a fiasco. Only four of the aircraft found their target and of these just one achieved any measure of success, and that no more than a near miss which caused minor hull damage.

Thanks to the efforts of the dockyard workers who had first arrived in Kaafjord at the beginning of October the intricate repair programme was completed by mid-March and on the 15th the great battleship moved down the fjord under her own steam for the first time in nearly six months. But although operational again, the scars left by the Royal Navy's midget submarines had not been totally eradicated and *Tirpitz*'s maximum speed was now permanently restricted to 27 knots, which meant she was no longer fast enough to out-run Britain's *King George V* class battleships.

Plans had already been drawn up in London for a carrier sortie against the *Tirpitz* and the news that she was operational again brought a new urgency to the preparations which one historian has described as 'probably the most carefully planned, briefed and rehearsed strike undertaken by the Fleet Air Arm during the war'.* Training schedules were stepped up and a dummy range was built at Loch Eriboll in Sutherland so that the Navy's Barracuda dive-bombers could carry out practice attacks on an anchored British battleship.

The task force for Operation Tungsten, as the sortie was code-named, included two fleet carriers, *Victorious* and *Furious*, four escort carriers, *Emperor*, *Fencer*, *Searcher* and *Pursuer*, together with the battleships *Duke of York* and *Anson*, three cruisers and twelve destroyers. The attack was set for dawn on 4 April and the ships left their Scottish base on 30 March, the two battleships and the *Victorious* being first diverted northwards to act as a covering force for convoy JW-58 which had left Loch Ewe three days earlier.

---

* *Carrier Operations in World War II*, J.D. Brown, Ian Allan, 1968, Vol 1, p 41.

On 1 April, however, Admiral Fraser received an Ultra intercept from the Admiralty which revealed a vital piece of intelligence — the *Tirpitz*'s steam trials, due to take place that day, had been postponed for 48 hours. The unexpected delay meant that the convoy was no longer in danger of a surface attack. But, even better, there was now a good chance of catching the battleship steaming up the fjord in relatively open water instead of trying to bomb her inside the heavily defended anchorage in which she normally lay. It was an opportunity too good to miss and, bringing forward the date of Operation Tungsten to 3 April, Fraser recalled the *Victorious* and the two battleships and headed for the launch position some 120 miles north-west of Kaafjord.

The first strike of 21 Barracudas, escorted by an assortment of 40 Corsair, Hellcat and Wildcat fighters, took off at 04.30 and arrived over the target an hour later, just as the 19 Barracudas of the second strike were leaving the *Victorious*. The machines caught the *Tirpitz* by surprise and the Fleet Air Arm pilots made the most of their opportunities, the fighters swooping down to strafe the decks and unprotected flak positions with machine-gun and cannon fire while the Barracudas executed a textbook dive-bombing attack from 3,000 feet. The carefully planned and rehearsed strike was all over within the space of a single minute. An hour later, as the battleship's crew were picking up the pieces and struggling to bring the fires under control, the second wave of Barracudas appeared overhead and their anguish was repeated.

For the loss of only four aircraft the Royal Navy had scored a stunning victory, a triumph that would have been even more complete had the Barracudas been capable of carrying larger bombs than their standard 1600-pound AP weapons. Fourteen bombs had struck the target causing serious damage in all parts of the ship. Her keel plates were buckled and a list to starboard was mute evidence of serious flooding, while her upper decks were in total shambles. 122 men had been killed and a further 316 wounded. Yet, thanks to her armour and the relatively small bombs employed in the raid, the *Tirpitz* was still seaworthy. She was, however, certainly not operational. The British estimated that the necessary repairs would take at least six months to complete, while Doenitz, more pessimistically, took the view that her seagoing days were over. Although the repair gangs began work immediately the Admiralty in Berlin agreed with the C-in-C's verdict. Accepting that the battleship would never go to sea again, the former pride of the *Kriegsmarine* was reduced to the ignominious role of a floating battery.

Having been denied the total destruction of the *Tirpitz* on this occasion, the Fleet Air Arm continued its attempts to sink the battleship. The Home Fleet carriers sailed again on 12 April but thick cloud forced Fraser to abandon the attack. A further strike, planned for 28 May, also had to be cancelled due to adverse weather conditions. July, however, saw Operation Mascot in which 45 Barracudas from a three-carrier task force swooped on Kaafjord in a virtual repeat of the April sortie. But this time the German defences reacted swiftly to the challenge and when the aircraft reached the target they found it obliterated by a dense smokescreen and, forced to drop their bombs blind, no hits were secured.

The tide of war was now moving rapidly against Germany and the fate of the *Tirpitz* was merely one of many problems which faced the naval high command. The Allies had landed in Normandy on 6 June, 1944, and Hitler was already pressing Doenitz to take action against the invasion armada in the Channel, a task that was by now completely beyond the Navy's resources. Meanwhile the situation in the east was deteriorating daily and the unfortunate Doenitz also found himself facing an urgent demand to send 10,000 sailors to fight alongside their comrades in the *Wehrmacht* on the Russian front. In July, however, he at least had the satisfaction of seeing the Führer eating his words. For in a desperate attempt to guard the seaward flank of the German Army as it began its long retreat westwards, Hitler agreed to reinstate the battleships *Lützow* and *Scheer*, together with the cruiser *Prinz Eugen* – all previously serving in the Baltic as training ships – to combat duties as part of Battle Force Two under the command of the *Lützow*'s former captain, Vice-Admiral August Thiele. The Führer's 'irrevocable decision' had lasted just eighteen months.

Operation Goodwood, a strike by aircraft from the carriers *Formidable*, *Furious* and *Indefatigable*, finally proved that the Fleet Air Arm had neither the machines nor the weapons necessary to sink a heavily armoured vessel like the *Tirpitz*. A total of four attacks were launched against the battleship between 22 and 29 August, but, despite the absence of *Luftwaffe* fighters, the German defences, notably an impenetrable smokescreen, proved to be extremely effective. In addition, and for the first time, the *Tirpitz* used her 15-inch guns for barrage firing. Nevertheless two hits were obtained by the Navy's pilots, although one, a 1600-pound bomb which pierced the armoured deck of the battleship, failed to explode. This time, however, the Royal Navy paid for its temerity. The escort carrier *Nabob* was torpedoed by the *U-354* and, although she managed to limp back to Britain, she was subsequently written off as a constructive total loss. Three days later Swordfish aircraft from her sister-carrier, the *Vindex*, caught and sank the U-boat responsible.

At the end of August, realizing that the Fleet Air Arm could not produce the required results, the Allied Joint Chiefs of Staff passed the problem of the *Tirpitz* over to the RAF which not only had the right aircraft for the task but also possessed a weapon that could penetrate and smash the battleship's massive armour – the 6-ton, 21-foot-long Tallboy bomb initially designed to destroy the ferro-concrete walls of Germany's Ruhr dams. On 11 September thirty-eight Lancaster bombers from 9 and 617 Squadrons, together with a single Mosquito weather reconnaissance aircraft, left Lossiemouth to fly to Russia from where the attack was to be launched. One was forced to return to base and six others crashed on landing, but the remainder touched down safely and, after a tedious three-day delay, a total of twenty-seven operational Lancasters — the twenty-eighth machine carried film cameras instead of bombs — lined up on the Soviet airfield at Yagodnik and, led by Wing Commander J.B. Tait, climbed away into the dawn sky and formed up for the four-hour flight to Kaafjord. Twenty carried the massive 12,000-pound Tallboy bomb, one to each Lancaster, while the other seven were loaded with 500-pound Johnny Walker mines, a weapon specifically designed for attacks on armoured ships moored in shallow waters.

The Lancasters made their approach from the south-east at 12,000 feet but the German defences were on the alert and the bombers were still some thirty miles from their target when the first wisps of vapour curled from the smoke generators surrounding the *Tirpitz*. Within seconds dense clouds of choking black smoke were billowing around the battleship and by the time the Lancasters arrived overhead only the tips of the *Tirpitz*'s mastheads were visible above the man-made murk. Nevertheless they provided a more than adequate target indicator and, as Tait's machine roared over the otherwise invisible battleship a Tallboy was released from its bomb-bay. The other pilots, unable to see the target as the rising smoke swallowed even the mastheads, dropped their bombs at random and, pursued by enemy flak, headed back eastwards to Yagodnik.

Although Tait and his aircrews claimed no hits the raid had been unexpectedly successful. A Tallboy, thought to have been the one dropped by Tait's own Lancaster, had struck the *Tirpitz*'s bows and blown an enormous 150 square-foot hole in the hull at waterline level causing extensive flooding. Two near-misses had created chaos amidships and, as an added bonus, the battleship's main engines had seized up. Captain Wolf Junge, who had taken over command of the ship from Hans Meyer four months earlier, sent an urgent report to Doenitz in which he submitted that the battleship should be removed from the active list. But the Grand Admiral refused to consider the idea and gave orders for the crippled vessel to be taken to Tromsö two hundred miles to the south.

The weary repair gangs got to work again and on 15 October, with her bows patched and her engines restored to some kind of life, the *Tirpitz* steamed through The Leads at a stately, if funereal, seven knots surrounded by every escort ship, large and small, that Navy Group North could lay its hands on. Yet, despite the very real risk of attack by British carrier aircraft, not a single *Luftwaffe* fighter flew overhead to provide air cover.

A new berth was found for the wounded fugitive under the lee of Haaköy Island a few miles from the small Norwegian town of Tromsö where the shallow waters of the fjord would ensure that, even if sunk, the battleship's turrets would remain above water and her 15-inch guns could still be used against hostile forces. As work began on strengthening the anti-aircraft defences at Tromsö, two flak ships were moved into the fjord to provide more immediate protection.

So far as the Royal Air Force was concerned the arrival of the *Tirpitz* in Tromsö was good news, for her new home was within range of the Lancaster's base at Lossiemouth and Bomber Command did not wait long to exploit its freshly gained advantage. A fortnight later, on 29 October, thirty six bombers, accompanied by the usual film-unit machine, took off and headed for Sweden where they made use of neutral air space to form up in readiness for a concentrated mass attack on the battleship. Weather conditions turned against them en route, however, and just thirty seconds before they reached the dropping zone a thick bank of cloud suddenly obliterated the target. It was, of course, too late to abandon the mission and, aiming blindly with little hope of success, the bomb doors of the Lancasters opened and a total of thirty-two Tallboys tumbled out of the skies.

The pilots were disappointed but not surprised by their failure to score a direct hit, yet, as it happened, the attack effectively brought the *Tirpitz*'s lack-lustre career to an end. For a near-miss inflicted serious damage to the port propeller shaft and rudder which, in turn, led to serious flooding in the stern section of the vessel. The battleship, now incapable of steaming under her own power, was finished. Yet, ironically, neither side was apparently willing to allow the corpse to rest in peace. The *Kriegsmarine* called in dredgers to push sand under the battleship's keel to prevent her from sinking completely out of sight while the *Luftwaffe*, in an inexplicable change of heart, sent Major Ehrler and a squadron of fighters to the nearby airfield at Bardufoss. For the very first time in her career the *Tirpitz* had been allocated a *Luftwaffe* unit of her very own. It was unfortunate that it had arrived a year too late!

Captain Junge left the battleship on 4 November and command of the *Tirpitz* passed to Robert Weber, the vessel's former Gunnery Officer. Weber was the flagship's fourth captain in as many years. He was also destined to be her last, for on 12 November, barely a week after his appointment, Wing Commander Tait's Lancasters returned to Tromsö. This time they finished the task which they had set themselves some four months earlier.

The approach of the bombers was first reported to the *Tirpitz* at 07.30. An hour later, having brought the battleship's crew to action stations, Captain Weber telephoned Major Ehrler at Bardufoss and asked him to scramble his fighters. By 09.38 the Lancasters were only fifteen miles away and the *Tirpitz* opened fire with her main armament, laying down a barrage which Weber hoped would deter even the bravest of pilots. But the bomber crews seemed unconcerned and the roar of the Lancaster engines thundered and echoed around the steep-walled fjord as they began their attack run.

One of the 6-ton Tallboy bombs struck turret *Bruno* while a second smashed through the armoured deck amidships and exploded deep inside the bowels of the battleship. The blast-wave from two others, which had near-missed the beam, peeled back the hull plating like the opened lid of a sardine tin. The *Tirpitz*, her guns still blazing, lurched sharply to port, and, almost before anyone had had time to gather their breath and assess the damage, the magazine under turret *Caesar* erupted in a sheet of white flame. The great ship, mortally wounded, slowly turned turtle, leaving her keel exposed above water as her superstructure grounded on the bottom of the shallow fjord. Yet, despite the battleship's urgent call for immediate assistance over an hour earlier, not a single *Luftwaffe* fighter arrived to defend her from the enemy's bombers.

Like Ernst Lindemann of the *Bismarck* and Fritz Hintze of the *Scharnhorst*, Captain Weber died with his ship, together with some seven hundred members of the crew. As the Lancasters faded into the distance an armada of small boats from Tromsö hurried to the upturned wreck in a frantic search for survivors. But few had remained alive for more than a few agonized minutes in the ice-cold waters of the fjord and most of the bodies dragged from the sea were already dead from exposure. The following day, however, rescue teams used blow-torches to cut through the exposed keel plating and bring out eighty-seven fortunate men who had been trapped in the lowest compartments of the ship when she turned over. But not all were so lucky. A junior officer and two seamen were located in an air-pocket deep inside the hull. Their tapping signals were acknowledged but without the necessary drilling equipment to burrow down into the debris it was impossible to get them out and the rescuers had to leave them to die in the damp darkness of their armoured tomb.

While the Royal Air Force was busy destroying the *Tirpitz*, the Russian Army was equally busy decimating the *Wehrmacht* and driving the Germans into the Baltic, a process that had begun in August when Soviet forces had reached the Gulf of Riga. By the beginning of October, 1944, Vice-Admiral Thiele's Battle Group Two was fiercely engaged in the struggle to prevent Stalin's troops from seizing the Sorve Peninsula and the *Lützow*, together with the *Prinz Eugen*, took part in a series of bombardment operations that were instrumental in keeping the Russians at bay for several weeks. When the two ships had to return to Gdynia to replenish their exhausted ammunition stocks the task was taken over by the *Admiral Scheer* and the cruiser *Hipper*, both of whom soon came under heavy air attack from Soviet high altitude bombers and torpedo planes. Fortunately for the battleship and her consort, the Red Air Force could not match the skills of their British counterparts and, despite the intensity of the attacks, the *Scheer* emerged undamaged.

Overwhelmed by sheer force of numbers, the German Army was finally forced to withdraw from its positions at the end of November and both the *Lützow*, now returned to the fray, and the *Scheer* provided artillery and flak cover for the little ships that carried out the Dunkirk-style evacuation. The heroism of the *Kriegsmarine* sailors was noted by the field commander, General Guderian, who sent an appreciatory signal to Doenitz: 'Having concluded the evacuation operations from Sorve, I feel myself impelled to… convey my thanks and those of the entire Army of the East to all members of the navy for the outstanding and self-sacrificing support they have given us.' Less formal, but equally sincere, was the response of the German troops in Gdynia when the *Scheer* returned for refuelling. A party of wounded soldiers who had been snatched to safety by the navy came up the gangways and, with tears in their eyes, shook the hands of the sailors who had helped to rescue them. 'Thank you,' was all they could say. 'Thank you.'

On 18 December the old battleship *Schleswig Holstein*, a veteran survivor of the 1919 *Reichsmarine*, was bombed by the RAF while anchored at Gdynia and, after thirty-six years of service that had spanned two world wars, her operational career was brought to an end by the enemy. She had, however, one more task to perform. On 21 March, 1945, when the Russians had reached the very gates of the town, the venerable old lady was towed into the harbour entrance and scuttled as a blockship. Her sister-ship *Schlesien*, which had spent most of the war engaged on training duties, was sunk by air-dropped mines off Swinemünde in the final days of the war.

Meanwhile the two surviving pocket-battleships, *Lützow* and *Scheer*, continued their inshore bombardment campaign to relieve Russian pressure on the *Wehrmacht* as it reeled before the onslaught of the Red Army. On 20 January, 1945, the Soviet war machine broke through on a 50-mile front in East Prussia. Although Doenitz promised Hitler that the navy would do all in its power to evacuate civilian refugees, he stressed that the ongoing operations in support of the army must continue to take priority. Yet, even at this crisis-point in the history of the Third Reich, the Grand Admiral saw fit to renew his complaints about the lack of co-operation which the *Kriegsmarine* was receiving from the *Luftwaffe*. The sinking of the liner *Wilhelm Gustloff*, a disaster that cost the lives of more than 7,000 refugees, prompted him to grumble: 'Russian submarines are able to operate at will in the Baltic Sea for the simple reason that no German aircraft are there to attack them', an excuse that served to conceal the fact that the navy, despite more than five years of war, had still failed to organize and train adequate anti-submarine forces.

Operations on the seaward flank of the army continued throughout January and February, 1945, with the *Scheer* at one point firing at land targets twenty-two miles inside the Russian lines. But the military situation was now so serious that the *Kriegsmarine* could do little to halt the Russian juggernaut. Memel finally fell in February, its occupation by the Red Army delayed for several weeks by the power and accuracy of the *Lutzow*'s 11-inch guns. There was, however, a certain irony in the situation for Hitler had travelled to Memel aboard the *Lützow*, then known as the *Deutschland*, when the town was ceded to Germany on 23 March, 1939. Now that same battleship was playing a leading role in the last-ditch stand to save the ancient Baltic port from the clutches of another invader.

At the beginning of March the *Scheer* was forced to withdraw from the battle. Her gun barrels, worn smooth by weeks of bombardment operations, needed relining and, with 800 refugees and 200 wounded soldiers aboard, she left Gdynia for a refit in the naval dockyard at Kiel. But even her return passage was not without incident for, on three separate occasions, she was taken close inshore to deter Russian artillery units from harassing the unending columns of refugees fleeing westwards to escape the brutalities of the advancing Red Army.

Soon after the battleship's arrival in Kiel a signal was received from the headquarters of Navy Group North announcing that Admiral Schniewind intended to inspect the ship, a formality that seemed oddly out of place at a time when the armed forces of the Third Reich were disintegrating on all fronts and Germany was close to total collapse. Anxious to create a good impression, the *Scheer*'s captain scoured the bomb-scarred dockyard for paint only to discover that no tins of regulation grey remained. At the last minute, however, several hundred drums of violet-blue paint were found in an old store shed and, donning their oldest overalls, the battleship's crew went to work with their brushes. Schniewind's comments when he stepped out of his Mercedes staff car and saw the apparition were, unfortunately, not recorded.

Kiel had been a routine target for the RAF since the earliest days of the war and the British stepped up their air attacks as the Russians launched their final offensive in East Prussia. The cruiser *Hipper* was hit on 3 April and again on the night of 9/10 April. This latter raid, a mass attack by 591 Lancaster bombers, also brought disaster to the *Scheer* which was berthed in the old inner basin of the dockyard. A cluster of bombs near-missed the pocket-battleship. The blast as they exploded shattered her lightly armoured hull and she sank within minutes. Fortunately the major part of her crew were safely ashore in bomb-proof shelters when the raid took place, but thirty-two of the men who had remained aboard to maintain essential machinery and to operate the flak defences lost their lives.

On 27 March the *Gneisenau*, now no more than a disarmed and useless hulk, had been towed out to the entrance to Gdynia harbour and sunk alongside the *Schleswig-Holstein* as a blockship, an ignominious end to a fine ship. But her sacrifice merely served to underline the hoodoo of misfortune that had pursued her with such relentless determination throughout her career for it failed to stem the enemy's advance and the naval base, renamed Gotenhaven by the Germans, fell to the Russian Army twenty-four hours later. Danzig suffered the same fate two days later, both the *Lützow* and the *Prinz Eugen* using their guns with considerable effect in the final days of the siege.

With the loss of the *Admiral Scheer* at Kiel on 10 April the *Kriegsmarine* was now reduced to only one operational battleship, the apparently indestructible *Lützow*. But having fought off a series of Russian attacks while providing cover to the armada of small ships which Admiral Kummetz had assembled to evacuate the troops cut-off on the Hela Peninsula, she too was finally withdrawn to Swinemünde to replenish her bunkers and take on more ammunition. On 13 April a force of 34 Lancasters attempted to bomb her in her new berth but the raid was aborted at the last minute due to cloud cover over the target area. Two nights later a similar attack by twenty Lancasters from 617 Squadron had to be called off for the same reason. The Squadron tried again twenty-four hours later and this time, with improved weather conditions, fifteen Lancasters dropped a lethal cargo of 6-ton Tallboys and 1,000-pound high-explosive bombs on Swinemünde. One Tallboy near-missed the battleship and, with her keel plating badly holed by the blast, the *Lützow* listed to port and settled gently on the bottom of the shallow *Kaiserfahrt* canal with her upperworks and gun turrets still showing above water. The former *Deutschland* was down but she was certainly not out. Her only casualties, some twenty dead and a similar number wounded, were all soldiers and not members of her crew. Although she would never go to sea again she was still of considerable military value as a heavy artillery battery once the holes in her hull had been sealed and she had been brought back on to an even keel.

The battleship was ready for action by 27 April and the next day her forward 11-inch turret and four of her 5.9-inch secondary armament weapons opened fire on Russian tanks and infantry as they advanced towards the coast from the direction of Pasewalk. She was still engaging the enemy on the 30th when Adolf Hitler, unable to face up to the enormity of Germany's defeat, committed suicide in his Berlin bunker.

An electrical fire nearly put paid to the gallant efforts of the *Lützow*'s crew on the night of 1/2 May, still fighting valiantly to save the Third Reich despite the death of their Führer. Forced to abandon their land-locked ship, they sheltered behind some nearby trees as the flames swirled around the ready-use ammunition and detonated the shells lying scattered about the decks. Dawn revealed the extent of the damage she had suffered: her superstructure torn and twisted by the random explosion of her own shells, the electrical circuits burned out, and the forward 11-inch turret, blackened by flame, no longer operational. Without weapons there was nothing more the men of the *Lützow* could do and on the 3rd the survivors were taken back to Swinemünde in a naval motorboat.

The struggle, however, was not yet over, for the chance discovery of 3,000 rounds of 5.9-inch ammunition meant that the ship could continue the fight and the eager gunners, their eyes red-rimmed with exhaustion, hurried back to the canal to turn their weapons against the Russians once more. But by now the situation was beyond retrieval and, as the stranded battleship came within range of Soviet machine guns, it was time to bow to the inevitable. Shortly before midnight on the 3rd, the day on which Germany's military representatives met General Montgomery to negotiate a ceasefire and to accept the Allies' demand for unconditional surrender, orders were given to prepare the vessel for demolition. At 00.12 on 4 May, five days after the Führer's death, a series of tremendous explosions tore the *Lützow* apart.

Thirty hours later the OKW, acting under the authority of Grand Admiral Karl Doenitz, who had succeeded Hitler as Führer of the Third Reich, ordered all hostilities against Britain and the United States to cease immediately. The war was finally over and of Hitler's seven battleships not a single one had survived. It was a record of sacrifice that has rarely been matched in the history of naval warfare.

APPENDIX
HITLER'S BATTLESHIPS

	Deutschland [Lützow]	Admiral Scheer	Graf Spee	Gneisenau	Scharnhorst	Bismarck	Tirpitz
Laid down:	5 Feb 1929	26 June 1931	1 Oct 1932	Mar 1935	16 May 1935	1 July 1936	26 Oct 1936
Launched	19 May 1931	1 Apr 1933	30 June 1934	8 Dec 1936	3 Oct 1936	14 Feb 1939	1 Apr 1939
Commissioned	1 Apr 1933	12 Nov 1934	6 Jan 1936	21 May 1938	7 Jan 1939	29 Aug 1940	25 Jan 1941
Displacement (Standard)	11,700 tons	11,700 tons	12,100 tons	31,800 tons	31,800 tons	41,700 tons	42,900 tons
Displacement (Full load)	15,900 tons	15,900 tons	16,200 tons	38,900 tons	38,900 tons	50,900 tons	52,600 tons
Overall length (Feet)	616¾	616¾	616¾	771	771	822¾	822¾
Beam (Feet)	68	68	71¼	100	100	118¼	118¼
Draught (Feet)	19/23¼	19/23¼	19/24	27/32½	27/32½	28½/33½	29½/34¾
Main Armament	Six x 11″	Six x 11″	Six x 11″	Nine x 11″	Nine x 11″	Eight x 15″	Eight x 15″
Secondary Armament	Eight x 5.9″	Eight x 5.9″	Eight x 5.9″	Twelve x 5.9″	Twelve x 5.9″	Twelve x 5.9″	Twelve x 5.9″
Main anti aircraft armament	Six x 4.1″	Six x 4.1″	Six x 4.1″	Fourteen x 4.1″	Fourteen x 4.1″	Sixteen x 4.1″	Sixteen x 4.1″
Other weapons	Eight x 37mm Ten x 20mm	Six x 88mm	Six x 88mm	Sixteen x 37mm Fourteen x 20mm	Sixteen x 37mm Eighteen x 20mm	Sixteen x 37mm Thirty-six x 20mm	Sixteen x 37mm Seventy x 20mm
Torpedo tubes	Eight	Eight	Eight	Six	Six	Nil	Eight
Aircraft capacity	Two	Two	Two	Four	Four	Six	Six
Complement	1150	1124	1124	1754	1754	2065	2530
Engines:	MAN diesel 48,390 SHP	MAN diesel 52,050 SHP	MAN diesel 54,000 SHP	Brown-Boveri turbines 160,000 SHP	Brown-Boveri turbines 160,000 SHP	Brown-Boveri turbines 138,000 SHP	Brown-Boveri turbines 138,000 SHP
Speed — best (knots)	28	28.3	28.5	32	32	30.8	29
Built by:	Deutsche Werke Kiel	Marine Werft Wilhelmshaven	Marine Werft Wilhelmshaven	Deutsche Werke Kiel	Navy Yard Wilhelmshaven	Blohm & Voss Hamburg	Navy Yard Wilhemshaven
ARMOUR							
Belt [Inches]	3¼	4	4	12	12	12¾	12¾
Deck [Inches]	1½	1½	1½	4¼	4¼	4½	4½
Conning tower [Inches]	5½	5½	5½	14	14	14	14
Turrets — face [Inches]	5½	5½	5½	14¼	14¼	14	14
Turrets — side [Inches]	4	3	3	9¾	9¾	12½	12½
Main barbettes [Inches]	4	5	5	14	14	13½	13½
Secondary barbettes [Inches]	Shields only	Shields only	Shields only	6	6	8½	8½
Fate:	Scuttled after bomb damage 4 May 1945	Capsized after bombing 9 Apr 1945	Scuttled 17 Dec 1939	Scuttled as block-ship 27 Mar 1945	Sunk in action 26 Dec 1943	Sunk in action 27 May 1941	Sunk by RAF bombers 12 Nov 1944

BIBLIOGRAPHY

Escape of the Scharnhorst and Gneisenau, Peter Kemp, Ian Allen, London, 1975

Scharnhorst and Gneisenau, The Elusive Sisters, Richard Garrett, David & Charles, London, 1978

Fiasco, John Deane Potter, Heinemann, London, 1970

The Story of the Prinz Eugen, Fritz-Otto Busch, Robert Hale, London, 1960

Channel Dash, Terence Robertson, Evans, London, 1958

Panzerschiffe! Harry Woodman, (Feature in *Sea Classic* Magazine), Summer, 1985

Battle of the River Plate, Geoffrey Bennett, Ian Allan, London, 1972

Eclipse of the German Navy, Thaddeus V Tujela, Dent, London, 1958

Verdammte See (Hitler's Naval War), Cajus Bekker, Gerhard Stalling, Oldenburg, 1971

Swastika at Sea, Cajus Bekker, Kimber, London, 1954

Loss of the Bismarck, B. B. Schofield, Ian Allan, London, 1972

Battleship Bismarck, Baron von Mullenheim-Rechberg, NIP, Annapolis, 1980

Pursuit, Ludovic Kennedy, Collins, London, 1974

Struggle for the Sea, Grand-Admiral Erich Raeder, Kimber, London, 1959

Bomber Command War Diaries, Martin Middlebrook & Chris Everitt, Viking, London, 1985

Admiral of the Fleet Earl Beatty, Stephen Roskill, Collins, London, 1980

Our Admiral, Charles Beatty, W. H. Allen, London, 1980

Churchill and the Admirals, Stephen Roskill, Collins, London, 1977

Zehn Jahre und Zwanzig Tag, Grand Admiral Karl Doenitz, Atheneum Verlag, Bonn, 1958

Doenitz — the Last Fuehrer, Peter Padfield, Gollancz, London, 1984

Fraser of North Cape, Richard Humble, Routledge & Kegan Paul, London, 1983

73 North, Dudley Pope, Weidenfeld & Nicolson, London, 1958

Sailor at Sea, Vice-Admiral Harold Hickling, Kimber, London, 1965

Very Special Intelligence, Patrick Beesly, Hamish Hamilton, London, 1977

VCs of the Royal Navy, John Frayne Turner, Harrap, London, 1956

The Electron and Sea Power, Vice-Ad Sir Arthur Hezlet, Davies, London, 1975

Graf Spee, Michael Powell, Hodder & Stoughton, London, 1956

Prologue to a War, Ewart Brookes, Jarrolds, London, 1966

I was Graf Spee's Prisoner, Captain Patrick Dove, Cherry Tree Books, London, 1940

Under Three Flags, Geoffrey Jones, Kimber, London, 1973

Rise & Fall of the Third Reich, William Shirer, Secker & Warburg, London, 1959

Influence of Law on Sea Power, D. P. O'Connel, Manchester University Press, Manchester, 1975

Oppenheim's International Law, Edited Lauterpacht, 7th Edition, Longmans, London, 1948

INDEX